All about shrimps, crayfishes, and crabs in the freshwater aquarium

Uwe Werner

Procambarus clarkii is a North American river crayfish. In crayfishes the first of the three pairs of chelipeds (clawed feet) is enlarged for fighting or for seizing prey.

A colourful long-arm shrimp (*Macrobrachium rosenbergi*). In *Macrobrachium* species it is the second of the two pairs of chelipeds that s enlarged Photo: Sch. Nakano

A bright red mangrove crab (Sesarmidae gen. sp.). Here the first (and only) pair of chelipeds is large. Photo: Sch. Nakano

All pictures by Uwe Werner, if not mentioned otherwise

The following photographers, companies, and institutions contributed to this volume:

Aqua Magazine (Taiwan), Philippe Bacchet, Georgina Bond-Buckup, Ludwig Buckup, Keith Crandall, Olivier Gargominy, Michel Keijman, Chris Lukhaup, Burkhard Migge, Schuzo Nakano, Gustav Paulay, Jens Pinhard, Vanessa Pike-Russell, Joseph Poupin, Kai A. Quante, Rüdiger Riehl, Hans-Georg Rupp, William A. Tomey, Keoki Stender, Frank Schäfer, Erwin Schraml, Dirk Schrüfer, Ingo Seidel, Wolfgang Seign, Frank Teigler.

Aquarium Glaser GmbH,
Aquaristik Service Reuter,
Tropenparadies Oberhausen
***amtra* - Aquaristik GmbH**
Dr. med. vet. Markus Biffar,

Our hearty thanks for all their help.

AQUALOG: Rodgau: A.C.S.
All about shrimps, crayfishes, and crabs in the freshwater aquarium, brackish water aquarium, and paludarium, 2008
Uwe Werner
ISBN 978-3-936027-68-6

German edition: ISBN 978-3-936027-66-2

Texte und fachliche Bearbeitung:
Uwe Werner
Redaktion:
Dipl. Biol. Frank Schäfer
Titelgestaltung:
Aqualog Verlag A.C.S.

Druck, Satz, Verarbeitung:
Lithos: Aqualog Verlag A.C.S.
Layout: Frank Schäfer, Levin Locke
Druck: Rohland & more, Offenbach
Gedruckt auf EURO ART glänzend, 100% chlorfrei von PWA, umweltfreundlich.

Redaktionsanschrift:
Aqualog Verlag A.C.S. GmbH
Liebigstraße 1
D-63110 Rodgau
Fax: +49 (0) 6106 – 64 46 92

E-mail: info@aqualog.de
http://www.aqualog.de

PRINTED IN GERMANY

Cover photos

Front cover
Caridina sp. – a freshwater shrimp from Sulawesi (C. Lukhaup)
Back cover
Macrobrachium vollenhoveni (U. Werner), *Cambarus speciosus* (U. Werner), *Coenobita compressus* (F. Schäfer), *Geosesarma* sp. (F. Schäfer), *Cardisoma armatum* (F. Schäfer). Crystal-Red-Shrimp (Aqua Magazine), *Procambarus alleni* (U. Werner).

Contents

Acknowledgements

This book could not have appeared in its current form without the help of numerous crustacean experts who provided me with literature and other information. Accordingly I would like to express my heartfelt thanks to Chris Lukhaup, S. de Grave, Dirk Brandis, Dieter Schaller, and A. Broesing. A very special thank you is due, however, to Werner Klotz, who has identified numerous shrimp species so that we no longer need to rely on popular names. In addition I am grateful to Frank Schäfer, who has added a long overdue chapter on hermit and horseshoe crabs and revised the existing chapter on crabs.

Preface

Uwe Werner

Born in 1948, I have been an aquarist since my childhood, breeding characins and many other fishes, and developing a special interest in the cichlids of Central and South America. My first articles in periodicals and the publication of books followed, and since the beginning of the eighties I have been to the tropics many times to observe fishes in their natural habitats and to bring home a number of species.

My interest in freshwater crustaceans dates back to one of these trips, in 1985, when I found some nice freshwater shrimps in Guatemala, took some home, and kept them in my tanks. Later on I maintained other shrimp and crayfish species, bred some of them, and reported my experiences in periodicals, and soon was regarded as a specialist - without really being one.

It has always been - and still is - a problem for me accurately to identify the species kept. But more recently I have received help from numerous crustacean enthusiasts, so that the scientific names of many - albeit not all - species are now known. And in many cases the significance of these names as well.

River crab of the species *Sartoriana spinigera* from India.

The Australian crayfish *Cherax destructor* develops huge, powerful claws, but is a peaceful fellow.

Higher crustaceans and decapods

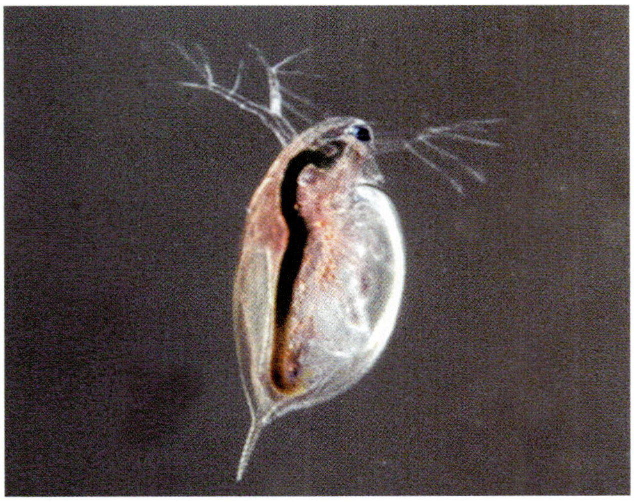

The water fleas, popular as live food, belong to the lower crustaceans. Photo: F. Schäfer

Assellus - this is the Water Hoglouse, *Assellus aquaticus*, which lives in fresh water - are likewise crustaceans. Photo: F. Schäfer

Higher crustaceans and decapods

The class of the crustaceans (Crustacea) consists of a number of different subclasses: for example, the water fleas (*Daphnia*) and copepods such as *Cyclops*, with which the aquarist will be familiar because they are used as fish food, and the fish lice (*Argulus*), which he knows as fish parasites. In addition to these and other lower crustaceans there is the subclass Malacostraca, which contains the so-called higher crustaceans, represented by about 18000 (!) different species, a number corresponding to about half of all known crustaceans. The higher crustaceans are distinguished by their high level of anatomical organisation, their astonishing variety of forms, and the wide range of different natural habitats they have conquered. Other reasons include their highly developed behaviour and - last but not least - their size. The so-called decapods (Decapoda) in this group are the largest living arthropods. There are giant Antarctic shrimp species with a length of 60 centimetres, giant Australian crayfish with spiny armour, Indo-Australian (marine) crabs with a carapace 40 centimetres wide, and giant Japanese spider crabs, living in the depths of the sea, whose walking legs span about three metres.

The order Decapoda is divided into two suborders: the Natantia (swimming crustaceans) and the Reptantia (walking/creeping crustaceans). To the Natantia belong all shrimp-like forms, normally called shrimps and prawns: crustaceans with a body deeper than wide and a thin shell, which are good swimmers, able to swim forwards using their pleopods. They have two pairs of claws, which in *Macrobrachium* species (long-arm shrimps) are enlarged to a different degree: the smaller, anterior claws are used for eating, and the larger, second pair for threatening and fighting. The Natantia include - *inter alia* - the freshwater shrimps of the families Atyidae and Palaemonidae.

The Reptantia include all the forms that primarily walk rather than swim and have a thick shell. They are divided into four groups:

1) The Astacidea, the lobster- or crayfish-like crustaceans, include, inter alia, the marine lobster family (Homaridae) and the true river crayfishes, usually called simply crayfishes. These have three pairs of claws, the first pair of which are always enlarged. Their body is less deep than wide and they walk forwards, but swim (using their pleon) only backwards. They are referred to three families: the Old World river crayfishes (Astacidae), the New World river crayfishes (Cambaridae) - both of which are represented by many genera and species in the northern hemisphere (northern-hemisphere river crayfishes) - and the Parastacidae, which live in the southern hemisphere (southern-hemisphere river crayfishes). The latter are distributed in southern South America, New Zealand, Australia/New Guinea, and Madagascar. The Australian crayfishes are generally regarded as a separate family, the Austroastacidae.

The Palinura - this is a spiny lobster, *Palinurus homarus*, from the Indian Ocean - do not include any freshwater species. Photo: I. Seidel

2. The Palinura or spiny lobsters comprise only marine species and have large, clawed antennae rather than large claws. Most species are very tasty, but cannot be kept in freshwater aquaria.

3. The Anomura are crayfishes with a large asymmetrical tail; they are a large group, rich in forms, and some species are of great interest to the freshwater aquarist. These include the Aeglidae from South America: elongated crustaceans, reminiscent of the river crayfishes, which live in the rivers and lakes of subtropical South America. During the breeding period the females of some species leave the water and congregate under stones or dead wood. From their eggs emerge completely developed young. The Paguridae (hermit crabs), which protect their abdomens in spiral shells, include a number of terrestrial species (genus *Coenobita*) that can be kept in the terrarium without difficulty. A very small number of species live in fresh and brackish water, but the majority are marine.

4. The Brachyura (the true crabs) have their abdomen folded beneath the greatly broadened anterior part of the body. They have only one pair of claws, which are greatly enlarged. They include the true freshwater crabs (Potamoidea), the mangrove crabs (Grapsidae), the running and fiddler crabs (Ocypodidae), and the land crabs *sensu stricto* (Gecarcinidae).

The horseshoe crabs also discussed briefly in this book do not belong to the crustaceans, despite their misleading name, but are actually more closely related to the arachnids.

The decapods, their exo- and endo-skeleton

The morphology and anatomy of crustaceans makes them interesting subjects for study. The body consists of two main parts: the immovable cephalothorax (combined head and thorax), which is elongate in shrimps and crayfishes but short and wide in crabs (Brachyura); and the pleon or abdomen, which can be moved backwards and forwards and ends in the telson, which in most cases is triangular, and beneath which we find the anus. An immediately noticeable feature is the pair of strongly-developed "arms" with claws on the anterior body. These are termed chelipeds (= "claw-feet") and are followed by four pairs of legs which serve for walking, and are called peraeopods (= "walking legs"). The chelipeds are, essentially, specialised walking-legs. Their penultimate segment forms a rigid, upward-pointing, finger-like element, against which closes a further, movable "finger". The chelipeds and legs each consist of seven segments (sometimes two are fused, such that only six can be counted), and these five pairs of legs have a combined total of ten "feet", hence the name Decapoda (= "ten-footers") given to the order. In front of the peraeopods we find the mouthparts, consisting of a pair of mandibles, two pairs of maxillae, and three pairs of maxillipeds (= "jaw-feet"), the posteriormost of which are of considerable size. The maxillipeds bear lateral appendages, which in part move the water for respiration and in part serve as gills.
On the abdomen we find limbs with a completely different structure, usually five pairs of so-called swimmerets or pleopods. These exhibit the original fissiped structure and are used for swimming, producing a current of water, and reproduction. They consist of a basal segment, on which are located two branches, one exterior and one interior (exopoid and endopoid).

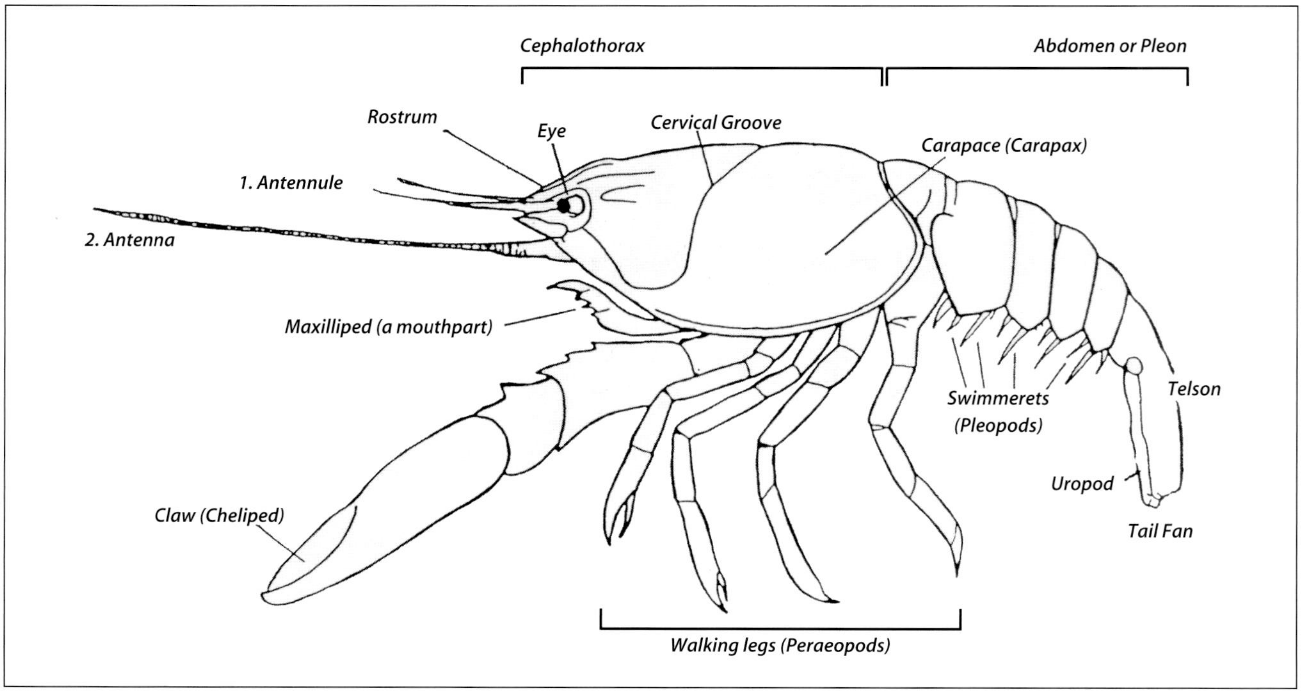

Generalised morphology of a crayfish, after Merrik & Lambert (1991).

The decapods, their exo- and endo-skeleton

Exuvia (moulted "shell") of a long-arm shrimp.

Originally all the limbs were built like this, but some have been modified for locomotion and feeding. Today the walking legs (peraeopods) consist almost entirely of the inner branch, while the outer has been reduced. On the basal part of the peraeopods there are multiple appendages that form gills. The mandibles and (in long-tailed forms) the posteriormost pleopods are highly specialised, the latter, together with the telson, forming the tail fan, and thus termed uropods (= "tail feet"). If a crayfish jerks its abdomen to and fro, the tail fan causes a sudden backward impetus, which crays often use to flee. In male river crayfishes and crabs the first two pairs of pleopods are modified for reproduction, forming tube-like copulatory organs that transmit the sperm. In addition, females carry the fertilised eggs and embryos around on their pleopods.

The body of the crustacean is covered by a hard skin (the cuticula), which is composed in part of calcium carbonate and thus forms a solid armour. The anterior part of the body and the gills, which are located on the sides, are covered by a shield-like structure, the carapace, creating two respiratory or gill chambers, one on each side. It serves as an exterior skeleton (exoskeleton), protecting the body tissue and the gills inside. In terrestrial forms the "ceiling" of the gill chamber contains finely ramified blood vessels and serves as a kind of "lung", enabling the animal to breathe air. Crustaceans with a lung of this type will suffocate in water that is low in oxygen if there is no possibility of taking up air.

In addition the muscles are attached to the inner surface of this armour. To this end, at least in larger crustaceans, excrescences are present on the inner surface such that the exterior skeleton is continued in places by an inner one (the endoskeleton). This is especially important for the gizzard, which is situated in the anterior part of the body and whose numerous muscles require firm attachment points. The cervical groove on the carapace represents the posterior edge of the head. In crabs a system of such grooves indicates the positions of certain organs. The anterior part of the carapace is pointed in shrimps and crayfishes, forming a more or less protruding rostrum. This corresponds to the margin of the forehead in crabs, and is flanked by "cut-outs" for the eyes, from which the movable eye-stalks with their bulging eyes protrude.

Growth and coloration

Because of their rigid carapace, crustaceans do not grow gradually, but in a series of steps associated with moulting. Each such step is signalled by the cessation of feeding. Stimulated by a hormone, the crustacean leaves its old shell, which has become too tight, within a few minutes, jerking violently to break free. Shrimps and crayfishes emerge from their old shell through a split in the neck. In crabs the back edge of the carapace splits along the line of the dorsum, and the dorsal armour is then lifted like the lid of a box, with the crab sliding out backwards.

The new shell, wrinkly and too large, then fills with water and tightens. And then, while it is still soft and lethargic, the crustacean grows, at the same time replacing limbs formerly lost, completely or at least in part (smaller in size). After the moult it initially lies about apathetically for some time, noticeably lighter-coloured than before. Eventually the usually still soft and defenceless animal gets to its feet with difficulty and seeks out shelter. It then hides for the next two or three days until the new carapace has hardened. Most of the necessary calcium carbonate is taken from the water via the gills, with part being stored before the moult in the stomach (or proventiculum) as paired gastroliths, initially small and flat, later shaped like a convex button. The empty shell (exuvia) is usually eaten by the newly-moulted crustacean in order to recycle the mineral salts it contains.

Crustaceans grow for as long as they live, but increasingly slowly, so older specimens moult less frequently than young. At the beginning of their independent lives young crustaceans may moult every few days, while young adults moult four or five times a year, and old individuals only once or twice. The glands that control moulting and the production of chitin are, incidentally, situated in the eye-stalks of the "ten-footers".

The coloration of crustaceans is composed of pigments embedded in the shell. Most of these are reddish, brownish, or bluish. But crustaceans are also able to change their colours: this happens (as in fish) in two different ways, gradually (controlled by hormones) or in a flash (controlled by the nervous system) by the expansion or contraction of certain pigment cells (chromatophores) in the underlying skin tissue. The coloration of smaller crustaceans may also be influenced by coloured (red or yellow) fat-balls inside the body or by the (green or blue) content of the gut. Crabs can also adapt their coloration to that of their surroundings, under the control of hormones secreted in the eye-stalks.

When crustaceans die, the albuminous pigment of the armour (astaxanthin) can break down more or less completely and at variable speed into its component albumen and pigments (carotenoids), so that the shell assumes an orange or red coloration. This happens particularly rapidly and intensely under the influence of heat, for example if they are dropped into boiling water.

Dwarf shrimps of the genus *Neocaridina* are not only capable of rapid physiological colour changes (*centre and bottom*) but can also readily be produced in specific colours by selective breeding. Red varieties (*top*) are particularly popular. All three photos show the same species, the so-called Red Cherry Dwarf Shrimp (*N. denticulata sinensis*).
Photos: F. Schäfer

Sex determination and reproduction

Sex determination and reproduction

It is not always easy to determine the sex of shrimps reliably, but usually possible with practice. Females generally have a broader pleon and the sides of the pleon segments extend further downward. In some groups the size and colour of the claws is different, most strikingly in the long-arm shrimps. In adult *Macrobrachium* the sexes are usually distinguishable at first glance, as the abdomen of the female is somewhat deeper by virtue of an additional egg-store above the gizzard, in which the eggs can clearly be seen, at least in the transparent species. Males as a rule develop longer, often thickened, chelipeds. It appears that the function of the long arms, which are a secondary sexual characteristic, is not (or not only) a matter of males needing to be better armed. Perhaps they are (also) an indication of strength, but it is more likely that the long arms are used to manipulate the female into a position favourable for copulation and thus stimulate her for that purpose. These shrimps can

The sexes are easy to differentiate in long-arm shrimps. Male (*above*) and female (*below*) of an as yet undetermined *Macrobrachium* species from northern Bengal (Coochbehar).

Photos: F. Schäfer

regularly be seen in pairs in a T-position, where the male approaches the female from the side and then keeps her in place by using one arm to block her escape forwards, and the other her retreat backwards.

Among the Atyidae males often have special appendages on their legs, for holding females. Dwarf-shrimp males are smaller and more slender than the females (see photos opposite: the bottom individual is a male, the middle one a female). Among the larger fan shrimps one pair of peraeopods is often noticeably thickened in males, as, for example, in *Atya gabonensis*. The pleopods are not very specialised, and although males do have a so-called appendix masculinus (male appendage) on the first pair of pleopods, this is barely visible in live specimens. Copulation often takes place quickly and mostly at night.

In river crayfishes the sperm packets are usually deposited on the ventral surface of the female and the eggs are fertilised externally after they emerge. River crayfishes also copulate belly to belly. Females of some related

In the Atyidae the sexual differences are not so noticeable: in lateral view it can be seen that in *Atya gabonensis* the male (*left*) has enlarged claws and a more strongly ridged carapace. Viewed from above, it can be seen that the male (*below*) is appreciably slighter in build. The latter character can be used to differentiate the sexes in almost all Atyidae.

Photos: F. Schäfer

groups have a special chamber (the annulus ventralis) or indentation (thelycium) on their underside, into which sperm packets can be deposited and stored for some time.

The sex of crabs is possible to determine by the shape and width of the abdomen: in females the pleon is very wide, oval, and occupies a large part of the posterior

Sex determination and reproduction

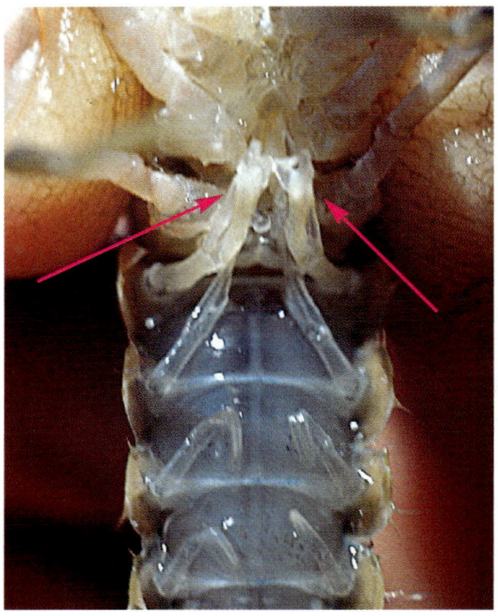

In northern-hemisphere crayfishes the sexes are easily distinguished. Females (*left*) lack the gonopods of the male (*centre*, indicated by magenta arrows). In southern-hemisphere crayfishes the sexes are most easily distinguished by the sexual openings, present only in females, on the third pair of peraeopods (*right*, indicated by yellow arrows). The gonopods of the males are small and inconspicuous.

body, while in males it is narrow and triangular. The genital openings are sometimes situated at the base of the third pair of legs in females, but further back in males, at the base of the fifth pair. In many crabs the genital openings of females are to be found on the third segment of the sternum.

The pleopods of male Brachyura and river crayfishes form the gonopods, by means of which the sperm packets are transferred onto or into the genital openings of females. Essentially, in male crabs all the other pairs of pleopods are atrophied. In females each pair of pleopods is developed and covered with copious bristles. Females also have glands which are used to attach the eggs to the pleopods - they carry the fertilised eggs and even the newly-hatched larvae or young around on their pleopods.

During copulation in crabs, the tips of the anterior gonopods are inserted into the female genital openings. To this end, both partners bend their pleon down and the female is usually turned onto her back. After the gonopods have been inserted, sperm masses are pumped into the female's genital openings. This may take some hours during which the crabs seem to be totally immune to disturbance. Many marine species are able to copulate only when the female has recently moulted and her shell is soft, as, once the shell has hardened, a kind of chalky grating blocks the genital opening. In crabs the eggs are fertilised in the genital ducts of the females.

Female

Male

Preserved Thailand Crabs (*Demanietta sirikit*) with pleon lifted so that the sexual characteristics can be seen.

Sex determination and reproduction, Modes of reproduction

In the Anomura (*Aegla* species and hermit crabs) the sexes are difficult to distinguish on the basis of external characteristics. The males often have larger claws, but this character is unreliable. The sexes can be reliably determined only by their sexual openings (3rd coxa: female, 5th coxa: male). In Aegla species it is also possible to check for the presence of gonopods (in which case the individual is a male), lifting the pleon (carefully!) to do so. In addition, hermit crabs will need to have left their "houses", and they don't do so willingly. Under no circumstances should any attempt be made to extract a hermit crab from its shell, as that would constitute cruelty, plain and simple. For this reason, if the intention is to breed hermit crabs then it is best to purchase several specimens of as different a size as possible (it seems that in terrestrial hermit crabs males grow larger than females) and with different-sized claws.

Macrobrachium female (the same species as on p. 11) with large eggs, an example of the specialised mode of reproduction.
Photo: F. Schäfer

Modes of reproduction

When it comes to the development of their eggs, decapods practise two completely different methods of reproduction. The first, specialised method, sometimes known as direct development, is found in all crayfishes but only some shrimps and crabs: the young become almost fully-formed inside the eggs, which are especially large and yolk-rich, and, after hatching from the eggshell, resemble their parents in all respects and need only to develop their sexual organs. They eat more or less the same food as adults, and, last but not least, are relatively large right from the start and grow fast, so that they have a good chance of surviving their first days of independent life. For all these reasons it is quite easy to breed these decapods under aquarium conditions. The eggs are not very numerous (their number depends on the size and condition of the female and may be up to 300) but rather large. The young crayfishes are tended by their mother, feeding voraciously on all types of foods and growing rapidly.

The second, more basic or primitive type of reproduction, is known as indirect development. This mode of reproduction is found in marine decapods and species that lay their eggs in brackish or salt water, as is the case in many shrimps and crabs. The eggs develop into tiny larvae which have only few body segments and limbs. The most simple larval form is called the nauplius, which has three pairs of limbs and is hardly ever seen in decapods. Almost all decapods instead start life as zoea larvae, which look like primitive shrimps. In the course of a number of moults they develop a greater number of body segments and limbs and change into fully-formed crustaceans. All the larval stages usually have highly specialised environmental requirements that may vary at each successive developmental stage. They often travel enormous distances across a variety of marine regions, before returning as juveniles to rivers or coastal regions. Hence it requires a huge amount of effort to rear them under aquarium conditions aand this is probably not feasible for hobbyists. And Nature allows for considerable losses: females of some species that practice this primitive method of reproduction produce several hundred thousand (!) eggs.

Macrobrachium (long-arm shrimp) female (*M. tenellum*, the Chocó Shrimp) with small eggs, an example of the primitive mode of reproduction.

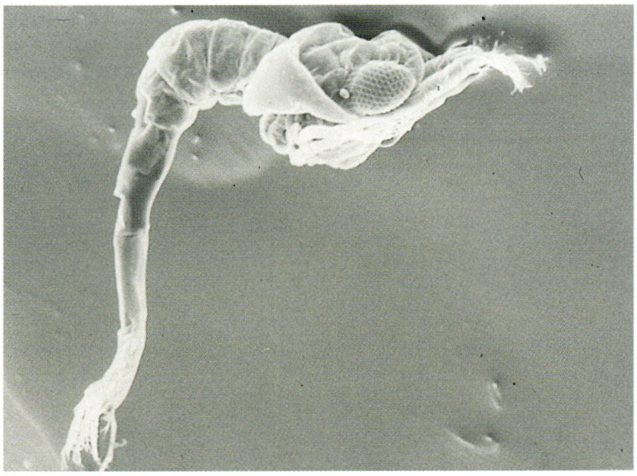
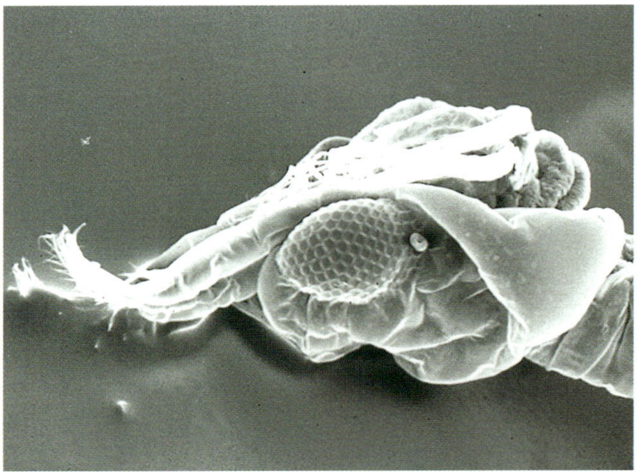
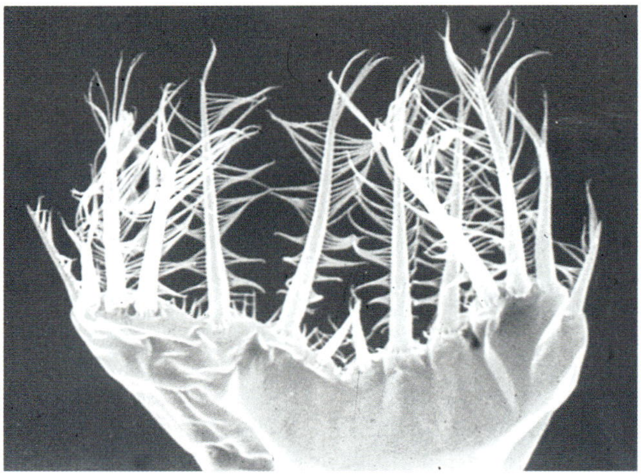
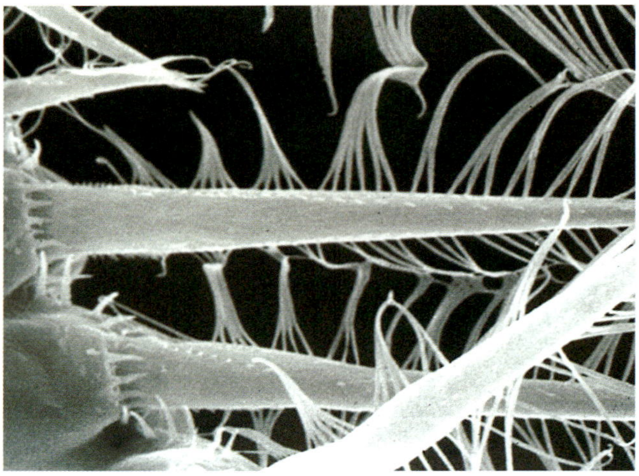

Electron-microscope photos of zoëa larvae of *Macrobrachium tenellum* from Colombia, showing the habitus (the legs are directed forwards), the head with faceted eyes, the tail fan, and details of the latter. Photos: R. Riehl

Zoëa larvae of *Uca ecuadoriensis*, a fiddler crab.

In crabs the final larval stage, following the various zoëa stages, is termed the megalopa stage. Photos: H.-G. Rupp

Sensory organs

Sensory organs

The eyes of decapods are mostly, but not always, located on eye stalks, and are complex or faceted - this can even be seen in photos of zoea larvae taken with an electron microscope - and very efficient. In crabs in particular they are highly developed: in some species there are up to thirty thousand individual eyes (ommatids) on each eye-stalk,

Fiddler crab with facetted eyes on extremely long stalks, no feeding claw and a large "fiddle". Photo: Sch. Nakano

while in others there are "only" seven thousand facets. The poorest sight is found in some crayfish larvae, which depend on a mere twenty sight cells. Crustaceans from deep waters or cave-dwelling species may have atrophied eyes. In such cases the animals orientate principally by their senses of touch and smell.

Crustaceans are able to detect not only different degrees of brightness, but also shapes and colours. Not for nothing are many species so colourful, and their claws strikingly large or intensely coloured. Their field of vision should also be mentioned - it comprises 360 degrees, so they can rely on complete all-round vision. Besides which, they can also detect stationary objects. These abilities give rise to others: some crustaceans, above all certain crabs, are able to find their way using the travel and position of the sun and perhaps also the moon, so that they can undertake long migrations. They can also detect potential dangers from a long way away: a person, for example, can be spotted from a distance of about 19 metres, giving the crab enough time to make its escape.

On the head there are two small and one large pairs of antennae. In shrimps and crayfishes these are particularly conspicuous, growing to about as long as the body, whereas in most crabs they are weakly developed. In addition, in crabs the first pair of antennae can be folded and concealed in special grooves beneath the rostrum, so that they can barely be seen. The first or basal segment of each of the first (smaller) antennae contains an organ of balance (statocyst). This consists of a kind of small bag of skin which is filled with water from outside and in which are embedded so-called statoliths, which are either manufactured by the crustacean or taken in from outside

Crabs can distinguish colours and it is not without reason that they are often very colourful. This land crab, *Cardisoma armatum*, is feeding on a (frozen) fish. The various claws are used to pass food to the mandibles.

(usually grains of sand). When they moult, they lose these as well as the shell, and have to make or take in new ones. The function of these statoliths can be easily explained: as the crustacean leans in any direction, they press against sensory hairs, indicating its orientation to the animal. Crustaceans can also detect rotation by virtue of the inertial mass of the statoliths.

Mouthparts of a Mediterranean land crab of the genus *Potamon*.
Photo: B. Migge

The larger or "second" antennae can be directed not only forwards and to both sides, but also completely backwards. They are used for orientation and enable the crustacean to move safely in any form of reduced light dictated by the time of day (evening, night) or the environment (in caves, under stones). In addition, fine sensory hairs on the mouthparts, claws, peraeopods, and abdomen provide exceptional sensitivity to the slightest tactile stimuli.

The senses of smell and taste depend on numerous tubular cells (aesthetasks) that are located on the first antennae and which are sensitive to substances dissolved in water, and perhaps also to air-borne smells. Further organs of taste are to be found on the ends of the peraeopods, and, of course, on the mouthparts.

Respiration, circulation, digestion

Most crustaceans breathe by means of gills. In shrimps and crayfishes these are clustered or tufted (trichobranchia), consisting of a shaft from which extend numerous small cylindrical appendages. The gills of crabs consist of double rows of close-packed plates (phyllobranchia). The water needed for gas exchange flows in through a number of ventrally-located openings between the edge of the carapace and the leg insertions, flowing out again via forward-opening gill slits in shrimps and crayfishes, while crabs have a wide outlet in the mouth region. Gas exchange takes place via the fine gill membranes. The gill lamellae contain haemolymph which carries oxygen to the organs and gives off CO_2.

The heart is whitish in live individuals and is located in front of the posterior edge of the cephalothorax, contained in a kind of sac, the pericardium. There are no veins, just four slit-like openings that act like valves, opening and closing as the heart expands and contracts. Two large arteries run from the heart, one forwards to the head, the other backwards to supply the pleon. Both are open-ended and the blood is then further distributed via interstices in the tissues until it is eventually sucked back in by the heart (open circulation).

The food is in most cases seized by the claws and passed to the mouthparts. The maxillipeds hold the food, and pieces are then cut off by the hard, powerful mandibles, sometimes with the aid of other mouthparts. These pieces are passed through the mouth opening and then enter the anterior part of the gut, which consists largely of a gigantic gizzard. This contains numerous variably-shaped chitinous teeth that chop up the food and mix it with digestive enzymes. In the rear part of the gizzard complex filter systems remove indigestible components and transport them to the mid-gut, from where they are excreted.

The digestible material is transported into the central gut glands, lateral sac-like appendages behind the gizzard, which extend throughout the anterior body and function much like our liver. It is here that the actual digestion and uptake of substances takes place. The end-products of metabolism are excreted via nephritic ducts which end near the second antennae, i.e. on the head (!). Most of these excreta are urinary compounds such as ammonia, ammonium salts, etc. These substances are also in part excreted via the gills.

This *Macrobrachium tenellum* from Guatemala is loosening fine particles from a food tablet.

Atyids: shrimps of the genus *Caridina* and related species

In the sub-order of long-tailed shrimp-like crustaceans (Natantia) we find two families which are particularly interesting for the aquarist, i.e. the freshwater shrimps (Atyidae) and - from the super-family Palaemonoidea - the Palaemonidae, to which belong, for example the shrimps of the Baltic Sea and the *Macrobrachium* species.

The Atyids represent an, evolutionarily speaking, very old family of shrimps and include mainly freshwater species. A number of them are found in Asia and Africa, others in South America. They have been classified in 15 different genera containing about 160 species. Typical features of some atyids include, according to E. &. U. LEIENDECKER (1982), "a brush-like pilosity of both pairs of claw-bearing legs and a tendency to reduction of the rostrum, expressed to a greater or lesser extent depending on the genus concerned". In other words, the usually delicate claws of these shrimps have been transformed into heavily bristled "hands", and the pointed "nose" is often short. In other Atyids, here termed the *Caridina* group, the claws are only tiny. The genus name *Caridina* is derived from the Greek and means "small crustaceans", while the genus name *Neocaridina* signifies "new *Caridina*".

The members of the *Caridina* group measure from two to four centimetres and are found in tropical Africa, tropical and subtropical parts of Asia, and the islands of the western Pacific. As far as the number of species is concerned, the genus *Caridina* MILNE-EDWARDS, 1839 is one of the largest in the family, with more than 120 species, while at present the most closely related genus, *Neocaridina* KUBO, 1938, contains 9 species (with a total of 10 subspecies. However, of these only two species (and perhaps a third) imported for the aquarium hobby have been positively identified to date. The two genera differ only slightly, specifically in the form of the inner branch (endopodite) of the first pair of pleopods in the male, a character unlikely to be of any relevance to the ordinary aquarist. In *Neocaridina* the endopodite is broad and pear-shaped, while in *Caridina*, on the other hand, it is narrow and leaf-like and tapers towards its end. In addition in both genera there is a small process on the endopodite which is equipped with a number of fine hooks and termed the appendix interna. In *Neocaridina* this process is sited on the part of the endopodite closest to the body (proximal), while in *Caridina* it is on the part of the endopodite furthest from the body (distal) (KLOTZ, 2004). There are other genera of dwarf shrimps - *Sinodina*, *Paracaridina*, and *Halocaridina* - but little is known about them.

Unfortunately only a small number of these dwarf shrimps have as yet been identified, and so the following text uses popular names that have become more or less generally accepted.

These shrimps are invariably completely harmless, quite unable to inflict any damage with their tiny claws. It is, instead, the shrimps that are at risk of falling prey to fishes, and it is not only when they moult and are temporarily soft as butter that they are in danger of being nibbled or devoured completely. Their young are also a welcome snack for fishes - despite being astonishingly quick and nimble they have little chance of growing on in an aquarium populated by fishes, even small fishes. In addition it is the case that when kept with lively, active fishes, for example small characins or poeciliids, these shrimps spend most of their time hiding, so it makes sense to keep them by themselves. The only fishes that make good companions for these mini-shrimps are loricariid catfishes of the genera *Ancistrus* and *Otocinclus*. Even though it is occasionally stated otherwise, small and half-grown *Ancistrus* will not harm these shrimps.

Dwarf shrimps are attractive and completely harmless aquarium inhabitants. This is the "Deep Red" cultivated form of the "Red Cherry", photographed in the tank of U. Waelti.
Photo: F. Schäfer

Ancistrus sp. L144 Photo: F. Schäfer

Atyids: shrimps of the genus *Caridina* and related species

These shrimps are, however, best kept with their own kind. Anyone who doesn't mind taking a little trouble over water changes can keep them in aquaria with a volume of as little as 10 to 20 litres. If there is plenty of fine-leaved vegetation and a vigorous growth of algae (i.e. if the tank is sited in as light a spot as possible) then very little effort will be needed as regards maintenance. Scrupulous cleanliness is not at all advisable, as the shrimps will feed on algae (even tuft and thread algae - it is possible to buy "algae stones" in the trade) as well as plant and animal detritus, and won't really feel at home until a layer of mulm has developed. Foods can include (crumbled) flake, (crushed) food tablets, granules, frozen *Cyclops* and algae. These shrimps particularly like hamster and/or rabbit pellets, probably because they contain a high vegetable component. For the same reason they should also regularly be offered the leaves of deciduous trees such as oak and beech, and this will help avoid moulting problems. Fresh green leaves should not be used, only dry, dead leaves collected in autumn and winter. In addition they can be given scalded lettuce, slices or chunks of cucumber, potato, carrot, capsicum, cauliflower, melon, dandelion, and banana.

It is even possible to do without a filter given regular water changes, though there should be at least a degree of water movement, which can be achieved using an air diffuser. Alternatively a small, air-powered sponge filter can be used, this will not put the young at risk of being sucked in to their doom, but will ensure constantly clear water and also provide the shrimps with an additional food source.

One additional important point: these shrimps are sociable creatures and in the wild live together in densely-populated colonies, and for this reason they shouldn't be kept in ones and twos.

There are no special requirements as regards water parameters, but even so it is important to find out the origin of the shrimps and/or the water parameters they enjoy in the natural habitat. As a general rule of thumb, better results will be obtained for almost all species at slightly acid to neutral pH values (6.5 - 7.2) and a low level of hardness (up to around 8 °dGH) than where they are maintained in hard water with a high pH. The hardness appears to be of less importance than the pH; at least the majority of species can also be kept successfully, and even bred, at a total hardness of up to 20 °dGH and a carbonate hardness of 11 °KH. The maintenance temperature appears to be more important, and, given the natural distribution of these shrimps, should not be too high, especially in the long term. The optimal temperature range appears to lie between 23 and 25 °C, but in the long term the species from subtropical Asia should be kept even cooler (17-20 °C). If the temperature rises too high then some species at least will cease breeding, while others may even die.

Dwarf loricariid catfishes - this is *Otocinclus hasemani* - are excellent companion fishes for dwarf shrimps. Photo: F. Schäfer

Atyids: shrimps of the genus *Caridina* and related species

However, short-term, not too extreme temperature fluctuations are well tolerated by the majority of species. And slight temperature fluctuations, as part of the day-night cycle, may even encourage willingness to breed.

Always bear in mind the fact that all shrimps are sensitive to all metal compounds and will react badly to the least trace of copper. For this reason water that has stood for any length of time in copper piping should be avoided, as should medications containing copper. Note too that other, fairly regular pollutants of the aquarium water (for example nitrogen and phosphorus compounds) are less well tolerated by shrimps than by fishes. Regular water maintenance, which is synonymous with regular partial water changes (avoiding excessive variation in water parameters), is thus essential if the shrimps are to be kept healthy and perhaps bred. However, the feeding of hamster or rabbit pellets containing lucerne, hay, and/or cereals, which contain traces of copper (regardless of what it says on the packet), is also essential. A certain amount of this metal is required by the shrimps for the synthesis of their blood pigment, haemocyanin (cf. KLOTZ, 2006).

Occasionally unwanted "tenants" may turn up in the shrimp aquarium, apparently predating on the young shrimps so that the originally numerous brood noticeably declines in numbers. These unwelcome visitors are aquatic mites, small round to oval creatures measuring around 1 mm and able to move through the water with astonishing speed. By preference they like to rest on the plants and feed on rotting plant material, but they also lurk in the corners of the aquarium or sit quietly on this or that object. If the water is agitated then some of them often trap a little air beneath their hard armour so that they float at the surface and take some time to manage to return to the open water below. Their reproductive rate is extraordinarily high and they proliferate rapidly. It is an unending and laborious task to remove them from the shrimp aquarium. It is possible to siphon them out through a small-diameter tube with some success, without endangering the baby shrimps, as the latter are strong enough to withstand the slight suction and as a rule are not sucked in as well. But even when you think you have removed all these aquatic mites - which actually ought to be possible in an aquarium with a bare glass bottom if the plants and other décor objects are replaced with others - then within a week the first individuals of a new plague put in an appearance. Hence if the rearing of young shrimps is desired, it is perhaps a better idea to transfer a few adult shrimps to a new breeding set-up, and clear out the old aquarium at your leisure.

Most of the *Caridina* species that are offered for aquarium maintenance practice the specialised mode of reproduction - which means that they produce relatively large eggs from which hatch fully-formed young shrimps.

Caridina shrimp female (a bee shrimp) with her large eggs, an example of the specialised mode of reproduction.

Atyids: shrimps of the genus *Caridina* and related species

As a rule they can be bred without problem - and, in fact, not only at high temperatures (up to 27 °C), but also in cooler water (18 to 21 °C). Females, which have a special "brood chamber" for their eggs on the abdomen, can be recognised by their stockier, deeper bodies, while males are more slender and have longer swimmerets.

The eggs are round, ranging from 20 to 30 in number, and can be seen through the carapace when the light is from behind. They develop over a period of 28 to 33 days, eventually hatching into not larvae but well-developed young shrimps that have already gone through all the larval stages in the egg, so that it is easy to raise them. Moreover they don't need any special feeding if they are kept in an "old", well-planted aquarium with a dense growth of algae. However, the aquarium filter can be rinsed in aquarium water and a small amount of the "ooze" released put back into the aquarium. The tiny shrimps will greedily fall upon the particulate organic material and the micro-organisms it contains. An added benefit is that the adults do not eat their young. The latter attain sexual maturity within 3 to 6 months.

The best-known shrimp in the *Caridina* group is the attractively coloured "Zebra Shrimp" or "Bee Shrimp" which is generally known as *Caridina* "serrata" and whose coloration is highly variable. It is imported from Hong Kong - as are a number of other freshwater shrimps - and hence the correct name of the species

Male of the species formerly known as the Bee Shrimp, but now usually known as the Coloured Shrimp because it is more boldly coloured than the Bee Shrimp.

may be something quite different. Most probably it is a local form or subspecies of *C. cantonensis Yu*, 1938 - the specific name relates to its origins. According to a recent revision of the genus there is, in fact, a so-called "*serrata*-group" of closely related, morphologically similar species, which includes *C. cantonensis*, *C. sphyrapoda*, *C. nanoensis*, *C. apodosis*, *C. yulinica*, *C. wumingensis*, and *C. mutata*, as well as *C. serrata*. Also very similar is a recently described species named *Caridina trifasciata* Yam & Cai, 2003 (= three-striped *Caridina*). Nearly all of them are known from limited distributions, live mainly in running water and avoid brackish water. The water for their maintenance should be rather soft and slightly acid (pH 6.8).

The Bee Shrimp, presented as *Caridina* sp. III in the previous edition of this book, is a sturdily built little shrimp with a short rostrum, in which males measure around 25, females about 35 mm total length. Only the tail fan is slightly orange, otherwise there is no orange or yellow colour present. There are white bands or blotches on the posterior part of the brown back, but - unlike in the Bumblebee Shrimp - these are not very clearly separated from one another. There is no dorsal stripe. The females are larger than the males and more compact in build, plus the abdomen is much down-curved. In egg-carrying females the coloration becomes intensified, and otherwise transparent areas then become white.

Since 1996 bright red-and-white colour variants, selectively bred in Japan, have been sold as *Caridina* sp. "Crystal Red". These are mutants derived from the Bee Shrimp, and hence are merely selectively-bred colour forms of that species. According to Bitter (2006) the Japanese Suzuki discovered odd red-and-white coloured specimens among normally coloured Bee Shrimps and used these as the parent stock to create pure-strain populations of his "Crystal Red Bee Shrimp". Yamagishi subsequently in-crossed black-and-white striped Bee Shrimps (see below) and in one instance produced live, fertile offspring, now known as the Red Bee Shrimp. In Japan there are classification standards for these shrimps, established by Pisces Publishers. The highest class contains the practically pure white shrimps known in Japan as Mosura, with the additional epithet of Brilliant if the head is intense white. Even more coveted are individuals with a double Hinomaru spot resembling a one-way street sign. These too are included in the highest class, followed by specimens with a Hinomaru spot at the front and an ordinary spot behind it; then, again a class lower, "multi-band" and "three-band" shrimps, whose quality is determined by how clearly the bands are defined.

Atyids: shrimps of the genus *Caridina* and related species

The breeding of the Crystal Red has become a hobby within the hobby. Photos: Aqua Magazine, Taiwan

Atyids: shrimps of the genus *Caridina* and related species

The Crystal Red can be bred for colour or markings.

Photos: Aqua Magazine, Taiwan

Atyids: shrimps of the genus *Caridina* and related species

It is possible to pay a small fortune for some cultivars of the Crystal Red, though there are frequent changes in what constitutes the "latest rage".
Photos: Aqua Magazine, Taiwan

Atyids: shrimps of the genus *Caridina* and related species

There are, however, other unclassified forms, in which, for example, the red is so dominant that there are only narrow white bands and no spots on the body, and others in which the white bands are particularly broad and solid in their colour. In addition there is a form in which the red coloration is replaced by a clear, warm brown.

All the forms mentioned grow to only around 2.5 cm long, at least in the case of males (females grow slightly larger) and either don't occur in the wild at all, or only rarely and then only as single specimens.

Their young are not all the same colour as the coloration is recessive. Thus selective breeding is required to retain the brilliant colours! Moreover, they should be fed "colour foods" containing carotene. These shrimps are far less productive than other species and they cease breeding at all at temperatures in excess of 25 °C. On the other hand they will temporarily tolerate low temperatures (around 10 °C), apparently without any ill effects.

Crystal Red from a strain with a lot of red.

According to KARGE (in: KLOTZ & KARGE, 2005), a completely white form purportedly selected for breeding in 1983 produced light blue (!) eggs and white offspring. Even when she was kept together with wild-coloured Bee Shrimps there were purportedly no wild-coloured young among the offspring of this white mother! Breeding white forms presents problems, however, as egg-carrying females often drop their eggs for no apparent reason or the larvae die. In addition, these shrimps appear to undergo morphological change. Under the microscope it can be seen that white Bee Shrimps still have a typical "bee rostrum", but the short stylocerite (a spiny process on the first basal segment of the second pair of antennae), which constitutes a distinctive character of the *serrata* group, is noticeably longer. Occasionally additional dwarf shrimps are imported which belong to the genera *Caridina* and *Neocaridina*. In the following list the relationship to the Bee Shrimp becomes progressively less close from beginning to end.

Caridina cf. *breviata* NG & CAI, 2000 (termed *Caridina* sp. IV in previous editions of this book) is in fact similar to the Bee Shrimp, but shorter and more stockily built - the Latin specific name means "shortened" - and with a total length of 20 mm in males and around 25 mm in females is also somewhat smaller. It doesn't normally exhibit any white spots, though egg-bearing females, which re generally more intensely coloured, may temporarily exhibit white spots. The three clearly delineated bands on the body, the first of which can sometimes merge dorsally with a spot in the eye region, are red-brown to dark brown, and the spaces between light and transparent. There are no yellow or orange areas.

Bumblebee Shrimp, *Caridina cf. breviata.*

Because of its coloration German-speaking aquarists call this shrimp the Bumblebee Shrimp, but this popular name is not in general use in English-speaking countries, where the *Caridina* group of banded shrimps are known collectively as bee shrimps, and, depending on their appearance, termed "Bee Shrimp X" where X is the classification number for the particular variant.

If the Bumblebee Shrimp is viewed under the microscope, the high degree of variation in the dentition of the rostrum is noticeable. There are specimens with a short rostrum with no serrae (saw-like teeth) at all and individuals with up to 14 serrae on the upper surface and up to two on the underside. In addition, in some Bumblebee Shrimps the stylocerite (the spiny process on the first basal segment of the second pair of antennae) is unusually long, extending to the end of the first basal segment of the antennae. If various strains are examined then it becomes apparent that the name Bumblebee Shrimp actually covers two different species, with the individuals with a long stylocerite and weak rostral dentition probably belonging to the southern Chinese species *Caridina breviata* (cf. KLOTZ in: KARGE & KLOTZ, 2005).

The Back-Stripe Shrimp (termed *Caridina* sp. I in previous editions and also known as the Colourful-Tail Shrimp) is probably *Caridina fernandoi* ARUDPRAGASAM & COSTA, 1962 (Fernando's Back-Stripe Shrimp). The specific name is an honorific. The species is endemic to Sri Lanka, where it lives in the lowlands and, along with the sympatric and syntopic (in the same water) *Caridina simoni*, is one of the most widespread species found there. It grows to barely 2 cm long and is distinguished morphologically from the Bee Shrimp by virtue of having a long rostrum covered in fine bristles, a stouter body (the cephalothorax and the abdomen are more powerfully built so that these shrimps look stockier), and the (rather variable) coloration: the armour is brown to black, with the underside of the body lighter than the dorsum. Specimens with a greenish base coloration are known from the area around Seelagama. In addition these shrimps can supposedly match their coloration to that of the substrate. All forms virtually invariably exhibit a longitudinal band on the dorsum; this may be more or less prominent depending on mood, and is light yellow in gravid females. By contrast, juveniles and males are more transparent (cf. KARGE in: KARGE & KLOTZ, 2004).

Back-Stripe Shrimp, *Caridina fernandoi*.

The Tiger Shrimp or Black Tiger Shrimp (termed *Caridina* sp. V in previous editions) is slightly more elongate than the species mentioned thus far and can also be distinguished from the Bee Shrimp by the quite different form of one of the male sexual characters, the endopod. These shrimps are easily recognisable by the yellowish-transparent body adorned with five narrow but prominent brown diagonal stripes, especially on the posterior part. Two of these stripes run forwards, three backwards. In addition there is a dark spot at the base of the tail. This species too has an orange-tinged tail fan. While even large males measure only around 25 mm, females may attain a total length of almost 35 mm. This also has an effect on their productivity: females can release 50 young shrimps every six weeks!

Tiger Shrimp, *Caridina* sp.

This species frequently and regularly undergoes mutations as regards its coloration. Some individuals have a fairly vivid yellow base coloration, but bluish or even intense blue specimens regularly occur, especially among juveniles. These have been selectively bred to produce more or less pure strains. Thus as well as the "black" form there is also a Blue Tiger Shrimp, which is

Tiger Shrimps can be rather variable.

Atyids: shrimps of the genus *Caridina* and related species

Blue Tiger Shrimps are very popular.

essentially patterned in the same way as the normal form; in other words it too has a striped body but with a dark blue base colour. A further remarkable feature of this form is its pink or yellow eyes, which create an attractive contrast with the blue colour of the armour.

The Spotted Shrimp (also termed *Caridina* sp. II in previous editions) may likewise be a mutated form of the Tiger Shrimp. It is a faint orange brown in colour. The rear parts of the body in particular are adorned with irregularly distributed black spots, perhaps rudiments of the striped pattern seen in the Tiger Shrimp.

Spotted Shrimps are also in fact a "sport" of the Tiger Shrimp.

Red-coloured aquarium occupants are particularly popular with aquarists, and this applies equally to freshwater crustaceans. Hence it is no wonder that one small red dwarf shrimp has experienced a real boom, especially as it is exceptionally easy to breed. It is known as the Red Cherry Dwarf Shrimp or Fire Dwarf Shrimp. The correct scientific name has been kindly supplied, as for other species, by Werner Klotz, to whom we are suitably grateful for his help! It is *Neocaridina denticulata sinensis* (Kemp, 1918); the specific name relates to the rostrum and signifies "toothed", while the subspecific name refers to its origin (China). The name is not restricted to the red form of the species, and in the wild it occurs chiefly as a greyish -brown form, though red individuals do occur, and it is these that have been selectively bred to produce more or less pure strains. All the colour forms have the same typical stripe pattern on the body.

It is reported that small numbers of the red mutation were discovered by somebody collecting fish food in pools in Taiwan. The species originally derived from eastern Asia but has been spread over large parts of China and has even reached Hawaii. In China, where it has become a threat to the native shrimps, it is mainly introduced, while it is thought that the shrimps in Hawaii were intended as food. The endemic (found there and nowhere else) Hawaiian shrimp species *Atyoida bisulcata* Randall, 1840 - the specific name means "with two shields or armours", possibly referring to the armour of the carapace and of the abdomen - also appears to be endangered as a result. In this regard it is important to be aware that the species can survive in temperate climatic zones and populations have allegedly even survived the winter in garden ponds with a surface layer of ice. For this reason care must be taken to avoid these shrimps escaping into our own native waters. It would be absolutely criminal to release them, but it is also important to dispose of waste water and aquatic plants from shrimp aquaria in such a way that no shrimps escape into the wild (cf. Klotz, 2004).

The Red Cherry Dwarf Shrimp" is the most hardy and easy-to-breed of all the species of its group presented here. It tolerates hard water and pH values above neutral, and reacts less negatively to prolonged high and - as already mentioned - low temperatures. It is, nevertheless, best maintained at around 23 to 25 °C. In the summer it can even be kept in the garden pond - always provided it cannot escape into other waters - and this supposedly results in deep red coloration in the females.

It is probable that the light of the sun has a beneficial effect, either directly or indirectly (ie via the food) on the coloration.

Atyids: shrimps of the genus *Caridina* and related species

The Red Cherry Dwarf Shrimp (*Neocaridina denticulata sinensis*) is one of the most popular and easy-to-keep shrimps.

Almost all the stocks available in Europe originate from Taiwan, but they are also bred in Germany and other European countries. It is sometimes stated that the shrimps are not, do not become, or do not remain the promised red, but as long as the colourless wild form isn't in-crossed the shrimps do remain red and also pass on their coloration to their offspring. It is, however, important to realise that the red is a fatty pigment that is stored in the cells of the body and needs to be externally supplemented via the food. The necessary red pigments (carotenoids) can be provided via carrots, sweet red peppers, or *Cyclops*, as well as by various types of flake and granular food enriched with carotenoids. This food is not normally harmful. Certain types of carotene are even converted into vitamin A by the organism. Nevertheless, it is normally sufficient to provide a varied diet of frozen food and vegetables in order for the requisite amounts of carotenoids to be taken up. If, despite appropriate feeding, these dwarf shrimps exhibit no red coloration, then the environmental conditions must be incorrect. Note, however, that only females become bright red, while males exhibit only a pale red coloration. This is no bad thing as it makes it very easy to distinguish the sexes in these little shrimps, where females attain only 25 mm.

This species too belongs to the specialised reproductive type. At around 25 °C the 20 to 40 eggs, approximately 1 mm across, hatch after around four weeks into fully-formed young shrimps, which look just like their parents but, at barely 2 mm total length, are of course much smaller. The adults do not predate on their young, and in a long-established aquarium with mulm on the bottom, Java moss and algae, the latter will find adequate food to grow on to sexual maturity within three months. Unlike in other species the eggs are not dark but light (yellowish), or greenish in a second population (?). They are produced in the neck of the female, where they show through as a light spot. Once the yellowish eggs are being carried beneath the abdomen the spot in the neck disappears.

There are other dwarf shrimps with different striking coloration recommended for maintenance in the aquarium. The first of these is *Neocaridina* cf. *zhangjiajiensis* CAI, 1996 - previously C. sp. "White Pearl", the White Pearl Dwarf Shrimp, or the White Egg Dwarf Shrimp, again apparently a mutation of a differently coloured (in this case brownish) species. The scientific specific name relates to the provenance of the type material. Originally the form was thought to be a colourless, but not albino, mutation of *Neocaridina denticulata*, to which the Red Cherry is also assigned. However, KLOTZ has established that the male sex organs can be clearly distinguished from those of *N. denticulata* by the form of the endopods; specifically the endopods of the first pair of pleopods possess a stout,

Atyids: shrimps of the genus *Caridina* and related species

The White Pearl Shrimp, *Neocaridina cf. zhangjiajiensis.*

keel-like appendage, and this means that this must be a distinct species closely related to *Neocaridina zhangjiajiensis* or perhaps that species itself. *N. zhangjiajiensis* was described from a body of water near the city of Dayong in central China (cf. KLOTZ in: KARGE & KLOTZ, 2004/2005).

The White Pearl Shrimp grows to 20 mm (male) or 25 mm (female) long and has black eyes. The body is invariably transparent, often glass-clear, but sometimes also milky white. In addition there is a whitish streak on the back, often barely apparent. Now and then individuals of a shimmering light bluish colour occur among broods of young. A striking feature - and the reason for the popular names - is the snow-white eggs, which are carried in the neck of the female and can be clearly seen through her as armour as a compact white spot. In addition the newly-hatched, not yet fully developed embryos are whitish, but exhibit the black eyes at an early stage.

The White Pearl Dwarf Shrimp tolerates hard water (up to 25 °dGH) and a pH up to at least 7.5 without problem and can be kept and bred at temperatures between 20 and 28 °C. It can be regarded as hardy and undemanding, easy to keep and breed. In addition, it is not at all timid, rarely hides, and hence is almost constantly on view. It is possible to achieve 40 juveniles every four to six weeks. Hence it is no surprise that these shrimps are particularly recommended for aquarists who have not yet accumulated any experience with dwarf shrimps.

Another strikingly coloured shrimp, this time from India, deserves to be covered in detail here, namely the Green Dwarf Shrimp, which, again following W. KLOTZ, is better termed *Caridina cf. babaulti*. KLOTZ has discovered that the material used for the original description of *C. babaulti* BOUVIER, 1918 - the specific name is an honorific. probably includes specimens of two very similar species, which can, however, be differentiated by the size of their eggs. In addition, the Green Dwarf Shrimps available in the hobby differ from BOUVIER'S specimens, and also from the type material of a subspecies from Iraq named *C. babaulti basrensis* (after the town of Basra, the type locality), by the number of spines on the fold of the tail fan and the number of spines on the terminal limb (dactylus) of the fifth pair of peraeopods, so that it is probably a further, as yet undescribed, subspecies. KLOTZ therefore suggests for the time being using the name with the addition of cf. (cf.=compare) (cf. KLOTZ in: KARGE & KLOTZ, 2004).

The Green Dwarf Shrimp, *Caridina cf. babaulti.*

The exact provenance of the aquarium-hobby specimens is unknown. In the wild the species is widely distributed from Burma (Myanmar) across the Indian subcontinent to Iraq. There is also a form of this species living in the water-supply system in Karachi in Pakistan!

Initially dealers and aquarists used the designation Caridina ceylanica for the Green Dwarf Shrimp. The name ceylanica means "from Ceylon" and was based on the assumption that they originated from Ceylon (nowadays Sri Lanka). But there isn't actually any species of this name at all! There is, however, a very similar-sounding Latin name with the same meaning - *Caridina zeylanica* ARUDPRAGASAM & COSTA, 1962 - and that species does actually occur in Sri Lanka. But it has a rostrum that extends far beyond the tip of the base of the antennae, while in *C.* cf. *babaulti* the rostrum extends only to the third segment and not noticeably past the base. In addition, *C. zeylanica* is found exclusively in brackish-water areas in Sri Lanka and females carry a large number of small eggs, indicating that the young must undergo a planktonic brackish-water stage such as is familiar from the Amano Shrimp. Reproduction in completely fresh water thus seems highly unlikely.

Atyids: shrimps of the genus *Caridina* and related species

A characteristic feature of *Caridina* cf. *babaulti* is the very long rostrum, as well as a dorsal stripe with no cross-banding. Compared to the species discussed previously, this shrimp is also more elongate in form, with this applying chiefly to males, as females as usual appear somewhat plumper on account of the brood chamber for the eggs. The species also grows comparatively large: males supposedly can attain 35 mm in total length, and females even as much as 40 mm! When it comes to breeding this species represents a special case. Specifically, on the one hand it produces up to 60 relatively large eggs, but doesn't give birth to fully developed young shrimps, instead releasing larvae that develop into juvenile shrimps via six different planktonic larval stages. But because all this takes place in fresh water, the species is relatively easy to breed in fresh water (cf. Klotz in: Karge & Klotz, 2004).

Because of their brilliant, even somewhat artificial-looking light green coloration, these shrimps have created quite a furore, but the light green base colour is far from a constant characteristic. Depending on mood the colour can also tend strongly towards brown, blue, transparent, or orange. Purportedly even blue-green to ink-blue individuals sometimes occur. These shrimps are said to be able to change colour rapidly, and they appear to match themselves to their surroundings and exhibit bolder colours against a darker background.

This species too is extremely tolerant as regards water parameters: it tolerates hard alkaline water just as well as the "Red Cherry" and also withstands higher temperatures better than the dwarf shrimps most closely related to the bee shrimp. It is, however, advisable to keep them in heavily vegetated tanks with very bright lighting, where they will normally also breed readily.

Not to be confused with the Black *Caridina*: the Black Tiger Shrimp, a cultivated form of the Tiger Shrimp, discussed in detail on pp. 25-26.
Photo: K. A. Quante

Occasionally another form, very closely related to this species, is sold as the Black *Caridina*. It has fine longitudinal banding on the body, but has never become truly black in my aquaria, instead mainly brownish, sometimes even reddish with light dorsal stripes visible. Individual specimens exhibit randomly sited dark spots on the body.

The species sometimes sold as the Black *Caridina* is a close relative of the Green Dwarf Shrimp, but despite its name it is often reddish in colour.

The Amano Shrimp, also known in the hobby as *Caridina japonica*, is also sold as the Algae Shrimp, the Yamamoto Shrimp, or the Japanese Shrimp. We will have to get used to a change in its scientific name: as recently as 2006 it turned out that *C. japonica* is a junior synonym of *Caridina multidentata* Stimpson, 1860. The specific name means "many-toothed" and refers to the high number of serrae on the rostrum. Even though the Amano Shrimp is not very colourful, it has become quite popular

The Amano Shrimp - this is a female - can be recognised by the characteristic spots and lines. Photo: Sch. Nakano

because it is an algae-eater par excellence. It eats even tough and firmly attached algae, and also feeds on plant detritus. It is imported from Japan and has a transparent or milky body, adorned with small brownish spots arranged in rows. Females are deeper-bodied and larger - they grow to about 6 cm - and are easily recognised by the distinctive brood chamber on the abdomen.

These shrimps are very tolerant as regards water temperature (which may range from 20 to 28°C), hardness, and pH, but, unlike the species discussed earlier, they prefer harder alkaline water. Use of medications always poses a risk. If conditions are to their liking they often swim in the open water.

The Amano Shrimp practices the primitive mode of reproduction. The incubation time for its up to 2000 eggs is about six weeks at a temperature range of 23 to 27 °C and a pH of between 5.8 and 8.0. The larvae subsequently released measure no more than 1 to 1.5 mm and should be transferred to brackish water with a salt content of 1.6 % and fed the tiniest of foods (Liquifry, Micromin, Protogen-Granulat, or the like). In the course of four weeks and several moults and stages, the larvae develop into young shrimps that can be slowly acclimated to fresh water.

There is another as yet unidentified species that is very similar in appearance but lacks spots. In addition the dentition of the rostrum is completely different. These shrimps, termed *Caridina* sp. cf. *japonica* in the previous

Caridina sp. *cf. multidentata* (? *C. sumatrensis*) is largely uniformly coloured. The upper photo shows a female, the lower a male.

edition of this book, probably belong to the *Caridina weberi* species assemblage. However they are not in fact *C. weberi* De Man, 1892 (the specific name is an honorific) sensu stricto (ie the species itself) as a number of the serrae on the rostrum are situated posterior to the margin of the eye and this is not the case in *C. weberi*. Perhaps they are instead *Caridina sumatrensis* De Man, 1892, from Malaysia. The specific name in this case refers to the origin of the type material. This species too produces numerous small grey-green eggs.

There are at least two species of unusual form known as Rhinoceros Shrimps, characterised by an elongate body and a particularly long and pointed rostrum that extends past the base of the antennae. The first to become known was the Red Rhinoceros Shrimp, which has now been identified as *Caridina gracilirostris* De Man, 1892 (in the previous edition of this book it was listed as *C. serratirostris*). The Latin specific name means "with a slender rostrum". The species belongs to the *Caridina nilotica* species group. The body is mainly transparent as glass, with only the rostrum, the telson, and the underside of the abdomen coloured red. In addition there are fine red cross-bands running across the dorsum.

This species inhabits large parts of the Indo-Pacific region and is distributed across Madagascar and India, Sri Lanka and south-east Asia to Australia. It occurs in brackish coastal lagoons and river estuaries where the water has very little or no current. Like *C. multidentata* the species produces countless small grey-green eggs that hatch into tiny larvae whose first developmental stages apparently take place in brackish water or the sea. As yet there are no reports known of successful breeding in the aquarium (cf. Klotz, 2004).

A second "primitive" species, sold as the Yellow Rhinoceros Shrimp, has the scientific name *Xiphocaris elongata*. The genus name is part Greek, part Latin in its derivation, and signifies "with a sword-like keel", while the Latin specific name means "elongate". *Hyppolyte elongata* and *Oplophorus americana* are synonyms. At first glance it looks very similar to the Red Rhinoceros Shrimp, but when it is examined under the microscope distinct differences are apparent in the form of the rostrum, tail, and limbs. For this reason the species occupies a special position in the family Atyidae, and perhaps should even be removed from that family and placed in a separate family - the Xiphocaridae - of its own.

The up to 5 cm long species is native to the islands of the Greater and Lesser Antilles in the Caribbean region, where adult specimens are encountered in small groups in open water in the immediate vicinity of the banks of

Atyids: shrimps of the genus *Caridina* and related species

The Red Rhinoceros Shrimp, *Caridina gracilirostris*, is regularly imported from India. The photo shows an egg-carrying female. The body in this species is transparent; the attractive blue coloration in the photo derives from the camera flash. Photo: F. Schäfer

The yellow Rhinoceros Shrimp, *Xiphocaris elongata*, which comes from South America, looks almost identical. The individual in the photo originated from Brazil. Photo: F. Schäfer

rivers. It is thus a swimming shrimp which isn't restricted to the substrate but usually swims in the open water. The females release their larvae to drift away in the natural current. They can survive only in the sea or in brackish water, and after passing through various developmental stages eventually migrate back into fresh water. Young individuals are often found in brackish water, no doubt on their way back. While breeding in the aquarium thus appears unlikely, at least given current techniques, the adult specimens imported have proved extremely decorative, lively, confident, and hardy. They have no special demands as regards water chemistry and also tolerate high temperatures without problem. Water parameters have been recorded for a biotope in the Dominican Republic, where the species occurs in the upper course of the Rio Yassica at 30 to 31 °C, a pH of around 8, and a conductivity of 355-451 (cf. KLOTZ in: KARGE & KLOTZ, 2004/2005).

Caridina seems to be a genus of "old" species, from which the *Atya* split off at a later date. Hence it is no surprise that there are intermediate forms which have the scientists scratching their heads. For example, there are a number of species in which the claws take a variety of forms within one and the same species: specifically, on the one hand they may have long feathery bristles that can be spread out to capture planktonic food, and on the other claws with short bristles for browsing food attached to a solid substrate. For a while they were assigned to the genus *Ortmannia* but the latter is now included in *Caridina*.

One of these species, which probably won't remain in the genus *Caridina* in the long term, is named *Caridina atyoides*. Its specific name relates to its being a member of the Atyidae. The species lives in the mountain regions of Bali and, because of its relatively large size and its body

Atyids: shrimps of the genus *Caridina* and related species

Caridina atyoides may not be very colourful, but systematically it is a very interesting species. Photo: C. Lukhaup

form, at first glance appears to belong in the genus *Atya*. However, closer study of the peraeopods and the claws (cf. KLOTZ, 2004) has revealed that it accords better with the genus *Caridina*, as currently defined, unless a new genus were to be erected especially for it. To date the species has probably been imported only once - brought back privately - from the mountain regions of Bali. At least one specimen lived for almost 10 years in the aquarium.

"Small" Atyids are also found in the European region: *Atyaephyra desmarestii* (MILLET, 1832) - the genus name signifies "with an *Atya*-like form", the specific name is an honorific - is a shrimp that was originally found in fresh and brackish waters in southern Europe and northern Africa, but in 1909 appeared for the first time in the Dortmund-Ems Canal and has subsequently shown up in the in the Rhine, the Mittelland Canal, the rivers Leine (near Hannover), Havel (near Berlin), and Lippe (and in the Lippe Canal). It has even been reported from the Netherlands and Belgium. Its preference for canals has led to its being commonly referred to as the Canal Shrimp. The species is usually translucent, but brown or blue shades are possible and it is able to change its colour just as other species do. Females of this "mini-shrimp" grow to 35 mm long, a good centimetre longer than males. The species seems to live no longer than a year and a half and should be kept in cold water, even though it tolerates temperatures up to 25 °C for a short time. They will eat algae and small aquatic organisms, and also flake food. In the wild, females carry up to 1500 eggs from the beginning of April until the end of August. Juveniles of about 6 mm can be found from June onwards, and attain about 2 cm by the end of the year.

Atyaephyra desmarestii is also known as the Canal Shrimp.

Atyids: fan shrimps

The family Atyidae also includes the so-called fan shrimps or radar shrimps, in which the fingers of the claws are transformed into bristled "hands". In these shrimps both the anterior and the posterior finger of each claw are set with fine bristles forming a semicircular fan, and when the bristles of both claws are used in combination they create a circular food-collecting apparatus which when open resembles a radar dish, but which can also be folded shut. In the aquarium these shrimps can be observed extending their bristled hands to capture anything edible or to grip food - as in a closed hand - while passing it to the mouth.

From this it can be deduced that these species originate from fast-flowing, or at least moving water, where as a rule they will not need to hunt for food but simply find a suitable elevated spot where they can extend their hands in front of and above themselves like parabolic antennae, in order to capture fine particles of plankton.

In the aquarium, of course, you will be able to observe this behaviour only if the filter return produces a suitably strong current. Otherwise the shrimps will search for food on the bottom, falling on any edible material and grasping it with their hands. They will not take large morsels, so it is best to feed *Artemia* nauplii, pond plankton, and fine flake food. They will eagerly feed on food tablets that slowly disintegrate into tiny pieces when softened by the water.

Micratya poeyi, blue variant. Photo: C. Lukhaup

To date only two small species of these fan or radar shrimps are known that correspond in size to the majority of the *Caridina* species. The first of these is *Micratya poeyi* (GUÉRIN-MÉNEVILLE, 1855), which is distributed on the Caribbean islands as well as in Costa

Atya gabonensis with outstretched fans.

Rica and Panama and has been brought back privately from Cuba. It attains a body length of only 20 mm. The genus name signifies "small *Atya*", while the specific name is an honorific. It was originally described as an *Atya*, but in 1913 BOUVIER assigned it to a specially erected a genus of its own, which to date remains monotypic, i.e.

Micratya poeyi, brown variant Photo: C. Lukhaup

it is represented by just this one species. In the wild it can be found on the bottom among dead leaves and stones in faster-flowing watercourses, while in more slowly-flowing water it frequents plant roots in the bank region. In both cases the species uses its outspread collecting-fans to filter fine plankton from the water. Interestingly, these shrimps can exhibit three different colour patterns: there are individuals with yellowish or bluish-white cross-bands on an orange-brown background; others with a light dorsal stripe; and yet others that are uniform reddish to dark brown in colour. Unfortunately the species belongs to the primitive reproductive type, which means that it cannot be bred in completely fresh water in the aquarium (cf. KARGE in: KARGE & KLOTZ, 2004).

Potimirim potimirim Photo: C. Lukhaup

A further dwarf fan shrimp with very slender anterior pairs of legs originates from Brazil and, along with four other New World shrimps, belongs to the genus *Potimirim* HOLTHUIS, 1954. The genus and specific names are the same, so that it is termed *Potimirim potimirim* (MÜLLER, 1881). It is whitish in colour and, with a body length of only 16 to 17 mm is even smaller than the previous species. Like the latter it belongs to the primitive reproductive type. Its larvae drift away into brackish water where they develop further and eventually migrate back into flowing fresh water. When maintained in the aquarium shrimps of this species will seek for food on the bottom or any algae-covered surface, just like *Caridina*. It is as yet unclear whether this is natural behaviour or indicative that the current in the aquarium is inadequate to trigger plankton capture with the outspread fans (cf. KLOTZ in: KARGE & KLOTZ, 2005).

The members of the genus *Atyopsis* are significantly larger. The genus name means "like *Atya* in appearance" and the taxon belongs to the Eucyphidea genus group. One species, *Atyopsis moluccensis* - the specific name refers to its distribution in the Moluccas - is regularly imported for aquarium maintenance. *A. moluccensis* (DE HAAN, 1849) grows to at least 6 cm long in females, around 8 cm in males or even larger. It has been variously described as *A. gustavi*, *A. armata*, and *A. dentirostris* and confused with the almost identically-coloured shrimp *A. spinipes* (whose specific name means "bristle-foot"). However, *A. moluccensis* possesses a slender rostrum with 7-16 serrae, while *A. spinipes*, by contrast, has a short rostrum with 2-6 such "teeth". In other respects the two species are indistinguishable from one another as they are identical in form and coloration. Importations almost always consist of a mixture of both species!

Atyopsis moluccensis

That apart, *A. moluccensis* is reputedly found not only in the Moluccas, but also on many islands in south-east Asia as well as on the mainland. It remains unclear whether differently coloured but anatomically identical individuals are simply colour variants or local forms, or should be regarded as distinct species.

An aberrantly patterned *Atyopsis*. Is this a colour variant of *A. moluccensis* or a separate species?

Atyopsis moluccensis is in great demand on account of its coloration, but it is not so much the colour itself as the ability to change colour that is the attraction. Young specimens always have a light dorsal band running from the rostrum to the beautiful fan-like tail. Despite reports to the contrary, this band does not disappear in older specimens, though it may become less prominent in time. In addition these shrimps can change their colour in minutes, apparently randomly, but perhaps depending on mood or in response to light levels or their surroundings. Sometimes they are marbled yellowish-brown, more often intense dark brown and sometimes even brown-red or red. Perhaps some observant aquarist who keeps records will be able to

Atyids: fan shrimps

In *Atyopsis moluccensis* the male grows significantly larger than the female. The photo shows a pair.

This *A. moluccensis* is using its fan-like "hands" to search the bottom for food.

make some kind of sense of this chamaeleon-like behaviour...

It must be said that these shrimps are not exactly elegant creatures. The general impression is, on the contrary, that the high, heavy shell is quite a burden, and follows the slow movements of the legs only with difficulty and sometimes jerkily. Their appearance of clumsiness is also due to the short rostrum, which is significantly shorter than that of the Palaemonids (which will be discussed later), and to the fact that the head and the body are not separate, but, so to speak, melded into one another. The impression that there is not much life in these animals is reinforced by the small eyes, which are located close to the head and not on long eye-stalks as in other shrimps.

In male fan shrimps - this is *Atyopsis moluccensis* - the first pair of peraeopods (i.e. the pair immediately behind the clawed arms) are thickened.

Atyopsis moluccensis, a female with a vivid golden dorsal band.

This impression is reinforced further by the short legs, three pairs of which are sited rather far forward, so that the rear part of the body seems to be dragged along behind. Nevertheless these shrimps climb with great agility, at least under water. Sometimes you will find them, clinging to a few strands of algae on the vertical

Atyoida pilipes

panes of the tank, or hanging upside-down on a floating plant leaf, with no obvious clue as to how they got there. Hence you should never underestimate their climbing abilities and bear in mind that they may clamber out of the tank!

A second Asian species, *Atyoida pilipes* (Newport, 1847), is now being more frequently imported. The genus name again means "*Atya*-like", and the specific name "hairy foot". This shrimp comes from the Philippines, the Lesser Sunda Islands, and other Pacific islands north to Rota (in the Marianas), south to Rapa (in the Tubuai Islands), and west to Mangareva (in the Gambier Islands), but is not known from the Asian mainland. It primarily inhabits small, sometimes overgrown, mountain streams up to an altitude of more than 300 metres; these streams are often no more than 3 metres wide, with a bottom of sand, gravel, or rock, and form repeated broader pools, and sometimes even small waterfalls or rapids.

The water temperature ranges between 25 and 26 °C.

Atyoida pilipes filtering.

Atyids: fan shrimps

The fan bristles on the hands of *Atyoida pilipes* are black, and this is particularly noticeable when the fans are folded.

In the Philippines these shrimps are called Koros, hence the English name "Koras Shrimp" (and French "Saltarelle Koros"). Their economic importance is small, but they are sold fresh or dried, and eaten or used as animal food.

The Latin name pilipes (= "hairy foot") is very appropriate, as the fan bristles on the hands are black, creating a dark spot when the shrimp closes its hand to grip. Apropos of which, it is interesting to note that this species includes specimens with two different claw forms. The majority of individuals have fan-hands without actual "palms". The bristles are thus sited on two basal segments of approximately equal width. Hands of this type are termed atyoid and in all probability are used primarily to filter plankton from the water (this is termed filter-feeding). There are, however, also individuals that do develop something rather like a palm, against which the other "finger" of the claw closes. Both basal elements bear bristles. It is thought that this type of hand can be used not only for filtering the water but also for brushing the substrate (filter-feeding and sweeping). Furthermore, it is as yet unknown whether the different types of hand are sex-specific or represent adaptations to particular habitats or seasonal variations in the natural biotopes.

In *Atyoida pilipes* the rostrum is noticeable down-curved and has only one, more rarely two or three, inferior serrae - if it has any at all. Beneath the rostrum the carapace has a blunt tip. On the posterior part there are a number of not particularly large, rigid serrae. The species appears to attain a total length of only around 4 cm. The base colour is a plain grey-white, but the back and flanks are attractively spotted with red-brown. In many individuals the individual segments of the abdomen exhibit particularly bold markings laterally at their lower ends. Between the spots, especially on the back, these shrimps are very finely speckled with brown, red, and blue.

The closely related species *Atyoida bisulcata* Randall, 1840, whose specific name means "with two furrows", develops as many as three different types of hand. The third form has broad hands and short fingers, and the bristles are greatly abbreviated. These are termed caridinoid hands and it is thought that they are used for selective scraping or picking of the substrate.

In this shrimp the rostrum is horizontal and normally has no interior serrae at all. Beneath the rostrum the carapace has a sharp tip. On the posterior part there are 2-7 striking - i.e. large - rigid serrae.

Atyids: fan shrimps

Atyoida bisulcata Photo: K. Stender

This fan shrimp (*Atya scabra*) was collected in the Grijalva drainage in southern Mexico. Photo: M. Keijman

Females attain a total length of around 50 mm, while males remain smaller. On the basis of tissue studies pointing to hermaphroditism and in view of the fact that numerous males but only a few females have been recorded in collections, it is thought that this is a hermaphroditic species in which the male gonads ripen earlier than the female - the term for this is protandry. In other words, a large number of the young - or maybe even all - are initially male, and later some of them develop into females. It may well be that *A. pilipes* is also a protandrous species.

As regards reproduction, it appears certain that the larvae develop only in the sea. The zoëa larvae will in fact hatch in standing water, but they fail to develop further, and die. In the wild, after the young have reached the post-larval stage they return upstream into fresh water. It is thus unlikely that breeding is feasible in the aquarium.

Atyoida bisulcata occurs in Oceania in the Hawaii Islands, where it lives in cool mountain waters up to an altitude of more than 540 metres. According to EDMONDSON (1936: cited in CHACE, 1993) the optimal temperature range lies between 20 and 26 °C, while the pH can vary between 8 and 9. According to ULLMAN (1967: cited in CHACE, 1993) the species exhibits no aberrant behaviour at temperatures between 15.5 and 29 °C and pH values between 6.5 and 9.

There are further atyids to be found in the New World, both on the mainland and in the islands of the Caribbean. I have myself found a brown-marbled shrimp of this group in Honduras, another in Lake Catemaco in the Papaloapan system in southern Mexico, and yet another in the Grijalva system in the highlands of southern Mexico. All these locations are on the Atlantic side of Central America. In addition there are photos of a similarly-patterned species from Brazil, but with no details of the precise locality. KLOTZ (cf. KARGE & KLOTZ, 2004) has identified a species, very similar in appearance to those mentioned above, as *Atya margaritacea* MILNE-EDWARDS, 1864 (the specific name means "pearly"). This species lives along the Pacific coast of Central and South America from California to Peru. Although, like *A. margaritacea*, the shrimps I discovered in Central America do not have any distinct furrowing of the carapace and are very similar in their form and markings, they cannot in fact be that species as I found them on the other side of Central America.

This colour variant of *Atya scabra* was initially erroneously identified as *A. margaritacea*. Photo: C. Lukhaup

Atyids: fan shrimps

Fan shrimps of the species *Atya scabra* are found in the mountain streams of Honduras (Atlantic slope), and are even cultivated for the cooking pot.

It has now become clear that the shrimps I collected are actually *Atya scabra* (LEACH, 1815). The specific name signifies "rough", and relates to the fact that the legs and the carapace are covered in countless small bumps and denticles. The rostrum, however, has no serrae on either its upper edge or its underside. The fingers of the two chelipeds have regular bunches of long hairs at their tips, but the following three pairs of peraeopods, the first of which are particularly thickened, are even more striking. Specifically, all three bear blunt-ended but nevertheless clearly protruding spines or nodules. The male sexual appendages are located on the inner branches of the second pair of pleopods and have the appearance of broad, sac- or bladder-like lobes covered in slender, curved spines. They are the only morphological characteristic that accurately differentiates males and females.

The species may have either a greenish or brownish base colour. The pattern consists of three bold dark elements that are almost invariably visible: first of all there is a dark spot or cross-band immediately behind the rostrum; then a second band on the posterior edge of the carapace; and finally, a third on the anterior half of the sixth abdominal segment, extending to the edge of the latter. In addition, the anterior parts of the thickened peraeopods are dark to above the first joint, so that the shrimps appear to be wearing dark socks.

Atya scabra, a specimen from Brazil. Photo: F. Teigler

This is a species that occurs on both sides of the Atlantic, with a distribution extending from the coastal waters of West Africa to the Caribbean region and from the coast of Mexico to Brazil. I have myself encountered these shrimps in Atlantic-slope mountain streams in Honduras, where back in the 1980s an agricultural research station was involved in cultivating them and breeding them for the cooking pot. The species primarily inhabits areas of strong current in rivers and streams up to an altitude of around 120 metres. Here they live beneath or between the water-washed rocks of the habitat. They are not found in areas where the water is calm. It also appears that when their environment changes - during the dry season, for example - and is no longer optimal to their requirements, they migrate into areas of their native waters that are more to their liking.

The *Atya* species most commonly offered for sale, *Atya gabonensis* GIEBEL, 1875 - the specific name refers to its occurrence in Gabon - is found both in West Africa and eastern South America; specifically in African waters from Senegal south to the Congo, and along the American east coast from Venezuela to Brazil. These shrimps live in rocky and stony rivers and streams upstream to their headwaters, where they are able to anchor themselves to the bottom using their powerful, spiny peraeopods, the first pair of which are enormously enlarged in males. They simultaneously extend their fan-hands, spread wide and resembling radar dishes, against

Atya gabonensis - in this case a beige-coloured individual - taking food from the bottom.

Atyids: fan shrimps

Blue specimens of *Atya gabonensis* are particularly attractive. Photo: F. Schäfer

the current, and use them to filter drifting plankton from the water. In the aquarium, however, these shrimps will also take food from the bottom, grabbing it with their partially folded fan-hands.

In *Atya gabonensis* the dorsal armour is ridged and furrowed, but otherwise both cephalothorax and abdomen are smooth. The legs are set with dark "warts", which are particularly strongly developed in males. Because this species can grow to as much as 15 cm long it is sometimes known as the Monster Shrimp. Usually, however, it is sold as the Cameroon Shrimp, Blue Fan Shrimp, or Giant African Freshwater Shrimp.

These shrimps are strikingly attractive and can change their colour in the same way as *A. moluccensis*. Juveniles are often bluish to light blue, while adults are usually bluish-grey or brownish, sometimes even yellowish, with a pink or bluish tinge. In the aquarium occasional individuals have been recorded as changing colour to white, while black specimens have been discovered in the wild. These shrimps appear particularly light in colour (flesh-coloured to pink) after moulting. Apparently they are also able to change their coloration depending on their mood or as an adaptation to light conditions in their environment. In these shrimps (as in *Atyopsis moluccensis*) the females remain significantly smaller than the males.

There are so far no reports of the completely successful breeding of the "primitive" *Atyopsis* and *Atya* species. GÖTHEL (1986) observed that females of *A. moluccensis* carried several hundred eggs, from which tiny larvae hatched after 22 days, their size ranging from 1.8 to 1.9 millimetres. They were translucent and swam head-down in the water, moving backwards. Unfortunately they all died, probably not only due to the wrong kind of food, but apparently also because they were unable to moult without difficulty. It may be that these problems resulted from too much nitrate in the water, which should therefore be changed as often as possible.

According to NG & CHIA (1994) the larvae develop in the brackish estuaries of rivers and in the sea, but even under natural conditions only a few of the million of larvae hatched return to the rivers and highland brooks as fully developed shrimps. It must be emphasised that today's human pollution of the lower reaches of rivers represents an additional problem for the survival of these species.

Shrimps

Palaemonids: long-arm shrimps

The genus *Macrobrachium* (long-arm shrimps) belongs to a closely-related group of genera which also includes *Leander*, *Palaemonetes*, and *Palaemon*, which will be familiar, at least by name, to hobbyists specialising in marine aquaria. *Macrobrachium* live in rivers and are distributed all over the world, and there are so many species that it is almost impossible to identify them. Many look very similar, no matter whether they come from West Africa, Asia, Central or South America.

As well as the small species there are very large ones that attain a body length of 20 or even 30 cm. In their native countries they are prized as delicacies for the table and are hunted with spears, cast-nets, and even just bare hands. I must admit that I have caught and eaten several different species in Central America!

These long-arm shrimps are true freshwater creatures which do not need to be kept in either brackish or hard water, and are sometimes found in habitats which are extremely poor in minerals, for example in regions where the delicate discus cichlid is also found. In Central America I have found these shrimps in water with a carbonate and general hardness of between 6 and 18 °KH/°dGH. Temperatures vary, depending on geography and season, between 23 and 34°C. Thus these accommodating and hardy shrimps have no special requirements. Nevertheless they will appreciate numerous hiding-places, e.g. among stones, plants and dead tree leaves used for decoration. In the wild, they utilise crannies between boulders and are to be found among the thick layers of dead leaves on the bottom, and are also fond of hiding in narrow cracks in the wood or beneath the bark of dead trees that have fallen into the water. There are, moreover, species which remain hidden for most of the day and come out only at feeding time or in the evening, and others which live on the bottom, but are quite active throughout the day, clambering all over the tank searching for anything edible. Yet others like to swim in the open water.

Most long-arm shrimps are not as colourful as the saltwater shrimps of the coral reefs, but more or less modestly coloured. They are nevertheless interesting by virtue of their bizarre faces with a long rostrum and greatly-projecting beady eyes positioned on so-called eye-stalks, and because of their long antennae and nimble, match-like, legs, the joints of which can be strikingly coloured - red, for example. It is really an amazing spectacle to watch these apparently motionless animals, which in reality are almost constantly occupied cleaning themselves with their nearly invisible limbs. This "toilet" may produce an element of comedy: it is most amusing to see a short leg run across an eye

In Central America long-arm shrimps are regarded as a delicacy. Even children hunt them eagerly.

like a hand, while at the same time the abdomen is bent forward and the animal starts scratching its posterior with another leg!

In the aquarium - a shallow tank with a volume of between 100 and 200 litres and the largest possible bottom area is quite adequate for keeping species which attain a body length of about 12 cm - these shrimps will have no problem making themselves at home. Soon each will have selected its favourite place, which in most cases will be an elevated "perch" not far from shelter, from which it dexterously climbs down when you offer food!

As their natural food consists first and foremost of carrion, they above all like dead meaty material (frozen bloodworm and brine shrimp, chopped beef heart, fish, etc.). But they also readily eat manufactured food tablets, and should be given those that are vegetable-based, as in the wild these shrimps also eat decaying plant material, algae, and fresh young shoots. They skilfully seize these food tablets and turn them round in their short, brush-like hands, feeding on the tiny particles thus loosened. Some people keep these shrimps because they feed on algae, and are said to eat even the firmly-attached types, but at the same time do not harm higher plants. The amount of algae they eat depends, of course, on the species and number of shrimps - and it is foolish to expect miracles. In addition, most *Macrobrachium* will eat snails, and not only ramshorn snails, but also Malaysian live-bearing snails (*Melanoides tuberculata*).

Like all other crustaceans they find their food by smell and approach it rapidly, excitedly feeling about with their antennae. Once they have taken their prey - which, if necessary, they vigorously defend against conspecifics or fishes - they carry it to a sheltered place. Not that they are at all timid - you will be able to observe them without difficulty most of the time. But they do fear competition from other occupants of the tank. These, by the way, shouldn't be too small. If you consider the size of your *Macrobrachium* and the fact that their generic name means "long-arm", not to mention the strong claws in which the arms terminate, then you can well imagine that they may take small fishes by surprise during the night although this is in fact rather rare - perhaps because it doesn't equate with their natural feeding behaviour. On the other hand they frequently fight with conspecifics and these quarrels often end in the loss of a leg or a claw, even though it is rare for one of the combatants to be killed. Plus, as already mentioned, lost limbs, will be replaced without problem at the next moult.

A good supply of food and frequent water changes will encourage growth and the moulting this necessitates, and which they signal by stopping feeding and going into hiding. For this reason their tank should be provided with roots, stones, and plants, and not just for aesthetic reasons alone.

In addition these shrimps only seldom swim, and are thus hardly ever found in open water, instead leading a substrate-orientated life. They are skilful climbers, and where their legs cannot grip, they use their swimmerets for propulsion, gliding up the smooth vertical glass, so it is important to cover their aquarium tightly. If danger threatens they stop for a moment, lifting their claws in a threatening manner. If they need to flee, they suddenly flick backwards, zigzagging away lightning-fast to safety.

Because *Macrobrachium* contains both large species and small, and males develop chelipeds of variable length and thickness, I have previously tried to categorise the species using these characters. I have now abandoned this strategy as there is simply too much overlap, and instead I will differentiate them here only by the modes of reproduction already described on page 13, with the "swimming shrimps" (those that tend to swim in open water) as a third group.

The primitive reproductive type consists of species that produce a very large number of tiny eggs which hatch into larvae, barely visible to the naked eye, after 10 days to three weeks. They float head-down in the water and move with a hopping motion. Their eyes are large, but, unlike those of adults, immobile. Unfortunately it is rarely possible to provide them with suitable food, so that they usually survive only till about the fourth day and then die within a few hours. In the wild they are carried by the current to brackish water or the open sea, where they pass through numerous developmental stages before returning to fresh water as fully-formed shrimps. The young of these species can thus be reared only with great effort - if at all.

Preserved zoea larvae of *Macrobrachium tenellum* have been photographed with an electron microscope by Dr. R. Riehl (University of Düsseldorf), whom I would like to thank for this favour. His pictures (see page 14) are very informative and show that the larvae lack pleopods at this stage and still use their forward-pointing peraeopods (visible in the two upper photos), which are not yet completely developed, for locomotion. They also already use their telson, whose broad "stem" is equipped with filigree "feathers", for jerky, hopping movement. The body is already armoured, and its posterior part segmented, as in adults, to facilitate movement. Their giant faceted eyes guarantee a wide field of vision. The larvae of *Macrobrachium* species are largely predatory, feeding on small planktonic organisms.

Palaemonids: long-arm shrimps

In south-east Asia, as here at Pak Chong in central Thailand, *Macrobrachium* shrimps are the subject of intensive fisheries and aquaculture.
Photo: D. Schrüfer

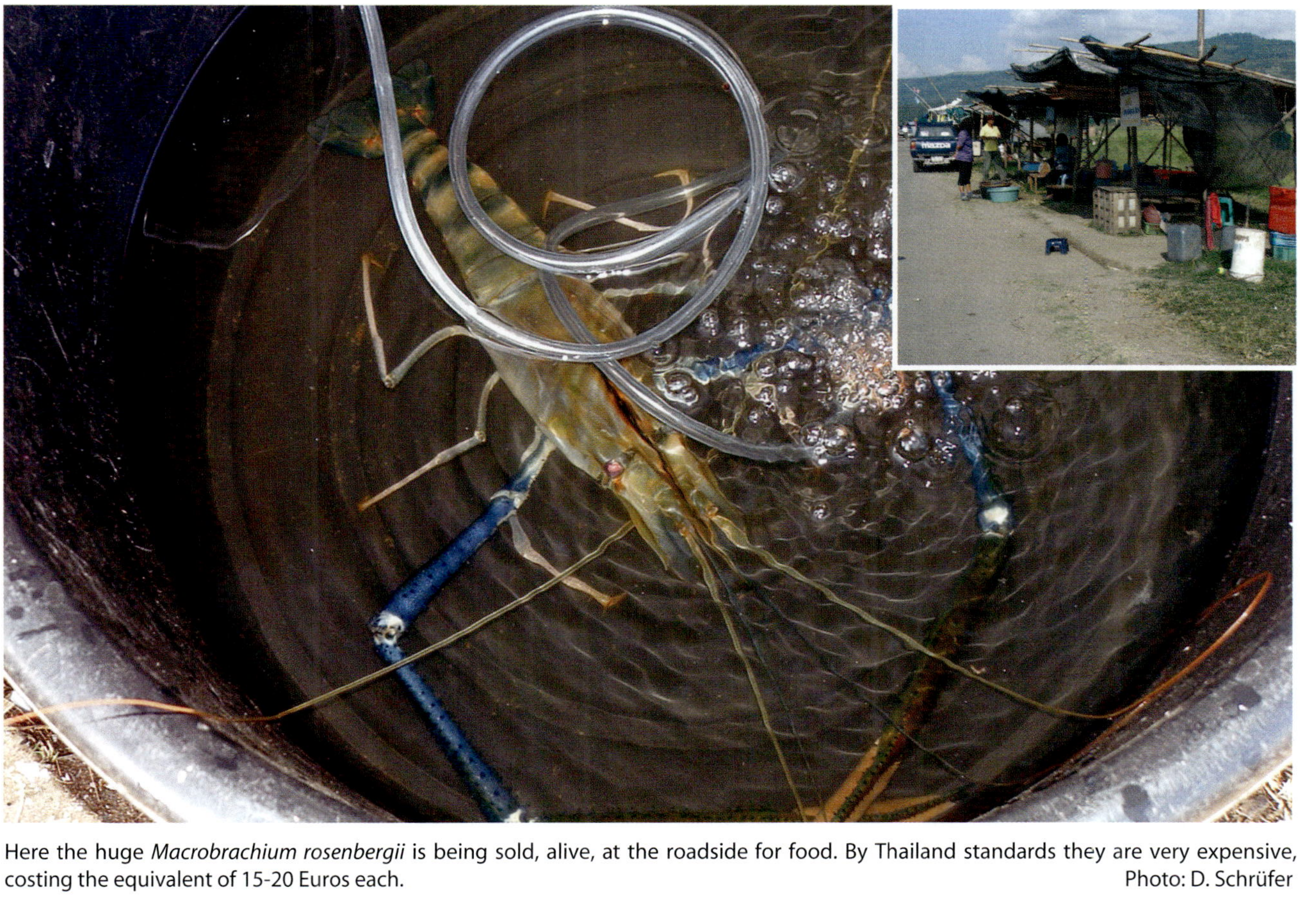

Here the huge *Macrobrachium rosenbergii* is being sold, alive, at the roadside for food. By Thailand standards they are very expensive, costing the equivalent of 15-20 Euros each.
Photo: D. Schrüfer

Palaemonids: long-arm shrimps

Macrobrachium carcinus, the Signal-Stripe Shrimp (left a juvenile, right an adult), is bred commercially for food. The specimens in the photos are from southern Mexico, Atlantic slope.

If the newly-released larvae are not too small, they can be fed with newly-hatched brine shrimp. In most cases this food will be too big, and it will be necessary to experiment with tinier items such as slipper animalcules, rotifers, micro-eels (*Panagrellus silusiae*), milk-powder (!), "Liquifry", or powdered flake food. Care must be taken to avoid the water becoming cloudy and polluted, and it is best to install a small, air-powered sponge filter that will trap the finest particles without sucking in the tiny larvae.

As with the atyids, the first moults, which begin about 24 hours after hatching, can also be a problem for these shrimp larvae and result in huge losses. However, those that survive for the first 14 days have a good chance of long-term survival. By this stage their initial whitish colour will be giving way to typical transparency, and by a size of about 12 mm the young will also have assumed the form of their parents. At the same time they stop swimming around and start leading a substrate-orientated life, just as their parents do, i.e. they prefer to remain on the bottom or explore the decor.

The professional breeding of *Macrobrachium* species that produce tiny eggs, i.e. the primitive reproductive type, was first achieved a few years ago. Most experiments have involved *Macrobrachium rosenbergii*, said to be the largest freshwater shrimp in the world. Its size is the more remarkable in that it is an annual species in which males live for only a year (or a little more) and grow - if they are kept in large rearing ponds - to sizes of 200 to 220 mm, whereas females seldom live longer than a year and reach 180 to 200 mm. The growth rate slows down after five or six months and is better if the population density is lower and the temperature higher. In addition, the shrimps grow better if cultivated in fresh rather than brackish water. In the wild *M. rosenbergii* may attain up to 30 centimetres in males and 25.5 in females.

In experiments performed with other *Macrobrachium* species as well, it was subsequently ascertained that sexually mature males are always ready for copulation, whereas females have to moult before mating. It is believed that females also then secrete special scents that attract males.

Fresh eggs of *Macrobrachium rosenbergii* are mostly orange-coloured, but soon become darker, turning to a greyish-green and, just before hatching, nearly black. In 1961, in Malaysia, it was discovered that the larvae of *M. rosenbergii* survive only if they are kept in sufficiently saline water. If the larvae hatch in completely fresh water, they are doomed to die, even though the adult shrimps often live in such water, more than 100 miles from the sea. In 1962 the first young shrimps were reared under laboratory conditions. Food size also seems to be significant: the particles must not be too small or the larvae will not accept them; on the other hand, they must not be too large either as the larvae will cling to them, sink to the bottom with them, and die there. For successfully raising larvae of *M. rosenbergii*, the food particles should be about one tenth of the body length of the larvae. They should be fed animal material, e.g. ground fish or egg yolk. At the same time, optimal water quality must be maintained and oxygen depletion avoided (Ling, 1977).

M. rosenbergii seems to be the most suitable *Macrobrachium* species for commercial breeding, but a Tahitian species called *M. lar*, in which full- grown individuals can be found in brackish water, is also suitable for breeding, especially in places where fresh water is difficult to obtain or expensive. In America, *M. carcinus* and *M. ohione* are being bred successfully. Unfortunately, individuals of the first species are rather aggressive towards each other, so that they can't be kept in large numbers in small pools, but on the other hand they tolerate cooler water than *M. rosenbergii*. *M. ohione* is hardy, but grows slowly and is not large enough to eat, so that in Louisiana these shrimps are used for bait. *M. carcinus* and *M. acanthurus* are found in Mexico, on the Atlantic slope in the Gulf of Mexico region, specifically in the federal states of Tamaulipas, Veracruz, Tabasco, and

Macrobrachium ohione Photo: C. Lukhaup

Campeche. On the Pacific slope there are two species, *M. americanum* and *M. tenellum*, which are distributed from Sinaloa in the north down to the frontier with Guatemala. The former species is more abundant in the north, the latter in the south. Other Mexican species, of little commercial interest, but which are nevertheless caught for food, are *M. olfersii*, *M. digueti*, *M. acanthochirus*, *M. michoacanus*, and *M. heterochirus* (see HANSON & GODWIN, 1977).

The species that practice the specialised mode of reproduction are easy to breed in the aquarium. They produce large eggs, which may number up to a hundred. Depending on the species, water temperature, aeration, and water movement they develop over a period of three to six weeks. It is advisable to isolate females carrying eggs after about two weeks.

Eventually they will release fully-formed young shrimps which they do not subsequently pursue as food. In fact some species at least practise a form of brood care, albeit somewhat passive, during the first few days. The female remains with her young, allows them to clamber onto her, and refrains from feeding of any type. This fasting apparently prevents the mother from preying on her own young. The latter can take Artemia nauplii and particles of flake or tablet food without difficulty, and grow on rapidly. They become sexually mature after only about three months.

The following pages are devoted, by way of example, to some of the shrimps of the genus *Macrobrachium* that are imported for the aquarium hobby from Central and South America, the Indian-Asian region, and Africa; in many cases the species names are unknown. The first of these are species with chelipeds of equal length, which normally live on the bottom, followed by species with differently developed chelipeds and which generally remain among cover of some type, and finally the palaemonids, which spend much of their time swimming in open water.

American species

The first of these is *Macrobrachium tenellum* (SMITH, 1871), a species with slender or dainty arms, as the Latin specific name (= "dainty") denotes. It was originally described as a *Palaemon*. *Palaemon longipes* LOCKINGTON, 1878 (the specific name means "long foot") is a synonym. Males attain a body length of at least 11.5 cm,

Macrobrachium tenellum, pair from western Colombia (Chocó).

while females remain somewhat smaller. The rostrum in *M. tenellum* is noticeably convex and has a long, untoothed area distally with only 1-3 sub-apical serrae. The eggs of this species are small - just 0.5 to 0.6 mm across.

Macrobrachium tenellum, juvenile.

Shrimps; Palaemonids: long-arm shrimps

American species with equal chelipeds

Macrobrachium tenellum, female Weibchen

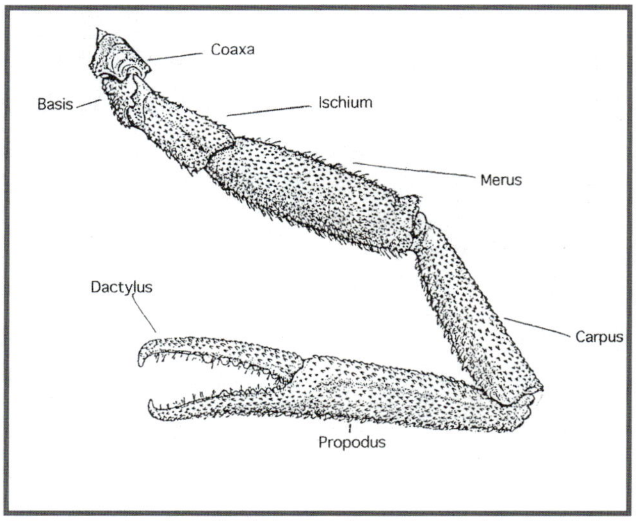

Cheliped of a *Macrobrachium* male with the individual elements labelled. *M. heterochirus*, after HOLTHUIS, 1952

M. tenellum is distributed along the Pacific (west) coast of Central and South America, from Baja California to northern Peru. This is the species that I termed the Guatemala Shrimp and the Chocó Shrimp in previous editions of this book. I have seen this species in Guatemala in a Pacific-slope river, the Rio Maria Linda; and in western Colombia in the so-called "Chocó", where I found it in exceptionally soft (0 °dGH, 3-3.5 °KH) and slightly acid (pH 5.5 to 6), warm (around 27 °C), clear water in a stream in the Baudo system near Pie de Pepé. The shrimps spent the day among the marginal vegetation and in the leaf litter that was frequently to be found in large aggregations.

Macrobrachium tenellum looks similar to *M. acanthurus*, a shrimp that lives in Atlantic-slope waters and will be discussed later. *M. tenellum* can be distinguished from *M. rathbunae*, with which it is sometimes found sympatric, by a longer rostrum, longer fingers on the second pair of claws, and a greater difference in length between the carpus and merus (see diagram) of this pair of legs. Juveniles and females in particular are very attractively coloured: the amber-coloured body is adorned with red-brown lines, sometimes bordered with yellow; and the joints of the legs and of the brown claws are red. In juveniles the chelipeds are still uniformly slender, even filigree, but the appearance of these shrimps alters noticeably in the course of time and from moult to moult. The males grow larger and develop long, powerful chelipeds, while both sexes become ever darker until they eventually appear almost uniform red-brown. The rostrum is particularly dark, the cephalothorax lighter, the pleon almost black. An irregularly-defined light band runs across the posterior part of the tail. The centre of the tail-fan is again dark, but by contrast the uropods are red-brown. The undersides of the arms are dark, but lighter on top. The actual claws are a bold dark brown.

In full-grown males the span of the chelipeds can exceed the length of the body. The chelipeds of females remain more slender and are also noticeably shorter. It is hard to say whether they are also less able to defend themselves than males. It is quite likely that the long chelipeds are something of a hindrance during skirmishes and certainly when it comes to mobility, and, of course, they also break off easily. The females appear nimbler in all respects. And even within the confines of the aquarium - my shrimps were kept in aquaria with a volume of 120 litres and a bottom area measuring 75 x 40 cm - the females were never injured by the males.

On the Atlantic slope of southern Mexico *M. tenellum* is replaced by *Macrobrachium acanthurus* (WIEGMANN, 1836). The specific name means "with a spinytail". Perhaps it

This juvenile Papaloapán Shrimp (*M. acanthurus*) has made its home in a snail shell.

American species with equal chelipeds

M. acanthurus, male

M. acanthurus is the Atlantic coast sibling species of *M. tenellum* and the African *M. macrobrachion.*

relates to the rostrum, which is not convex posteriorly and has more serrae than in *M. tenellum*. Thus there are, for example, two posterior to the margin of the eye, whereas *M. tenellum* has only one. In addition the large claws are more powerfully developed in comparison to *M. tenellum*.

In this species, referred to as the "Papaloapán Shrimp" in both previous editions of this book, adult males can be light blue, lighter on the belly and darker on the back. The tail fan is also dark. The undersides of the arms and legs are an intense blue, the claws brown. Young specimens are nearly colourless initially, later changing to a pale blue-grey, which is also the colour of adult females. The "Papaloapán Shrimp" lives a secretive life among the boulders of the river bottom. During the dry season the water is rather warm (27- 30 °C), slightly alkaline (pH about 7.5) and medium hard (4 to 11 °dGH; 4 to 13 °KH). There is virtually no submerse vegetation.

In southern Mexico, in the rivers of the Atlantic slope from the Rio Papaloapán down to the Usumacinta, my friends and I found another, very attractively patterned shrimp which also occurs in northern South America. This species, the Signal-Stripe Shrimp, has now been identified by W. Klotz as *Macrobrachium carcinus* (Linnaeus, 1857). It is distributed in fresh and brackish water in eastern (Atlantic coast) America from Florida to southern Brazil and is also found in the islands of the West Indies.

It offers a good example of how the same species is often recorded under a variety of names. *M. carcinus* was originally given the name *Poptipemavon* Marcgrave as long ago as 1648, but it wasn't until 1758 that it was correctly described, in Latin, by the father of binomial nomenclature, Carl von Linné. It was then given the name *Cancer carcinus* in line with modern rules of nomenclature, and stated to be "from the rivers of America" (in Americae fluviis). Both parts

American species with equal chelipeds

Macrobrachium carcinus, the Signal-Stripe Shrimp (additional photos on p. 44) has undergone a large number of name changes. This is a specimen from Honduras, photographed in the natural habitat.

of the name signify "crab". This shrimp probably also fits the description of the Astacus fluviatilis major chelis aculeatis (= "river crayfish with large prickly claws") SLOANE, 1725, which the latter discovered in Jamaica, which is thus the type locality.

A list of synonyms - *Squilla, Crangon, Amaericana major* - is cited by SEBA, 1761. GRONOVIUS described the species in 1764 as Astacus minor chelis denticulatis (= "small crayfish with denticulate claws"). In FERMIN, 1765 the species is named *Astacus major* (= "greater"); in FORSTER, 1771 it is again *Cancer carcinus*; in FABRICIUS, 1775 *Astacus carcinus*; in BROWNE, 1789 *Astacus 2*; and in HERBST, 1792 *Cancer* (*Astacus*) *Jamaicensis* (relating to its origin). After 1795 the genus name *Palaemon* (the name of a Greek god of the sea) was used, for example by WEBER, 1795, who refers to *Palaemon carcinus*, as well as by OLIVIER, 1811, who terms the species *Palaemon jamaicensis*. The above-mentioned genus names were used until 1872, so that the species was described as *Astacus* (*Palaemon*) *jamaicensis* VOIGT, 1836, *Palaemon brachydactylus* WIEGMANN, 1836 (= "short-arm"), *Palemon punctatus* RANDALL, 1840 (= "spotted"; alternative spelling of *Palaemon*), *Palemon brevicarpus* DE HAAN, 1849 (= "with a short carpus"), *Palaemon aztecus* (= "of the Aztecs", the former inhabitants of Mexico, so possibly denoting origin), *Palaemon Montezumae* DE SAUSSURE, 1857 (named after the last Aztec ruler), *Palaemon laminatus* VON MARTENS, 1869 (= "(armour-) plated"), and *Palaemon* (*Macrobrachium*) *Jamaicensis* VON MARTENS, 1869.

There then followed descriptions under the genus name *Bithynis* (which I cannot translate), namely *B. jamaicensis* POCOCK, 1889, *B. aztecus* YOUNG, 1900, and - with a question mark - *B. montezumae* YOUNG, 1900. Followed by a return to *Macrobrachium* or *Palaemon*, so that we find *Macrobrachium jamaicense* PEARSE, 1915, *Palemon ornatus* TORRALBAS, 1917 (= "decorated") (not *Palaemon orantus* OLIVIER, 1811), *Palaemon* (*Macroterocheir*) *jamaicensis* DE MAN, 1925, *Palaemon jamaicensis* f. *aztecus* PESTA, 1931, *Periclimenes* (?) *portoricensis* SCHMITT, 1933 (from its origin, Puerto Rico), and *Macrobrachium carcinus* HEDGPETH, 1949. HOLTHUIS, 1952, GEIJSKES, 1954, and CHACE & HOBBS, 1969 also used these names.

It is certainly also interesting that *M. carcinus* was formerly "lumped together" with a West African species, specifically *Macrobrachium vollenhovenii* (HERKLOTS, 1857). It is in fact the case that the *Macrobrachium* species which inhabit waters that empty into the Atlantic on the east coast of Central and South America, and which produce small eggs and larvae with brackish-water or marine stages, have a so-called sibling or sister species in West Africa. Examples of this are the species pairs *M. zariquiey* in Africa and *M. olfersii* in Central America, *M. felicinum* in Africa and *M. crenulatum* in Central America, and *M. vollenhovenii* in Africa and *M. carcinus* in Central and South America.

American species with equal chelipeds

M. carcinus has a narrow, slightly convex rostrum, with 11 to 14, evenly-distributed serrae (up to 16 in young specimens) and 3 or 4 on the underside. The armour of the thorax and abdomen is smooth, i.e. with no spines, except that the sides of the carapace may be rough in old males.

The second pair of peraeopods (chelipeds) are noticeably enlarged. The two fingers of the claws are narrow, only slightly flattened, and like the propodus, are set with fine spines, small on the upper surface, larger and somewhat further apart on the underside. On each cutting edge there is a large tooth and - between this tooth and the base of the finger - 2-4 smaller little teeth. The peraeopods are largely smooth, but the joints of the posterior three pairs are densely covered with fine bristles, at least in older individuals.

The markings of this species are very striking, as the carapace and abdomen exhibit broad yellow longitudinal stripes which, depending on age, create a more or less bold contrast with the otherwise darker body. The species can, however, vary from individual to individual in its coloration, depending on origin. The dark elements can be black-blue to brown, the lighter ones grey, pink-brown, cream, or lavender-coloured to various shades of yellow. The most variation is seen in the coloration of the olive or brownish claws. A particularly striking feature is the light whitish spots on the joints of the claws when the latter are slightly open, and the similarly patterned distal segments of the anterior peraeopods.

The sexes can be distinguished in *M. carcinus* of similar age on the basis of size, as females remain somewhat smaller. Moreover sexually mature females can be distinguished from males by their less powerfully developed chelipeds. In addition, the tips of the fingers do not overlap in females as is usually the case in sexually mature males, and in the latter a gap remains at the base of the fingers when the claws are closed, while in females the claws close together for their entire length. Plus the above-mentioned serration of the claws is not as strongly developed in females.

Male *M. carcinus* can attain more than 23 cm, females up to 17 cm. However females are sexually mature at a carapace length of less than 14 mm! In the wild *M. carcinus* supposedly breeds only from May to October (i.e. in the rainy season). The male is always ready to mate, while the female needs to moult before copulation. It appears that she then emits a scent to attract the male. The eggs are round in shape, very numerous, and very small, with a diameter of between 0.44 and 0.67 mm. Depending on the temperature and aeration the larvae, which are barely visible to the naked eye, hatch after 10 days to three weeks. They float head-down in the water and move with a hopping motion. Their eyes are large, but, unlike those of adults, immobile. Unfortunately it is rarely possible to provide them with suitable food, so that they usually survive only till about the fourth day and then die within a few hours. In the wild they are carried by the current to brackish water or the open sea, where they pass through numerous developmental stages before returning to fresh water as fully-formed shrimps.

M. carcinus is encountered in all possible water types. The species is found in the relatively slight current of the mouths of larger rivers but also in fast-flowing drainage channels, in the shelter or large rocks in reaches with seething water and beneath stones at the edge of deeper pools, and even in very small gullies. The altitude of these locations may extend up to around 700 metres, but if sufficient suitable hiding-places are available they may occur even further upstream.

The species is noticeably more active in the dark than by day. At the onset of darkness the shrimps leave their hiding-places and scurry around on the open bottom and they probably also negotiate shallow areas of rapids or cross very shallow or barely wet stretches in order to get from one pool to the next. Such activities are never seen by day; and they also never stray far from their hiding-places during the daytime (cf. CHACE & HOBBS, 1969).

The Jabuti Shrimp may be *Macrobrachium nattereri*.

During an expedition to Brazil I found other freshwater shrimps in the Tapajós drainage and in the Amazon south of Santarém. The small rivers or brooks that cross the road to Colonia Jabuti were teeming with waterlilies and other, submerse, plants. In places the banks were densely bordered with reeds and other marsh plants. The river bottom was soft, consisting of sand or a thick layer of

American species with equal chelipeds

The Jabuti Shrimp develops long, flattened chelipeds.

An attractive yellow-marbled male Palenque Shrimp, *Macrobrachium vicconi*.

dead leaves and wood. The biotope conditions were thus quite different from the stony rivers of Central America, and, of course, the water chemistry was different too. The water was tea-coloured and clear, with a pH of about 5.5 and no measurable general or carbonate hardness. And yet here too we found a shrimp species, which I decided to give the name "Jabuti Shrimp".

It now appears that the identification of this species as *Macrobrachium carcinus* in previous editions of this book was incorrect. Possibly it is instead *Macrobrachium nattereri* (HELLER, 1862) - the specific name is an honorific. The body of the Jabuti Shrimp is comparatively stout, the chelipeds are long in males, with especially broad, strong forearms. Both sexes develop a rather beautiful brown-red colour in the course of time, and a light stripe appears on the outer edges of the chelipeds. In addition, there is a lighter area on the head and a yellowish-white ring round the base of the tail fan. Unfortunately nothing is known about their reproductive biology.

In the Rio Otulum (in the Grijalva drainage), near the ruins of Palenque in southern Mexico, there lives another *Macrobrachium* which has now been described as *Macrobrachium vicconi* ROMÁN et al., 2000. The specific name is an honorific. It is supposedly similar to *M. quelchi* and *M. atabapense* in terms of its size and reproduction. The males of this Palenque Shrimp develop stronger and longer chelipeds than the females, but in both sexes exhibit an attractive black and yellow colour pattern. Males grow a little larger than females and attain a body length of about four centimetres. The deeper-bodied females grow to only about 3.5 centimetres.

The water in the natural habitat is hard with a pH of about 7.5, and the temperature varies seasonally from slightly above to a little below 25 °C. These shrimps can be kept in an aquarium of about 30 litres. When they are fully grown they look as if they are covered with brown powder, with

Female Palenque Shrimp, *Macrobrachium vicconi*, with eggs.

the fine spots on the carapace creating a dark marbled pattern. The colour pattern also includes black lines and a light longitudinal band on the back. Depending on age and condition, females of this species lay between 20 and 60 rather large eggs, from which hatch larvae that continue to feed on the remains of their yolk sac for a few days. After about three weeks they measure about four millimetres, by which time they are fully-formed, resembling their parents, and begin independent life. Unfortunately, this species has never been bred with complete success. In some cases a few young have appeared that were released without the

Macrobrachium vicconi can be recognised by its yellow claws even when young.

American species with equal chelipeds

Macrobrachium vicconi , male

knowledge of the breeder and grew up among the adults, but a larger number of fry have never been obtained from any female. In most cases the bulk of the eggs were lost, for unknown reasons, before the fry hatched or the larvae died. Luckily, this species has been brought back by a number of German and Dutch aquarists and is being kept in good numbers in the aquarium.

This species is very similar to *Macrobrachium brasiliense* Heller, 1862, which is occasionally imported from Peru and Colombia for the aquarium hobby. The male are said to grow to around 8.5 cm long. To date the imported stocks have been significantly smaller, however, at around 5 cm for males and 4 cm for females. *M. brasiliense* is reported to belong to the specialised reproductive type, but to date there have been no reports published regarding its breeding in the aquarium.

I found the following two species, portrayed in photos, in the Rio Trombetas in Brazil:

Trombetas Shrimp I, with long rostrum: form and dentition as well as the proportions of the large chelipeds suggest *M. amazonicum* (Heller, 1862). This species has relatively small eggs and was described from the entire Amazon region west to Peru.

Trombetas Shrimp II, with short rostrum: this may well be the widely distributed species *Macrobrachium nattereri* (Heller, 1862), and the body form and live coloration support this view. However, *M. ferreirai* Kensley & Walker, 1982 and *M. inpa* KENSLEY & WALKER, 1982 also look very similar.

Pair of *Macrobrachium brasiliense* from Colombia, the male in front.

Photo: F. Schäfer

Indo-Pacific species with equal chelipeds

Male Peacock Shrimp, *Palaemon concinnus*. The photo shows the species-specific black spot on the end of the tail and the peacock eye-spots.

Egg-carrying female Peacock Shrimp, *Palaemon concinnus*.

Indo-Pacific species with equal chelipeds

Indo-Pacific species

The "Peacock Shrimp" is transparent with a yellowish sheen on the back; males of this species grow to 7 cm long, while females remain 1-2 cm smaller. According to the researches of W. Klotz it is probably not a *Macrobrachium*, but a *Palaemon* species from the Indo-Pacific area, whose scientific name is *Palaemon concinnus* Dana, 1852. In this species the claws are - and remain - slender, which probably explains the specific name - the adjective concinnus means "slender" or "elegant". The two chelipeds are around the same length. The fingers of the claws bear fine hairs and the rostrum is long.

Palaemon concinnus, male

Adult specimens are recognisable by a narrow, dark-brown band and a dark spot in the interior of the sixth abdominal segment, i.e. immediately in front of the tail fan. In addition they exhibit a dark spot on both of the outer wings of the tail fan. These spots are not yet present in young specimens and are to be seen in adults only when they are in top condition. This also applies to the noticeably lighter (perhaps whitish is the best term) fingers of the male. Only in adult females are the lower points of the pleon attractively bordered with black and white. The eggs of this species are small (between 0.5 and 0.7 mm across) and light green initially, but change colour to grey as they develop.

These shrimps are almost always found near the coast, in river estuaries and shallow coastal lagoons - in other words they are inhabitants of brackish water. However, in some places they are also found in the sea and in fresh water, into which they migrate for a variable distance. It appears that adults at least are not found in salt water.

The medium-sized species *Macrobrachium lanchesteri* (De Man, 1911) has become known in the hobby as the "Glass Shrimp". The specific name is an honorific. Males attain a maximum total length of 5.5 cm. They cannot be distinguished from females on the basis of claw size, as the claws remain as small and slender as those of females. This means that these shrimps pose no real threat even to smaller fishes. The body is largely transparent with only a few brown lines patterning the carapace. The rostrum is long and has a (subapical) serra on the underside of its tip.

Macrobrachium lanchesteri, the Glass Shrimp, is frequently imported.
Photo: F. Teigler

This shrimp lives in the lowland regions of Thailand and Burma (Myanmar), where it is found in the rice fields - hence it is also sometimes known in English-speaking countries as the "Rice Field Prawn". In its native lands the rice farmers breed it for the cooking pot, so it is actually of some economic importance.

Macrobrachium lamarrei lamarrei, female from India.
Photo: C. Lukhaup

Macrobrachium lamarrei lamarrei (Milne-Edwards, 1837) is quite similar in appearance but can be distinguished by a longer rostrum, and is probably more frequently imported for aquarium maintenance than *M. lanchesteri.*

Indo-Pacific species with equal chelipeds

M. lanchesteri is a lowland species that in consequence enjoys higher temperatures and should be kept above 25 °C. If kept too cool it loses its glassy transparency and instead looks cloudy whitish, and sometimes it will quickly die if its requirement for warmth isn't met. On the other hand, it imposes no special demands as regards other water parameters. The eggs of this species are small, but not tiny, and thus *M. lanchesteri* has several times been bred successfully in the aquarium. Once released, the larvae should be fed the smallest plankton and freshly-hatched *Artemia* nauplii.

One of the most commonly maintained species in the hobby, the "Ring-Hand Shrimp", which belongs to the specialised reproductive type, has now been identified by S. De Grave as *Macrobrachium assamense* (Tiwari, 1859). It was originally described as *Palaemon assamensis*, with the specific name referring to its occurrence in Assam. There are two subspecies. *Macrobrachium assamense assamense* is widespread in the uplands of eastern Nepal, western Bengal, Assam, and Burma (Myanmar). The type locality is the Someswari River, which flows through the Garo Hills. The second subspecies was described from the Nerbudda River near Khetgaon as *M. assamense peninsularis*. It is found in the Satpura and Vindhya mountains in Madhya Pradesh. It appears that neither of the two forms occurs in the lowland plains. The first subspecies grows around a centimetre longer than the second, with males measuring 7 cm and females around 62 mm. The rostrum is longer and has more small serrae than in the second subspecies, whose chelipeds are somewhat thicker.

I invented the popular name in allusion to the colour pattern of the chelipeds of young individuals, which have black markings so that they appear to be wearing striped socks. But this is not always the case, and, in addition, not true of all individuals, as these shrimps too change colour considerably and repeatedly during their lives. Young shrimps are glassy or at least translucent, with faint lines on the body. Later the markings become denser and more intense, creating a brown marbled pattern. In well-coloured individuals the large, dark brown to black blotches, are surrounded by bright spots, while the rest of the carapace is brownish. From time to time individuals occur that are bright red, and for this reason this shrimp is also sometimes called *Macrobrachium* "Red Rusty". The red-brown coloration is not restricted to the (black and red) chelipeds! The latter are not particularly long in males, but are somewhat thickened. Both forms are exceptionally adaptable and recommended as aquarium occupants. They will readily breed from a total length of 45 mm (females) and 55 mm (males) upwards. The females lay large eggs with a diameter of around 2 mm, and - depending on the temperature, the water chemistry, and the air supply - take a period of around three weeks to develop into young shrimps that are perfect miniatures of their parents and can easily be reared in the freshwater aquarium.

The "Ring-Hand Shrimp" (*M. assamense*) often has attractive black-red ringed chelipeds, which are somewhat larger in males.

Indo-Pacific species with equal chelipeds

Dark-coloured male *M. assamense*.

Egg-carrying females of the Ring-Hand Shrimp become dark in colour so that the eggs can hardly be seen.

The eggs of the Ring-Hand Shrimp are large; they hatch into fully-formed young shrimps which are easy to rear.

Macrobrachium assamense belongs to the so-called *hendersoni* species group, whose members all exhibit a longitudinal groove on the large finger of the claws. This can best be seen with the naked eye in adult males, where the groove is coated with fine, fluffy hairs. A second species from this group is now also available, namely *Macrobrachium dayanum* (HENDERSON, 1893); in the juvenile stage this species exhibits similar "ring-hands" to those of *M. assamense* and the two species can be told apart only by examination under the microscope. If the rostrum is long and has more than five serrae on its lower margin then the shrimp is invariably *M. dayanum*.

Macrobrachium dayanum is very similar to *M. assamense*.
Photo: C. Lukhaup

The nine described species/subspecies of this group described to date can in fact be differentiated in most cases only by the length and serration of the rostrum and/or the relative proportions of the chelipeds. The species not previously mentioned are *M. hendersoni*, *M. hendersodayanum*, *M. platyrostris*, *M. cacharense*, *M. siwalikense*, and *M. cavernicola*. The last of these is worth mentioning as something of an oddity, as it leads a troglodytic existence, living in subterranean watercourses and flooded caves. The specific name means "cave-dweller".

M. hendersoni (DE MAN, 1906), from which the group takes its name, is occasionally seen in the aquarium trade as the Indian Shrimp. Its specific name is an honorific. It is not very easy to distinguish from the other species of its group

The species imported from Bengal as the "Spider Shrimp" is probably also *M. assamense*. Photo: F. Schäfer

Indo-Pacific species with equal chelipeds

Like the other species of the closely-related group that bears its name, *M. hendersoni* is very variable in its coloration and may even appear almost black.

Macrobrachium hendersoni, termed the "Indian Shrimp II" in previous editions.

as the very short, convex rostrum can be rather variable in its serration (5-11/2-3). Usually there are 5-7 serrae on the upper margin, generally with two of these behind the eye. Beneath the tip there are usually two serrae, so that the rostrum looks like a trident. The carapace is rough, the abdomen, by contrast, smooth. The chelipeds are equal in length (and usually these limbs are longer overall than the body), powerfully developed, and covered all over in tiny spines. The flattened claws and the fingers (which are always longitudinally grooved) are also coated in fine spines and hairs, and each finger has two powerful teeth.

Males of this species attain somewhat more than 5.5 cm total length. Juveniles and females are light-coloured, with a number of bluish-grey or dark olive stripes and spots. Innumerable tiny silvery dots are to be found all over the body. Males grow to a larger size, have longer and slightly thicker arms, and adopt a particularly dark coloration consisting of black-olive elements as soon as they become dominant. The claws are then almost completely black, and the posterior part of the body is dark marbled.

Macrobrachium idella, egg-carrying female.

Indo-Pacific species with equal chelipeds

Male *Macrobrachium idella*, referred to as Indian Shrimp I in previous editions, develop extremely long chelipeds.

Breeding poses no difficulties, but note that the species seems to be rather aggressive, at least towards conspecifics.

In India and Burma (Myanmar) this species inhabits exclusively running water and is found far into the interior at altitudes of between 300 and 1300 metres.

A second Indian Shrimp, of the primitive reproductive type, has also been imported. According to the researches of W. KLOTZ this shrimp is *Macrobrachium idella* (HILGENDORF, 1898). There are two subspecies, namely *M. idella idella* and *M. idella georgi*. In addition it is not quite certain whether or not *Macrobrachium idae* (HELLER, 1862) is identical with *M. idella*, as the two species differ only very slightly in the serration of the long rostrum and the power and length of the chelipeds.

For the time being I will assume that this shrimp is *M. idella*, a species that, depending on the sex, attains a body length of 5 to 7 cm. It occurs in southern India, western Madagascar, and even Tanganyika, and inhabits both rivers and still waters. Like *M. idea* this shrimp is regarded as a freshwater species, although both are sometimes also

Macrobrachium idae is occasionally imported from Sri Lanka for the aquarium hobby. It is very similar to *M. idella*. Photos: F. Schäfer

Indo-Pacific species with equal chelipeds

The Snowflake Shrimp, from India, was described as *Macrobrachium kulsiense* JAYACHANDRAN, MOHAN & RAJI, 2007 shortly before this new edition was printed. This specimen was "staged" against a dark substrate and using appropriate flash. Photo: F. Schäfer

encountered in brackish water. The chelipeds of females are short and slender, those of the male only slightly thicker, but extremely elongate and set with regular rows of fine spines. The claws are no broader than the chelipeds, the fingers narrow and equal in length. In addition the lower edges of the abdominal armour in sexually mature females are - and this is also the case in other species - marked alternately light and dark. The eggs of this species are brilliant white.

The dainty Snowflake Shrimp has only recently been scientifically described as *Macrobrachium kulsiense* JAYACHANDRAN, MOHAN & RAJI, 2007. It comes from eastern India and is now part of the standard range of the specialised pet trade. In the past it has been sold as *Macrobrachium luzifugem* or *M. banjare*, but it is now clear that it is neither of these species. It resembles *Macrobrachium mirabile* (KEMP, 1917) (which will be discussed later with the "swimming shrimps") from the Ganges delta and it seems likely that (like *M. mirabile*) it would be better assigned to a separate, specially erected genus. The two species are closely related to one another, although the Snowflake Shrimp appears to be more highly specialised.

The species is found from the Ganges delta to Burma (Myanmar) and in Thailand, where *M. mirabile* lives as well, but in each case in the upper reaches of rivers, which means it is better adapted to fresh water, and it also produces significantly larger eggs although it is smaller in size. The smaller females attain a length of up to 35 mm and are more stockily built than the up to 45 mm long males.

The new, currently valid, scientific name *kulsiense* relates to the type locality, the Kulsi River, a tributary of the Brahmaputra in northern India, where these shrimps constitute a food source for the local freshwater dolphins.

The popular name relates to its coloration. The sometimes more greenish- to brownish-, sometimes more whitish- to yellow-transparent base colour is covered with fine

Snowflake Shrimp, *Macrobrachium kulsiense*.

Indo-Pacific species with equal chelipeds

The Snowflake Shrimp can be quite active.

Snowflake Shrimp sitting on sand.

blackish and snow-white dots creating a pepper and salt pattern. This would be an excellent camouflage coloration over sandy bottoms, from which it can be assumed that this species is adapted to life in such habitats. In the aquarium their coloration looks most decorative against a uniformly dark background.

The species exhibits a series of striking characters. For example, the rostrum is exceptionally strongly convex and runs to a slender point anteriorly. The "palms" of the claws are slightly thickened and the claws of the second pair of chelipeds are without teeth. The peraeopods are slender and become noticeably longer posteriorly (cf. KLOTZ in: KARGE & KLOTZ, 2005).

These shrimps can be kept at a temperature of around 25 °C and a pH around 7; the water may - in fact should - be hard. However, this species tolerates sudden changes in water parameters badly. In addition they are shy and nervous and hence should have hiding-places available. The females produce large eggs, but totalling only between 15 and 20. Rearing the young is said to be relatively easy.

The Red Spotted Shrimp" is a large species from fresh water in Bengal. The individual in the photo originated from the River Ichamati. This shrimp too is imported for the aquarium hobby.

Indo-Pacific species with equal chelipeds

Macrobrachium cf. *equidens* JAYACHANDRAN, 1989 has been imported from Thailand for the aquarium hobby. In the wild at least it is not an inhabitant of completely fresh waters, but prefers brackish-water regions. Photo: F. Schäfer

This attractive, rather small (males around 7 cm in length, females 5 cm) *Macrobrachium* from Thailand has not yet been more specifically identified. For the time being it is termed *M.* sp. "Gold Arm" on account of the attractive gold marking on the chelipeds. Photo: F. Schäfer

African species with equal chelipeds

African species

Importations of ornamental fishes from West Africa again sometimes include *Macrobrachium*.

The arms and legs of the Guinea Long-Arm Shrimp are, like the body, brown or brown marbled, and the claws are comparatively broad. The species attains a body length of 13 cm. Unfortunately its identity remains a complete mystery.

I brought back from Ghana a species termed the Volta Shrimp on account of its origin, and which is probably *Macrobrachium dux* (LENZ, 1910). This shrimp, whose specific name translates as "leader", occurs in West Africa from Guinea to the Congo in relatively soft water and attains a total length of around 8 cm in males and 6 cm in females. The serration of the rostrum is striking, as both the posteriormost and the anteriormost serrae are somewhat further apart from the rest than the latter from one another. The chelipeds are slender and set with small spines, but lack any dense hair. On the anterior chelipeds there is a clearly discernible row of spines above and below, and these continue on each of the fingers. The fingers are noticeably shorter than the palm.

Juveniles of this species are more or less transparent, although the body is covered in tiny dark dots, producing an overall dusky appearance. However, most of the time these shrimps appear translucent-brown or reddish-brown, with a dark back and brown chelipeds, along whose outer edge runs a light stripe which continues on the lower finger of the claw. The chelipeds are long, but little thickened, so that the species looks rather delicate. In males the chelipeds are about a third longer than in females, which makes it easy to determine the sexes.

The species is purported to produce large eggs (around 2 mm in diameter), so that the species should be possible to breed in fresh water. However, to date there have been no reports of successful breeding.

Female Volta Shrimp, *Macrobrachium dux*.

Adult male of the Guinea Long-Arm Shrimp, imported from West Africa.

African species with equal chelipeds

An extremely dark-coloured, egg-bearing female of the Volta Shrimp, *Macrobrachium dux*, which I brought back from Ghana.

I have also seen large eggs in the species imported from the Democratic Republic of Congo and popularly known as the Zaire Shrimp, which in all probability is *Macrobrachium lujae* (De Man, 1912). The specific name refers to its occurrence in the Luja River. This species too lives in relatively soft water, and is also found in the interior of the country.

Pair of Zaire Shrimps, *Macrobrachium lujae*.

These shrimps are glassy-yellow when young, but soon a fine dark speckling appears, alternating with brown blotches to create an attractive marbled pattern. Breeding females in particular are dark, and their chelipeds almost black. The latter are short and thin, whereas those of the males are extremely long. Unfortunately, I haven't been able managed to breed this species successfully so far. I had two females which both carried eggs for some time, but one lost her eggs and the other died for unknown reasons before releasing her young.

Female Zaire Shrimp, *Macrobrachium lujae*.

An African species with slender chelipeds, imported from Guinea, is a sibling species to the American taxa *M. tenellum* (from the Pacific side) and *M. acanthurus* (from the Atlantic side). Its scientific name is *Macrobrachium macrobrachion* (Herklots, 1851). Its long arms are so striking that not only the genus name but also the specific name was chosen to reflect this. However, the chelipeds are not thickened although they are noticeably laterally compressed. The upper part of the arm in particular is set with stout teeth, set wide apart, on its upper and lower edges. The fingers of the claws are

African species with equal chelipeds

Male Zaire Shrimp, *Macrobrachium lujae.*

likewise flattened, short, and rounded anteriorly, such that they are spatulate in appearance. This brownish coloured species has a long rostrum, much prolonged anteriorly and strongly serrated. It is distributed in West Africa from Guinea to Angola and inhabits not only bodies of fresh water but also brackish regions.

Macrobrachium macrobrachion

The Lagos Shrimp turns up quite frequently in the pet trade. It is imported from Nigeria (Lagos) and I have also found it in Ghana. It was formerly sold as the "Laos Shrimp" and hence thought to be an Asian species! It has now been identified by D. Brandis as *Macrobrachium vollenhoveni* (Herklots, 1857). It can be found in West Africa from Senegal to Angola and was originally described as *Palaemon Vollenhoveni*. The specific name is an honorific. Synonyms are *Palaemon jamaicensis africanus*, *Palemon jamaicensis Vollenhoveni*, *Bithynis jamaicanus vollenhoveni*, *Palaemon* (*macrobrachium*) *jamaicanus angolensis*, *Palaemon* (*Parapalaemon*) *Vollenhoveni*, and *Palaemon* (*Macroterocheir*) *jamaicensis Herklotsii*. The names relating to Jamaica can be explained by the fact that *M. vollenhoveni* was once thought to be identical with the American species *M. carcinus* (qv), which is similar in form. But nowadays all the African *Macrobrachium* species are regarded as distinct and treated as separate from their sibling species in America.

Macrobrachium vollenhoveni attains a body size of 20 cm and develops particularly long claws, which are thicker in males than in females, but nevertheless slender and covered with small warty growths and somewhat larger spines. Along the upper edge of the arms there is a regular row of such spines. On top of the rostrum there are about a dozen very pointed serrae , and five on the underside. The claws are brilliant blue, while their bases and the ends of the forearms are yellow in young individuals. The rest of each arm is bluish in older specimens, and the upper edge of the otherwise grey forearm is yellow.

The females of this species attain at least 15 cm in length.

African species with equal chelipeds

Macrobrachium vollenhoveni is regularly exported from Nigeria for the aquarium hobby.

The similar-sounding names of the South-East Asian country Laos and the Nigerian coastal city of Lagos initially led to the false assumption that the Lagos Shrimp, *M. vollenhoveni*, originated from Asia.

African species with equal chelipeds

Their chelipeds are narrower and smaller in cross-section, but almost as long as those of the males. The numerous eggs are orange-coloured initially and so small that there seems little hope of breeding these shrimps successfully under aquarium conditions.

Their size alone dictates an aquarium of about 200 litres with a bottom area of about 100 x 60 or 120 x 50 centimetres for a group of three or four of these giant shrimps. In contrast to smaller species there is also a greater risk that they will prey on fishes, seizing them with their claws. Of course they will find it easier to catch fishes that are ill or cultivated forms with long tails that are not able to flee fast enough, and during the night they may take sleeping fishes by surprise.

In addition they eat a considerable amount of food: within a few minutes an adult specimen can shovel down three smelt (slender food fish, about 5 centimetres long, available frozen - but defrost before use).

Juvenile specimen of the Lagos Shrimp, *M. vollenhoveni*. Even at this age the species can be recognised by its yellow palms and blue fingers.

The identity of this shrimp species, occasionally imported from Cameroon, remains as yet undetermined. Photo: J. Pinhard

Full-grown pair of the *Macrobrachium* species from Cameroon. Photo: F. Schäfer

Palaemonids with unequal chelipeds

"Dwarf Macrobrachium"

Similar to *Macrobrachium* are the shrimps of the genera *Pseudopalaemon* and *Euryrhynchus*, which are occasionally imported to Europe as bycatches from South America, more precisely from the Amazon and the Rio Negro and are labelled as "dwarf *Macrobrachium*", because they share the habitus of the long-arm shrimps with the small size of the dwarf shrimps of the family Atyidae - in other words the *Caridina* group. They do in fact attain a body length of only two to three centimetres, but actually belong to the family Palaemonidae. In the five *Pseudopalaemon* species the chelipeds are slender and delicate; by contrast in the three known *Euryrhynchus* species they are powerful and often blue or green in colour. In both genera there are species that produce a reduced number of very large eggs per clutch, which suggests that on hatching the offspring must be well on their way towards independent life. This means they should be relatively easy to breed in the aquarium.

Euryrhynchus amazoniensis is now and then exported from Peru.
Photo: F. Schäfer

Palaemonids with chelipeds of differing size and form

There are, however, long-arm shrimps of a type in which males exhibit chelipeds of different size, that is, one is particularly strongly enlarged and thickened or broadened in various ways, and often equipped with spines. This is not regarded as being of taxonomic importance, ie these species are not assigned to a special taxon because of this peculiarity, but are "lumped together" with the other palaemonids, although their behaviour distinguishes them from the species with chelipeds of equal size. For this reason they are dealt with separately here.

From my personal observations shrimps of this type lead a secretive life "in the background", and in addition a number appear to be crepuscular or nocturnal. As a rule they choose a narrow retreat at the bottom, for example beneath a stone or a piece of wood, which they then excavate, carrying and pushing sand and fine gravel to the exit. This may explain the cushion of bristles around the thickened cheliped - protection when the latter is used for shifting sand. When the work is done, they spend most of their time peering from these dugouts, lying in wait for prey, which they seize in a quick dart, hurrying back to their caves immediately afterwards. Their method of reproduction is that of the less specialised species, producing very small eggs from which, after eight to ten days, hatch tiny larvae which are virtually impossible to raise under aquarium conditions.

This is also true of a species I have provisionally called the Chamaeleon Shrimp, which was previously believed to be *Macrobrachium pilimanus*, and which is related to, inter alia, *M. eriocheirum*. These species have relatively large eggs and release fairly well-developed larvae that can even be reared in the freshwater aquarium. But this is not the case with my Chamaeleon Shrimp. According to De Grave (pers. comm.), it is in fact *M. scabriculum* (Heller, 1862), a shrimp which is distributed in Sri Lanka, southern India, Singapore, and the Malaysian peninsula (including Tioman). There are other, older, suspect reports that the species also occurs in East Africa and Madagascar. The species is purportedly similar to *M. dolichodactylus*, a species which can be found in the same areas - and in East Africa!

Juvenile Chamaeleon Shrimps (*Macrobrachium scabriculum*) are usually bluish in colour.

Macrobrachium scabriculum, the Rough Long-Arm Shrimp - for such is the meaning of the specific name - has a very short rostrum with a convex upper surface with 12 to 15 serrae on its upper edge - five of them posterior to the margin of the eye - and one or three (but normally two) on the lower edge. The carapace is rough in that it is covered in tiny spines, and the telson is strongly developed. The two

Palaemonids with unequal chelipeds

Adult males of the Chamaeleon Shrimp (*Macrobrachium scabriculum*) develop a cushion of bristles around the thickened cheliped.

chelipeds can differ considerably in their size, with either the left or the right arm being the larger. The fingers of the claws are slender and considerably longer than the palm. Males can reach a body length of around 6.5 cm, while females attain barely 5 cm.

In juvenile shrimps of this type the chelipeds are slender and both the same length. In the course of time, one of the arms becomes longer and thicker - this is also true of females, even though their enlarged arm always remains significantly smaller than that of the male. Fine bristles then gradually develop around the forearm of the latter, forming a kind of cuff-like cushion, from which only the tips of the claws emerge. It should be added that the upper parts of the arms of adult specimens, the entire smaller arm, and all the anterior limbs (except the antennae and the peraeopods) are covered with conspicuous long bristles, resembling spines.

In the course of their lives these shrimps too alter their coloration considerably. In still-growing specimens the body and legs are sometimes marbled light brown, but more frequently grey-blue to sky blue, while the spots on the body become denser and more close-packed with time, eventually forming black-brown patches in adult specimens. Ultimate only a yellow-brown stripe remains from the rostrum across the carapace to the tail, becoming broader posteriorly. On the upper surface of the anterior part of the telson this band splits into a double stripe, the two parts sometimes linked. There are also light stripes on the outer edges of the telson and the upper carapace.

Male of a long-arm shrimp species caught in western Ecuador.

I have also found shrimps with a singe enlarged cheliped in South America, for example in western Ecuador, but I am not quite sure if the males and females I caught at the same place represent the same species. The females were carrying numerous very small eggs, so it doesn't seem likely that they can be bred under aquarium conditions.

Palaemonids with unequal chelipeds

This egg-carrying *Macrobrachium* female was caught at the same location in Ecuador as the male pictured on the previous page. But that does not necessarily mean they belong to the same species.

The previous editions of this book also mentioned the so-called "Cuban Shrimp" that M. KEIJMAN brought back from the northeast part of that Caribbean island. The same applies to a species brought back by G. VOSS from. The Cuban species at least is probably *Macrobrachium faustinum* (DE SAUSSURE, 1857), a species that, according to KLOTZ (in KLOTZ & KARGE, 2005), is supposedly similar in appearance to *M. crenulatum* - a species that also occurs - and *M. olfersii*. In all three species the chelipeds are set with robust spines, with those on the palms of the claws being coated with fine bristles.

In *M. faustinum* the rostrum is slightly convex and has no upward-pointing tip, extends to the base of the antennae; on its upper surface there are 13 to 15 evenly distributed serrae, with five or six posterior to the

Juvenile specimen of the Cuban Shrimp, *Macrobrachium faustinum*. Photo: M. Keijman

margin of the eye, and two to three on the underside. The chelipeds are very different in their degree of development in males. The fingers of the larger claw are somewhat longer than the palm and stand noticeably apart from one another, with each bearing a stout tooth posteriorly. The palm is much widened and possesses

This shrimp of unknown provenance, imported for the aquarium hobby, is very similar to *M. faustinum* and probably identical with that species. Photo: J. Pinhard

longitudinal rows of spines, particularly strongly developed on its edges and outer parts but covered by a dense "coat" of hairs on the inner region.

The coloration is almost transparent, yellowish to pink, with spots of the same colour or a reddish hue on the body; these are more numerous on the carapace in

Macrobrachium crenulatum Photo: C. Lukhaup

females. The rostrum is reddish on the lower part of its base. However, this coloration can supposedly vary considerably - and from this it can be assumed that at least some variations in coloration can be explained as adaptations to a light or dark background.

M. faustinum occurs in Cuba, on other West Indian islands off Central America, and from the southern United States (Florida) south to Venezuela. The species inhabits the lower courses rivers and is apparently restricted to calmer water and sandy areas, where it can

Palaemonids with unequal chelipeds

The identification of long-arm shrimps is a tricky business. This individual from Panama is either *M. digueti*, as suggested by its coloration (if from the Pacific side) or *M. olfersii* (Atlantic side), as suggested by the length of the serrated part of the carapace.

pursue a secretive existence beneath leaves, wood, and rocks. These shrimps hardly ever venture into flowing water, but they do, on the other hand, like to visit coastal regions as long as the sea there isn't too rough. They prefer to live over sandy bottoms where they utilise pieces of wood and coconut shells embedded in the sand as daytime hiding-places, coming out by night to hunt for food.

Males attain a body length of almost 8 cm, while females grow to only a good 6 cm long. In *M. faustinum* the male sexual appendages are located on the second pair of pleopods. The species breeds year-round, but females appear to carry eggs mainly in the first half of the year. The larvae have to pass through several developmental stages in salt water before migrating back into fresh water as fully developed young shrimps that are initially still completely transparent.

The species *M. crenulatum* Holthuis, 1950, mentioned above, probably derives its specific name - meaning notched or serrated - from the form of its claws, as the spines are not covered in a dense coat of hairs as in *M. digueti* and *M. olfersii*. This species inhabits fast-flowing waters in Panama and Venezuela, but is also found on the islands of the West Indies in the Caribbean region and is considered a freshwater species. It is supposedly relatively easy to distinguish from *M. faustinum* by its unbanded fingers. The body and claws are grey-blue, the posterior body more yellowish in colour. The claws are enlarged, broad and set with robust teeth, but are overall more elongate in form and not so balloon- or ball-shaped as in *M. olfersii* and *M. digueti*.

Macrobrachium olfersii (Wiegmann, 1836) is distributed on the east coast of the Americas in Florida and from southern Mexico to Brazil, and is again regarded as an inhabitant of fresh water. I have found the species in Atlantic Panama, in the Rio Changuinola, a large, during the dry season shallow but nevertheless fast-flowing clear-water river with a stony bottom (pH 7.0; hardness 3 °KH and °dGH; 26 °C), where the species occurs sympatric with *M. heterochirus*. V. Wambach brought the species back to Europe from a watercourse near Puerto Viejo de Talamanca in Atlantic Costa Rica. His collecting locality was not far from mine. *Macrobrachium digueti* (Bouvier, 1895) - the specific name is an honorific - is regarded as a sibling species, occurring on the Pacific side of the Americas from Baja California south to Ecuador.

Unfortunately a faunal exchange has taken place via the Panama Canal, so that nowadays the species is also to be found on the other side of the Americas (or at the

Palaemonids with unequal chelipeds

This male *Macrobrachium olfersii* originates from Talamanca in Costa Rica.

The construction of the Panama Canal breached the geographical barrier between the externally very similar *M. olfersii* (Atlantic side) and *M. digueti* (Pacific side). It is thus virtually impossible to determine to which of the two species this specimen from Changuinola, Panama (the Atlantic side) belongs.

Palaemonids with unequal chelipeds

A further specimen of *M. olfersii* from the Rio Changuinola.

very least this is a possibility), which rules out identification on the basis of provenance and instead makes detailed study of the morphology.

Macrobrachium olfersii possesses a straight, at most slightly downward-pointing rostrum with 12 to 15 evenly distributed upper serrae, 4 to 5 of which lie behind the eye. On its lower edge there are as a rule three, more rarely four serrae. The carapace and telson are smooth. As in the previous species the chelipeds are very dissimilar in form, ie one of the arms and the associated hand is significantly prolonged and thickened into a ball-shape. The fingers of the claws are so strongly curved that a gap remains between them when closed. The two large chelipeds and their fingers are set with numerous robust spines, above all on the outer faces of the claws. By contrast the inner faces of the fingers are coated in numerous dense-packed, fine bristles. According to SCHMITT (cited by HOLTHUIS, 1952) the species can supposedly leap through the air for around 30 cm and run as well as a quadruped animal.

The base coloration of *Macrobrachium olfersii* is a warm yellow or light ochre. The claws, body, and tail fan exhibit a variable dark pattern of brownish to greenish spotting and striping. Males of the species, which is regarded as comparatively peaceful and "well-behaved", grow to around 9 cm, while females attain only around 6.5 cm in length, but are sexually mature by around 3 cm. Because they lay tiny eggs with a diameter of only 0.4 to 0.6 mm, the species is unlikely to be possible to breed in the aquarium.

Macrobrachium heterochirus (WIEGMANN, 1836) is a large shrimp morphologically reminiscent of *M. carcinus*. Some individuals are brown, but by far the majority are uniform blue to blue-green or olive in colour. This species as a

This impressive male *Macrobrachium heterochirus* was also collected in the Changuinola.

Palaemonids with unequal chelipeds

Macrobrachium heterochirus, egg-bearing female from the Rio Changuinola.

rule exhibits a striking cross-banding of the posterior body, by virtue of the segments of the abdomen having dark edges. It occupies roughly the same distribution region as *M. carcinus*.

The rostrum of *M. heterochirus* has 10 to 13 serrae on its upper surface, three to four on the underside, and a slightly upward-curving anterior tip. The serrae differ from those of *M. carcinus* - the spaces between the posterior serrae are larger than those between the anterior - and the joints of the second pair of chelipeds have different proportions in terms of length. In *M. carcinus* the so-called carpus (lower arm) is significantly shorter than the merus (upper arm), while in *M. heterochirus* it is the same length or longer. In addition the second chelipeds are similar in form in males except that one of the arms is always noticeably longer. This is the reason for the Latinised Greek specific name, which signifies "with different hands".

The species attains a body length of at least 135 mm in males, while large females measure only a little over 70 mm. I have collected adult specimens in the crystal-clear, fast-flowing and rocky Rio Changuinola (already mentioned in connection with *M. olfersii*) in Atlantic-coast Panama, not far from the border with Costa Rica. This shrimp lives in fresh water in the eastern parts of Central and South America from Mexico to southern Brazil, and is also found in the islands of the West Indies.

The same group of species also includes *Macrobrachium hancocki* HOLTHUIS, 1950, a large shrimp resident in Costa Rica and on the Galapagos Islands, and whose specific name is an honorific. W. KLOTZ (2006) has described it as possibly the most attractive freshwater shrimp in the world. If maintenance conditions are to its liking the males should appear bright blue, while the females are instead brownish in colour, remain somewhat smaller, and, of course, don't develop the huge claws that are such an attractive feature of the males.

Macrobrachium hancocki, perhaps the most attractive shrimp in this group. Photo: C. Lukhaup

Swimming shrimps

Swimming shrimps - Palaemonids that frequently swim in the open water

There are additional shrimps (with rather short arms), which are here termed "swimming shrimps", rather than "floating shrimps" as in the first edition of this book, because that name is used for the species of the family Mysidaceae. Some of the latter may also have been imported, but that is not definite.

The swimming shrimps - the term has no taxonomic significance but provides the aquarist with a clue as to their maintenance - have in fact been imported as "Ghost Shrimps" from South and Central America, India, and Africa (Guinea, Zaire) and practice - as far as we know to date - the primitive mode of reproduction. One exception is *Palaemonetes ivonicus* (see p. 76), which is sometimes imported from Peru and Colombia and belongs to the specialised reproductive type, producing a small number of large eggs. Most species are small, always transparent, almost invisible shrimps lacking any markings. Even in a well-decorated aquarium they prefer to remain in the darkest corners. They appear to avoid the light, so perhaps they are crepuscular or nocturnal!

At night their behaviour changes: they come out of hiding, paddle about in the open water using their comparatively long swimmerets, and search for food, which in nature supposedly consists of tiny plankton. Accordingly they can be fed on brine shrimp nauplii, powdered flake food, or fine frozen food (for example *Cyclops*). Naturally the food should be added to the tank after the light has been switched off for a while. It is also important to ensure that the food is distributed and circulated by the aeration, because these crustaceans catch their food in the open water. This also means that they lead a less substrate-oriented life than many of their relatives.

These swimming shrimps are highly specialised in various ways: firstly, their eyes are extraordinarily large and probably also particularly mobile, which undoubtedly enables them to orientate effectively, even in the dark. Secondly, their swimmerets are extremely long. They paddle forwards with almost imperceptible movements, such that they seem almost to float. In fact, in West Africa there are swimming shrimps that can even swim on the spot, with their swimmerets angled at 90° to their sides! If, on the other hand, they swim rapidly, their movements sometimes seem rather clumsy. But in the event of danger they flee as fast as lightning, shooting away backwards with their tail fans spread wide and jerky contractions of their abdomens.

Swimming shrimps react with alarm to sudden changes in illumination, for example the switching on of the lighting, and will jump out of the tank if there is the tiniest gap in the cover glasses. For this reason it is advisable to plug the gaps required for airlines and filter pipes, and the feeding aperture, with filter floss or similar material.

Their transparency is undoubtedly to be regarded as a protective specialisation. And finally, almost all known species exhibit fine iridescent lines, composed of chromatophores, on the antennae and on the back. These probably serve to enable the shrimps to recognise each other and to keep close together, as they apparently live in large shoals in nature. This is, at least, what hobbyists have observed in Central America: GARBE was unable to take photos while diving in Cuban mountain rivers during the night because there were too many swimming shrimps, which had not been visible during the daytime. SCHALLER (pers. comm.) reports similar experiences in Madagascar.

Desmocaris trispinosa AURIVILLUS, 1898 (the specific name signifies "with three spines") can certainly be regarded as swimming shrimps. The genus *Desmocaris* SOLLAUD, 1911

Desmocaris trispinosa. This swimming shrimp from Guinea moves around in the open water, above all at night.

itself is to date monotypic - in other words it contains only this one species. It is sold as the Nigerian Swimming Shrimp in the trade and can be recognised by a supra-orbital serra on the carapace and the smooth surface of

The same species spends the day resting concealed among the plants.

The Blue Indian Shrimp has now been identified as *Macrobrachium mirabile*. The specific name means "wonderful" or "marvellous".

the telson. It inhabits fresh water in West and Central Africa and is said to feed on detritus, algae, and small invertebrates. In terms of behaviour it can be classed as exceptionally peaceful.

I also assign to the swimming shrimps a species I have termed the "Blue Indian Shrimp", as in both sexes (and particularly in males) the pleopods are long, such that when the shrimp swims forwards they frequently curve to the rear. And these shrimps like to swim a lot, and often backwards as well as forwards! Males of the species grow to around 4 cm long, while females can attain up to 6 cm.

Macrobrachium mirabile, male

W. KLOTZ has now discovered that this species is without doubt *Macrobrachium mirabile* (KEMP, 1917). It is largely transparent, although, depending on the angle of the light, its armour may shimmer with a more or less intense blue. The segments of the abdomen are clearly delineated by black spots that widen into black cross-bands on the posterior edge of each segment. The appendixes of the caudal segments are darker in the deeper-bodied females than in the males. The contents of the stomach and the internal organs are almost always visible through the carapace. Depending on what the shrimps have eaten they develop an often brilliant spot, sometimes more of a yellowish colour, sometimes orange or greenish.

A further characteristic feature of *M. mirabile* is the very short rostrum, which begins in the middle of the carapace, describes a high convex curve above the eyes, and then continues convexly downwards. On its upper margin there are 13 to 16 regularly spaced serrae, four to six of them behind the eye. Another peculiarity involves the fifth pair of peraeopods, which are longer than the preceding two pairs, so that some authors would prefer to transfer this species, together with the Snowflake Shrimp, qv., to a separate genus. While the latter species inhabits sections of water at higher altitudes within its range (which extends from the Ganges delta to Myanmar and Thailand), the morphologically very similar species *M. mirabile* lives in the same distribution region but at lower levels, and is regarded as a brackish-water species.

Swimming shrimps

Swimming female with eggs (the eggs are yellow!)

In consequence its pale greenish-yellow, sometimes bright yellow, and slightly oval eggs are small. According to Jayachandran (2001) their longer dimension measures 0.54 to 0.61 mm, but only 0.41 to 0.46 mm at the narrowest point. The incubation period of the eggs depends on the temperature and oxygen content of the water and takes 17 to 19 days. They hatch into tiny larvae that drift away with the current.

The swimming shrimps also include a small species that originates from Paraguay and is the first freshwater shrimp to be seen exhibiting the cleaning behaviour previously known only from marine species. Further study of this phenomenon is required, but an armoured catfish seemed very happy to be attended to by the small, barely 3 cm long shrimp. These shrimps are exceptionally frequently imported from Paraguay as so-called by-catches with small catfishes of the *Otocinclus* assemblage, but because of their unprepossessing and inconspicuous appearance apparently provoke no interest among hobbyists. The species has not yet been identified.

A small swimming shrimp from Paraguay (highlighted) cleans an armoured catfish. Photo: F. Schäfer

By contrast another member of the swimming shrimp group, which has been imported several times from Peru and Colombia, has now been identified as *Palaemonetes ivonicus* Holthuis, 1950, a species that is widely distributed in Amazonia. Three species of the genus are known from Amazonia: not only *P. ivonicus* but also the sibling species *P. carteri* Gordon, 1935 and *P. mercedae* Pereira, 1986. *P. mercedae* is a readily distinguishable species that can be told apart from the other two species by its smaller eventual size and various morphological characters (the relative sizes of the elements of the second pair of pleopods, form of the telson). In addition *P. mercedae* undergoes a much-abbreviated larval development. All three belong to the specialised reproductive type and should thus be readily breedable under aquarium conditions.

P. mercedae has to date not been imported - or at least has not been recognised, as all these glassy swimming shrimps are extremely similar in appearance.

In a very interesting work Garcia-Dávila, Megalhães & Guerrero (2005) discuss the variability of taxonomically relevant characters in seven comparative populations of *P. carteri* and *P. ivonicus*.

Palaemonetes ivonicus is regarded as a whitewater species sensu Sioli, while *P. carteri* is supposedly an inhabitant of black and clear water. Research using various statistical methods demonstrated that *P. carteri* and *P. ivonicus* cannot be unequivocally distinguished from one another by any of the methods employed. At the same time the seven populations investigated included three different phenotypes. It was also found that one of these phenotypes, identified by statistical evaluation of methods of measurement, may occur in both black and clear water as well as white water, so that it is not possible to differentiate the two nominal species on ecological grounds. However, Garcia-Dávila, Megalhães & Guerrero (2005) do not synonymise *P. carteri* with *P. ivonicus* as their results overall indicate that there may indeed be more than one species of this complex in Amazonia, but at the same time it is not at present possible to equate any of these shrimps unequivocally with either of the available taxa as currently defined.

Swimming shrimps

The swimming shrimps include the small, barely 4 cm long *Palaemonetes ivonicus*, in this case a specimen imported from Colombia.
Photo: F. Schäfer

Palaemonetes ivonicus has very large eggs, but only a small number. Photo: F. Schäfer

Swimming shrimps

From a quite practical, aquarium-hobby viewpoint, however, the outcome of this research is that it is at present quite impossible to separate these two nominal species from one another. For this reason only the name *Palaemonetes ivonicus* will be used here. In the event of any future synonymisation of the two forms, this name is the older and hence takes priority.

The aquarium maintenance of this shrimp is totally without problem. It is very peaceful and also breeds quite readily, although the number of the eggs is relatively small. The species is actually an omnivore but should nevertheless be given (frozen) mosquito larvae as often as possible, as field studies of a freshwater species of the genus from Spain (*Palaemonetes zariquieyi* Sollaud, 1939) demonstrated that around 20% of the stomach contents of specimens investigated in summer in every case consisted of red mosquito larvae (bloodworm) and worms (Pérez-Bote, 2006).

The genus *Palaemonetes* occurs worldwide at warm and temperate latitudes, where it inhabits both marine and freshwater biotopes. *P. varians* (Leach, 1814), a species that occurs along the Atlantic coastline of Europe and Africa, exhibits a high degree of adaptability to a salt content of between 0.5 and 100 % of the concentration normal for sea water, but dies in completely fresh water (Parry & Potts, 1965). It has been bred for several generations in an unheated aquarium with a salt content of around 20 g/l (Seign, 2005). The newly free-swimming larvae were fed using rotifers (*Brachionus*) and *Artemia* nauplii. The larvae could be left with the adults.

Palaemonetes varians Photo: W. Seign

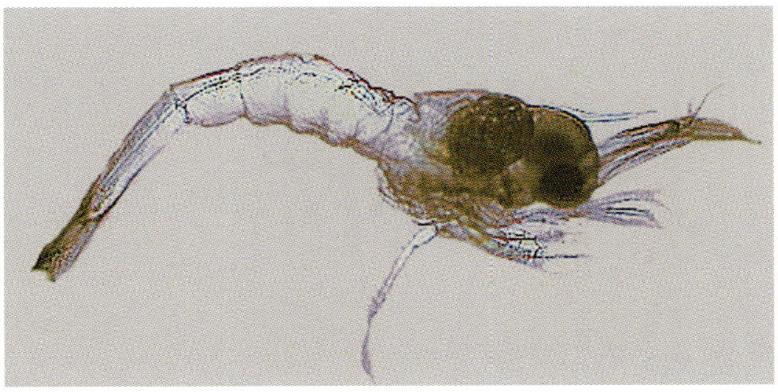

Palaemonetes varians, larva Photo: W. Seign

In southern Europe there is a widespread, but only locally common, freshwater species, *Palaemonetes antennarius* (H. Milne Edwards, 1837), which is regularly collected by aquarists, for example from Lake Garda. It too has been bred under aquarium conditions, with three larval and two post-larval stages so far described (Falciai & Palmerini, 2004).

Palaemonetes antennarius, a freshwater shrimp from Lake Garda. Photo: C. Lukhaup

European species

Our River Cray (*Astacus astacus*) has been almost eradicated by the crayfish disease introduced by American crayfishes.

Tropical crayfish species are the most suitable for aquarium maintenance, and European species are only very rarely maintained. In the first instance this is because all our native crays are strictly protected, so that only species bred for the table or imported are available. Secondly, it must be borne in mind that coldwater species cannot be kept in warm water all the tim. They need a winter rest period, during which the water temperature should drop to - depending on the species in question - well below 10°C and must be at this low level for several weeks at least. Unfortunately, there are no low-priced cooling units available for this purpose, whereas it is, on the other hand, quite inexpensive and easy to heat an aquarium. A third reason is that our native crays do not exhibit much activity during the wintertime, retiring to their hiding-places where they are of little decorative value.

Nevertheless it is important to be aware that three native European species do exist: the so-called Noble or River Cray, *Astacus astacus* Linné, 1758 (both parts of the scientific name signify crayfish); the Stone or Brook Cray, *Austropotamobius torrentium* (Schrank, 1903) (the genus name means roughly "southern river-dweller", the specific name refers to its occurrence in fast-flowing water); and the Drain or Culvert Cray, *Austropotamobius pallipes* Lereboullet, 1858 (pallipes =

Austropotamobius torrentinum Photo: C. Lukhaup

Austropotamobius pallipes Photo: C. Lukhaup

The Galician Swamp Cray, *Astacus leptodactylus*, develops powerful claws

"cloaked foot"). Only the last of these is found in Great Britain, where it is known as the Freshwater Cray. The genus *Astacus* was erected in 1775 by FABRICIUS, *Austropotamobius* by SKORIKOV in 1908.

Astacus astacus is reputedly very tasty and was distributed all over central Europe, with exception of the mountainous regions, during the 18th century. Unfortunately its numbers have been greatly reduced by the crayfish pestilence, and today it is considered an endangered species. *Austropotamobius torrentium* lives in mountainous areas, but is of no commercial importance. This is also true of *A. pallipes*.

The Galician Swamp Cray, *Astacus leptodactylus* ESCHHOLZ 1823, is occasionally imported from eastern Europe. It can be blue or brownish-olive in colour. Its body is covered in spines, and its claws are long and slender, hence the specific name (= "slender finger"). The underside is the same colour as the rest of the body. Just like *Astacus astacus* it has two hump-like post-orbital processes on the upper surface of the carapace, behind the eyes. Males are easily recognisable by their gonopods, and females by the genital openings at the base of the second pair of peraeopods. Females remain considerably smaller, are more sturdily built, and have a broader tail and smaller claws than males. The latter may grow to 18 centimetres in body length and can weigh more than 200 grams.

The species owes its popular name to its natural range,

Male Galician Swamp Cray: the photo shows the gonopods.

Galician Swamp Cray (*Astacus leptodactylus*)

Two males of the Galician Swamp Cray in battle.

namely Galicia, the northern slopes and foothills of the Carpathians, a region that today belongs mainly to Poland. But this cray is also found in other eastern European countries and in Turkey. It is unclear whether its natural range also includes eastern Austria or if it was introduced there by Man. All the populations in Germany are also attributable to Man.

There are four subspecies, and these live in brackish water some of the time! The species tolerates temperatures in the range between 7 and 22 °C, even 30 °C for short periods, but can be kept and bred only in spacious aquaria. These crays are omnivorous, feeding on anything edible including autumn leaves, thread algae, aquatic plants, snails, and aquatic insects. These largely crepuscular or completely nocturnal crayfishes are only mildly aggressive among themselves. Mating occurs in autumn at water temperatures of about 10 to 12 °C. The up to 400 eggs are laid some hours, or sometimes up to 14 days, after copulation. Their developmental rate is highly dependent on the prevailing temperature.

As a rule these battles do not lead to serious injury.

Northern-hemisphere crayfishes

American species: genus *Pacifastacus*

A small number of North American crayfishes belong to the subfamily Astacinae (but CROCKER & BARR,1968 place them in the subfamily Cambaroidinae) and the genus *Pacifastacus*. The genus name signifies "crayfish/astacid from the Pacific side" (i.e. of the Rocky Mountains). Members of the Astacinae and the genus *Pacifastacus* differ from the rest of the North American fluviatile crayfishes in that the males have no hooks on the ischium and the females have no special store for sperm, so that the latter is simply attached to the underside of the abdomen; hence fertilisation in these species is termed external. In addition there is no transverse seam on the telson. Moreover the gonopods in males are simpler in their structure; and finally, the genus can also be recognised by the form of the frontal process – specifically the latter invariably exhibits only a single pair of points, spines, or humps, and thus resembles a trident, although, depending on the species and the provenance of the individual this may not be particularly obvious. The two lateral tines of the trident at least are often rather blunt.

This can in fact be the case in the best-known species, the Signal Cray, *Pacifastacus leniusculus* (DANA, 1852):

With regard to the maintenance of American Crays, it is essential to point out that they represent a serious danger to our European crayfishes (*Astacus astacus, Austropotamobius torrentium*, and *A. pallipes*), as they can infect them with the so-called "crayfish pestilence", a fungal infection that was unknown in Europe until the Camber Cray (*Orconectes limosus*) was introduced here a good 100 years ago. Because, unlike the American crays, our native species had no immunity to the foreign pathogen, large numbers of them died. In fact they died out completely in some areas with only isolated populations surviving. And this happened only in Germany, but also in France, Spain, Sweden, Finland, and during the 1980s, apparently in Turkey as well. At the same time the American crays invaded the waters that had been home to the indigenous species, making it impossible, even now, to re-establish the native crays themselves. Because the American species remains a permanent carrier of the pathogen causing the disease, such attempts were doomed to failure from the start. It is thus absolutely essential to ensure that no American crays escape into European waters, which means that under no circumstances should they be released into the wild or even kept in outdoor ponds. Even the aquarium water in which American crays have been kept should not be tipped down the drain where it may eventually end up in natural waters!

The Signal Cray, a species of American origin, owes its popular name to the white markings on its claws.

Photo: Sch. Nakano

there are individuals with very pointed rostral tines and others where the tips are rather rounded. The natural distribution of *Pacifastacus leniusculus* is Canada and western North America, where it occurs in lakes and running water in the states of British Columbia, California, Idaho, Nevada, Oregon, and Washington. Because of its occurrence in California the Signal Cray is sometimes also known as the California River Cray. In terms of the form of the heavy carapace, the broad, robust abdomen, and the powerful claws, *P. leniusculus* is similar to the European *Astacus astacus*. As in the latter the armour lacks spines and is smooth, and this also applies to the claws. This character is also the reason for the Latin specific name (= "the little smooth one").

As in *Astacus astacus* the undersides of the claws are bright red - signal red, so to speak – although the popular name supposedly relates to the conspicuous white or whitish light blue patches on the joints of the claws, a feature not seen in *Astacus astacus*. In addition in the Signal Cray the bases of the legs are whitish and the underside of the body slightly bluish – in some individuals even sky blue in places. The upper surface of the Signal Cray is ochre-coloured to light brown.

As well as the nominate form *Pacifastacus leniusculus leniusculus* two subspecies have been described; these differ in the development of the postorbital ridges, that is the raised longitudinal areas of the carapace behind the eyes. In the nominate form *P. l. leniusculus* (pictured here) these ridges almost always taper to a spine-like point anteriorly. This point can be seen as a light spot in the photos. Immediately behind it there is in each case a separate, forward-pointing, shorter, light-coloured spine.

The acumen, the anterior tip of the head armour, is

Pacifastacus leniusculus, the Signal Cray, is a comparatively peaceful fellow. As long as its need for cool water temperatures is taken into account it can be readily maintained in the aquarium.

prolonged far forwards, narrow, and has pointed prongs. In *Pacifastacus leniusculus trowbridgii* the postorbital ridges are not pointed anteriorly and are followed by two separate humps with no points. The acumen is short and wide, and its prongs are blunt. In *Pacifastacus leniusculus klamathensis* the postorbital ridges again lack points; in addition they are only around half as long as in the preceding forms, slightly curved towards the very broad, short acumen, and lack any humps posteriorly. But because within any single population there may be individuals with different types of postorbital ridges and all the forms share the same distribution region, it is probable that at some stage they will be declared to be just a single, variable taxon.

Pacifastacus leniusculus is bred for the delicatessen trade in southern Germany at least, as this species is faster growing and less sensitive to higher temperatures than *Astacus astacus* and hence can be maintained in shallower ponds. In addition they are more tolerant of pollution of the water and very peaceful in their behaviour among themselves, so that they can be raised at a high population density. Perhaps their Latin specific name also relates to this characteristic, as leniusculus can be translated not only as "the little smooth one" but also as "the little gentle one"!

Male (above) and female of the Signal Cray.

Ponds for Signal Crays must be designed to be escape-proof, as these carriers of the crayfish pestilence must not be allowed to escape. This is eminently possible in the case of Signal Crays, which will, if the oxygen content of the water they live in is too low, leave it even by day and seek to survive the heat in cool, shady places. They can do this because as well as breathing via gills they also have a primitive lung, and as long as their body remains moist internally they can, if necessary, survive for weeks out of water. But they may also leave the water at night to feed and investigate their surroundings. Their nocturnal forays can cover a radius of several hundred metres.

The Signal Cray is crepuscular and nocturnal, and primarily vegetarian. It feeds mainly on algae, but also eats dead leaves, the roots of bushes, and both aquatic and marsh plants. A smaller part of its diet, up to around 10 %, also consists of animal protein, at least from its second year of life onwards. These crays will eat zooplankton, river shrimps, mosquito and other insect larvae, as well as carrion.

The claws of the Signal Cray, already mentioned above, are large and broad in both sexes and thus not a reliable method of sexing. The abdomen of the male is, however, always narrower and more elongate, and females – viewed from above – look bulkier overall. Even so they remain somewhat smaller than the males, which, from the age of four to five years onwards, can measure more than 15 cm from the tip of the rostrum to the end of the tail-fan, and tip the scales at over 200 grams. However, the most reliable method of determining sex is to turn the cray onto its back. Males have gonopods between the last pair of legs, pointing forwards like two bows; they are unmistakeable as, depending on the size of the male, their anterior part can measure more than a centimetre. These organs are lacking in females, in which it is possible to see the openings from which the eggs emerge, on the rear edge of the first segment of the third pair of legs from the rear. They are about twice the size of the sexual openings in males.

Signal Crays become sexually mature relatively late, which is in accord with their long lifespan. It is said that males become reproductively capable only at around a year and a half old, and females not until two and a half. The mating season of the Signal Cray begins when the water temperature drops in September. The males then seek out females, even during the day, seizing them and turning them onto their backs. Sexually receptive females are generally cooperative such that even smaller males are able to fertilise females of superior size. The male emits a whitish seminal fluid that hardens into little light-coloured rods in the water and adheres to the underside of the female.

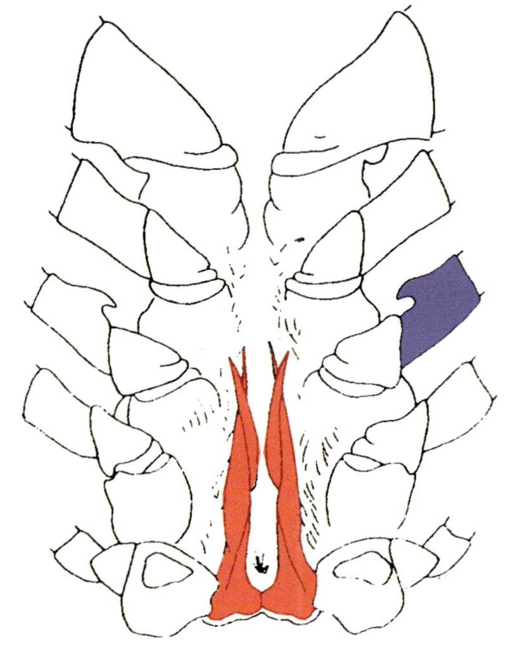

View of the ventral surface of *Orconectes limosus*. The first pair of pleopods is shown in red; the ischium, with hooks, on the third pair of peraeopods in blue. This colour coding permits comparison with the two adjacent drawings.

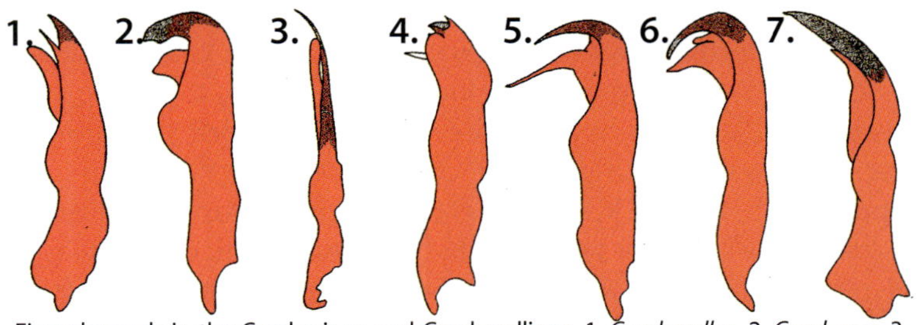

First pleopods in the Cambarinae and Cambarellinae. 1. *Cambarellus*, 2. *Cambarus*, 3. *Orconectes*, 4. *Procambarus*, 5. *Hobbseus*, 6. *Fallicambarus*, 7. *Faxonella*. In each case the left-hand pleopods of a sexually active male, with the hardened part shaded.

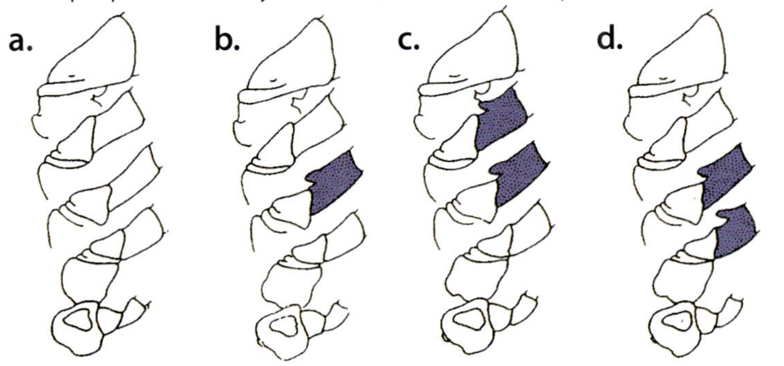

Peraeopods of male American crayfishes. a. without ischial hooks (*Pacifastacus*); b. with ischial hooks on the third pair of peraeopods (*Cambarus, Procambarus, Orconectes*); c. with ischial hooks on the second and third pair of peraeopods (*Cambarellus*); and d. with ischial hooks on the third and fourth pair of peraeopods (*Procambarus*).

All drawings after HOBBS, 1972 (modified)

However, it will be weeks yet before the eggs are laid. The females don't usually lay until February or even March. The eggs then rub against the sperm and are thus fertilised. The eggs have a diameter of approximately 2.5 mm and vary in colour between mid brown and blue-violet. Their number is dependent on the age and the size of the female and can be anywhere between 50 and 300. They adhere to the swimmerets of the female via fine threads and she can move them with the aid of the swimmerets. The developmental period of the eggs is highly dependent on the temperature and the oxygen supply, so that recorded data vary considerably. At an average temperature of 10 °C around 40 days should be required for development. The time from insemination to the release of the young crays can be six months, with 40 to 70 days of this representing the time required for the development the eggs and larvae. The female carries the larvae for around 10 days, during which they do not feed but are nourished by the remains of the yolk which they carry on their necks. But not all the young crays leave their mother simultaneously. Some of them sally forth but if necessary clamber back to the shelter of their mother's body, with their – usually nocturnal – forays getting longer and longer until eventually they stop returning to their mother and begin their independent life. They grow rapidly. While young Astacus astacus measure around 2 to 3 cm at the end of their first year of life, Signal Cray juveniles are already that large by July.

The Signal Cray is of only limited suitability for maintenance in the domestic aquarium as it cannot be kept at warm temperatures in the long term. It needs to be kept cool (and this applies to practically all North American crays) and if possible over-wintered at a temperature below 10 °C (i.e. in an unheated but frost-free shed or cellar), after which it can be transferred to a coldwater aquarium in which the temperature may rise to 22 °C, but not for long periods. At the same time strong aeration is essential. By contrast, feeding is no problem: these crays can be given vegetable-food tablets such are sold in the aquarium trade, as well as scalded spinach and/or lettuce, chicory, young nettle and dandelion leaves, flaked oats, and any type of aquatic plant from the garden pond.

American crayfishes of the subfamilies Cambarinae and Cambarellinae

The remaining Central and North American crays belong to the subfamilies Cambarellinae and Cambarinae which contain about 300 different species. These are assigned to the genera *Cambarus, Fallicambarus, Faxonella, Hobbseus, Orconectes, Procambarus*, and *Troglocambarus*. In terms of their reproduction these genera are the most highly specialised river crays of North America, as the males, which vacillate between a sexually inactive and a sexually active form, have evolved complex organs of insemination and possess so-called ischial hooks on the peraeopods, with which they attach themselves to the female during copulation in order to fertilise her with sperm. It is on the basis of the form of this character that these crays are assigned to the various genera listed above. All of them exhibit a tendency to internal insemination, unlike *Astacus, Pacifastacus*, and the Australian crays, which practice external fertilisation. Only those genera that are imported for aquarium maintenance will be discussed here.

These crays include large and small, aggressive and peaceful species, and both out-and-out plant-eaters and others that do not harm higher plants much if at all. They also come from different climatic zones, which means that their temperature requirements vary considerably. There is thus little point in generalising too much.

Even so, general statements can be made regarding the nutritional requirements of these crays (and all the other crayfishes discussed later). As they feed on carrion in the wild, their food needn't be "fresh". They voraciously devour the flesh of fish or mussels, as well as food tablets. They also readily accept any kind of frozen or commercially produced fish food (fish eggs, Mysis, bloodworm, sticks, pellets) and greedily feed on vegetable matter (frozen lettuce, spinach, Brussels sprouts). In addition all crays like to nibble on some types of twigs (willow, alder, oak, beech) and leaves (those of beech and oak are said to prevent fungal diseases). They should also be given material they can use for armour-building, for example unshelled shrimps or coarsely chopped fish complete with scales and bones.

American crayfishes of the genus *Orconectes* Cope, 1872

With around 90 described species the genus *Orconectes* is the most speciose genus of North American crays after *Procambarus* and *Cambarus*. Morphologically speaking they are highly evolved, but their behaviour is not particularly specialised. The first pleopods of the sexually active male form are spear-shaped and invariably end in two long, clearly visible prongs. These organs of fertilisation are straight or slightly curved, short or long, but always rather pointed, and the inner prong is hardened. Ischial hooks are usually found on the third, sometimes also the fourth, pair of peraeopods in the male.

American species: genus *Orconectes*

The Camber Cray, *Orconectes limosus*, was for a long the only species of the genus available in the aquarium hobby. It is the most commonplace large crayfish species in German waters, where it was introduced at the end of the 19th century as a food resource.

The majority of *Orconectes* species live further to the north than the other American crays, and a number even still occur in the catchment of the Great Lakes. The genus thus occupies a huge distribution region in the eastern and central parts of North America. From an aquarium viewpoint this means that as a rule *Orconectes* need to be kept cooler than the other American crays and that they should without fail be given a winter rest period of several weeks at low temperature (less than 15 °C).

A number of species are troglodytic, that is, they live in cave systems containing watercourses. This is reflected in the genus name: Orcus signifies "underworld" and nectes translates as "swimmer". As a consequence of their adaptation to a life in darkness a number of species have reduced pigmentation and atrophied eyes.

Orconectes inhabit waters that flow through lime-rich soil, which, of course, has an effect on the water parameters. In most cases the water is relatively hard with a high pH. Nevertheless all the species available to date can be maintained and bred without problem at a pH between 6.5 and 8.5 and a hardness of up to 20 °dGH.

At present probably only one *Orconectes* species is regularly available for aquarium maintenance, namely the Camber Cray, *Orconectes limosus* (RAFINESQUE, 1817). A month after its original description this species was described a second time as *Cambarus affinis*, which means that the latter name is a synonym. The species attains a body length of around 11 cm. Its Latin specific name (= "muddy") probably relates to its occurrence in swampy areas in the wild. Like other *Orconectes* it has a "warty" dorsal carapace, with spines on the sides of the head and a post-orbital ridge behind the eye. The striking brownish-red, vertically-elongate, blotches on the individual segments of the abdomen are a further diagnostic character. The tips of the claws may be studded with orange-red spines.

The species inhabits Atlantic slope drainages of North America from Maine south to the lower James River in Virginia. The Camber Cray was introduced into German rivers in 1890, and has subsequently conquered large parts of the drainages of the Rhine and Main, as well as rivers in Lower Saxony, and is now found in rivers, canals, lakes, and reservoirs.

These crayfishes survive our winters and hence should be kept in the garden pond only if there is absolutely no way they can escape. In any case, it is better to keep them in a cool aquarium. The water temperature can be allowed to rise to about 25 °C or more for short periods in summer. That apart, these crayfishes appreciate hard

Orconectes limosus Photo: B. Migge

water with an alkaline pH (above 7.2), and prefer a coarse gravel or pebble bottom rather than sand, with numerous hiding-places and clean, well-filtered water.

Orconectes limosus is also constantly active during the daytime. By dint of moulting, males alternate between two forms, one sexually active and the other sexually inactive. The former can most readily be recognised by its enlarged claws. In addition, such males have so-called ischial hooks on the third element of the middle pair of walking legs, which they use to anchor themselves to females.

The females are broader in form. There are as yet no reports of successful reproduction under aquarium conditions, though breeding should be possible. In the wild mating occurs in late autumn, but the females do not lay their 100 to 300, perhaps even 600, eggs until spring. The larvae hatch after four to six weeks, thereafter metamorphosing through two different larval stages (which shouldn't be fed) into fully-formed crays, which are tended by their mother for one or two weeks, gradually starting to live independently.

Orconectes maletae

A further species, which has now been identified as *Orconectes maletae* Walls, 1972, was first brought back by A. Nolte in the mid 1990s. It is found in the United States, in the Natchitoches and Sabine districts of Louisiana and in Upshure County in Texas. In the wild this Orconectes inhabits rocky stretches of rivers and streams.

The species can attain a body length of around 8 cm and, like the majority of members of the genus, is relatively plump in its form. It is strikingly patterned and hence can easily be recognised by its coloration: the body is unspotted, but the carapace is adorned with two broad, curved, bluish-grey bands. The first of these marks the posterior edge of the head and describes a kind of semicircular curve on its underside. The second extends along the posterior edge of the cephalothorax. The face too is bluish-grey, and each segment of the abdomen and the tail fan is delineated with brown. The most conspicuous characters are, however, the bright red spots behind the eyes (sometimes also on the back), the red tips to the claws, and the red markings on the middle joints of the peraeopods.

In the aquarium these crays have proved to be quite harmless fellows that can do no real damage by virtue of their small size, neither when they are kept together with smaller fishes, nor to plants. These crays are, however, rather quarrelsome among themselves, battling for order of rank and favourite spots in the aquarium. In some situations they may even kill weaker conspecifics or those that have just moulted. Nevertheless they can be maintained in relatively small aquaria with a bottom area of around 80 x 50 cm, as long as the container is provided with numerous caves. And it is quite possible to include hardier plants. An important factor in successful maintenance seems to be clean, well-filtered water, part of which should regularly be replaced with fresh. The water should also not be too soft and the pH should produce a slightly alkaline reaction.

Nolte also brought back *Orconectes holti* Cooper & Hobbs, 1980 in the mid 1990s. The specific name is once again an honorific. These crays are widespread in the south-eastern United States in the drainage of the Alabama River and have been recorded in the counties of Dallas, Lowndes, Montgomery, Perry, and Wilcox. The natural habitat is usually relatively slow-flowing waters with more often than not a sandy and/or muddy bottom, less frequently a stony substrate.

Orconectes holti attains around 9 cm in body length and in my view is a hardy and adaptable, but at the same time harmless little species, whose behaviour is similar

Orconectes holti

Orconectes placidus

Orconectes placidus

to that already described above for *O. maletae*. The body is short, broad, and strikingly patterned: the base coloration is a light sandy colour, somewhat darker only on the back, while the entire body, including the powerful claws and legs, is sprinkled with dark grey spots. These spots are irregular in shape and particularly large on the carapace and the anterior part of the broad claws, but by contrast rather small on the abdomen and telson. Sometimes they merge into one another. The tips of the claws are a striking red, but by contrast the joints of the peraeopods exhibit no red coloration.

To the best of my knowledge *Orconectes placidus* (HAGEN, 1870) was first imported by Friedrich BITTER in 2002. The specific name signifies "smooth", probably referring to the surface of the carapace. This cray, which attains around 8 cm, is relatively widespread in the south-east of the United States where it is found in various river drainages (Ohio River; Cumberland River; Duck River; Tennessee River) in the states of Illinois, Kentucky, and Tennessee, and in northern Alabama. According to descriptions of the natural habitat the species inhabits not so much fast-flowing but rather quiet, shallow, and mainly stony areas of water where it uses roots for shelter.

This is what can generally be termed a small, comparatively broad-built *Orconectes* with powerful claws and which can again be recognised by its striking pattern. The most prominent character is the broad striping of the carapace: above a narrow white margin a dark brown to green-brown stripe runs backwards describing an upward curve, and above it an olive band of similar width. In addition the sides of the head exhibit a light triangle that gives the impression of continuing as a light band on the chelipeds. The outer surfaces of the claws are dark green, so that there is a distinct contrast between the whitish underside and the lighter upper surface. In addition a dark band runs from side to side across the dorsum in the area of the cervical groove. The light brown claws become dark green towards their tips, while the tips themselves are yellow to orange.

Despite its overall brownish to ochre-coloured appear-

Orconectes durellii

It is not yet absolutely certain whether this crayfish is really *Orconectes pagei*.

ance *Orconectes durellii* BOUCHARD & BOUCHARD, 1995 - the specific name is an honorific - is well worth keeping as it is in fact a very active and lively little cray, which often occurs at relatively high population densities in the wild and hence can also be maintained in larger numbers in the aquarium – providing there are sufficient hiding-places available. These crays grow no larger than 7 cm and can be recognised by their very unusual stripe pattern. The upper surface of the head is somewhat darker than that of the carapace. A lighter, cream-coloured stripe begins beneath the eye and extends to the head groove. Beneath this there is a narrower, very dark stripe that broadens posterior to the cervical groove and runs across the dorsum in a lovely curve to the other side of the body. Further down there another, wider, light stripe that runs to the end of the carapace, but doesn't quite extend to its lower edge. The entire posterior body is brownish, the claws are particularly light in the area at the base of the fingers, then extremely dark brown, and finally light red at the tips.

Orconectes durellii inhabits clear, fast-flowing, small streams and rivers with boulders and dead wood on the bottom to provide hiding-places. Its distribution region includes the basin of the Green River as well as those of the rivers Cumberland and the Tennessee; in other words it is found in the American states of Kentucky and Tennessee. I am not entirely sure about the identity of a further *Orconectes* species but assume that it may be *Orconectes pagei* (TAYLOR & SABAJ, 1998). This species, whose name is an honorific, is said to inhabit small and medium-sized running waters with sandy bottoms in the counties of Henry, Benton, Carroll, and Henderson in Tennessee. I do not have any more detailed ecological data on the natural habitat.

This species can attain a total length of 6 cm and is an unassuming yellow-brown in colour, with darker brown spots on the legs and the claws, and two regular rows of spots extending from the posterior part of the carapace along the individual elements of the telson and tapering posteriorly. The tips of the claws are bright orange in colour.

American crayfishes of the genus *Procambarus* ORTMANN, 1905

The genus *Procambarus*, whose members are found mainly in the southern United States and in Mexico, are regarded as relatively primitive. In this genus the males have two to five small, spatulate, dish-like, or spine-shaped appendages on the first pleopods. The ischial hooks are found on the third or the third and fourth peraeopods of the male. The majority of the American crayfishes available in the aquarium trade are members of this genus.

One species worth keeping is the Cuban Cray, *Procambarus*

Male Cuban Cray, *Procambarus cubensis.*

cubensis ERICHSON, 1846. It attains 8-10 cm in length and its coloration can be variable and/or its coloration alter over time. Young crays are sky blue, medium-sized specimens usually grey-blue to grey-brown, larger and older individuals pale red-brown. The form shown here is the subspecies P. cubensis cubensis which is found in the Cuban lowlands. Its carapace is smooth and without spines, and it has two longitudinal postorbital ridges behind the eyes, a short rostrum with a single point, and slender claws.

Cuban Crays are not particularly aggressive. When first introduced into an aquarium these crays will, of course, fight for their caves, but the quarrelling is soon over. Within their caves they are find shelter in a strategically favourable spot which they create, at least in part, themselves, using sand, gravel and even pieces of wood to erect a wall, over which they are just able to see what is going on outside. If two crays meet outside in the aquarium they may raise their claws in threat, but in most cases the weaker individual retreats from the field of battle without any conflict taking place. If it comes to a fight the weaker crayfish may be thrown onto its back. If it is expedient to flee, it jerks backwards, whipping its tail forward, zigzagging lightning-fast to safety. But if the crayfishes know each other this happens only rarely. It should be added that the females are by no means afraid of the males, perhaps because they are bigger and quite capable of repulsing attacks and unwanted sexual advances on the part of males.

Sexual differences in the Cuban Cray, male above.

Mating in the Cuban Cray.

Female Cuban Cray with eggs/embryos on her pleopods.

Young Cuban Crays are often light blue in colour.

Newly hatched juvenile Cuban Cray.

The Cuban Crayfish can be used as an example of how to distinguish the sexes in crayfishes of the genus Procambarus. There are at least some species – including the Cuban Cray - in which the claws are so similar in all individuals that they do not indicate the sex reliably. Nevertheless the entire body of the male, and above all the abdomen, is more slender; as a result the body and claws seem to be longer - this can be seen more easily from above. Secondly, the males have so-called ischial hooks, about a millimetre long, on the fourth element of the third pair of peraeopods (males of P. clarkii have these hooks on the second and third pairs of peraeopods), and, behind the last pair of legs, the gonopods. The first and second pleopods in the male are curved forwards like a pair of bows, and form a kind of "stirrup", known as the petasma. They are used to transfer the sperm. Females lack them, but between the last and the second-last pair of peraeopods they have a whitish, oval plate with a diameter of 2-3 mm, the annulus ventralis, which is a characteristic of all the Cambaridae. In males it is so small as to be virtually unnoticeable.

The breeding behaviour of the American crayfishes can also be exemplified by the Cuban Cray. Mating often takes place following a water change. The male turns the female onto her back, while she indicates her readiness to mate by becoming rigid. During the act of copulation, which takes about ten minutes, both partners remain completely motionless and then separate without showing any further interest in each other.

Females with eggs can be transferred to another aquarium without hesitation. The eggs are round, with a diameter of about 1.5 to 2.0 millimetres, and hang like "bunches of grapes" of varying sizes beneath the abdomen, to which they are firmly attached. Their number ranges from 100 to 150, maybe even 300, but often not all of them develop for some reason, and are lost. They are greyish-green initially, but by the second or third day their colour will already have changed to a dark brown with a lighter "cap". Breeding females wave their pleopods to and fro, the more frequently the less the aquarium water is aerated. Well-oxygenated water seems important for the optimal development of the eggs. The future mother also keeps hidden most of the time, eating nothing. After 14 days the first newly-hatched young can be seen, still attached to the abdomen of their mother, leaving her by and by. The incubation time of the eggs depends largely on the prevailing conditions – 17 days at 26 °C, and 25 at 20 to 22 °C. It takes another three or four other days for all the young crayfishes to leave their mother.

The female does not hunt them for food, nor does she start feeding again until she has been put back with the other adult crays.

The size of the young is about 3 mm initially, and they are easily raised. As they don't show much interest in vegetarian food during the first weeks, it is best to offer them live Artemia nauplii, which they capture dexterously. After feeding the orange-coloured shrimps can be seen inside their bodies. They will also eat microworm, Cyclops, and Grindal worm. They must have food constantly available as otherwise they will eat each other. As they grow quickly there are always some that have just moulted, and it is difficult to provide enough hiding-places to prevent cannibalism completely. At the age of about four weeks the young will already have attained a length of over 2 cm and be noticeably blue in colour.

The species most frequently seen in the trade is *Procambarus clarkii* (Girard, 1852). The scientific specific name is an honorific, while it is popularly known as the Louisiana Swamp Cray, reflecting its (original) provenance. But this crayfish is far more widespread than its name implies, occurring from southern Illinois to northern Mexico (Chihuahua, Coahuila, Nuevo Léon, Sonora) and Escambia County in Florida. In addition it has been introduced in Virginia and Hawaii. There are even feral populations of P. clarkii in Japan, and for some years also in southern Europe (southern France, Spain). Moreover the species has been introduced into rice fields in Asia, where in some places it has multiplied to plague proportions, burrowing holes through dams and leaving the rice paddies high and dry. For a long time P. clarkii has been imported from Asia for the delicatessen trade and as an ornamental cray for aquarium maintenance.

Procambarus clarkii, blue variant

The result is that the *Procambarus clarkii* nowadays offered in the specialist trade come in a whole variety of colours. First of all there is the dark red natural form, originally the only type offered for sale until by and by occasional red and blue coloured specimens turned up too. These occur in wild-living populations as well, and I personally find them particularly attractive in appearance. But nowadays there are additional colour variants, which, as far as I know, have been line-bred in Asia from mutations and now breed true.

The form most frequently offered for sale is a brilliant light blue or white-blue, with almost no reddish elements at all in the coloration and thus somewhat "artificial" in its appearance, although the small thickenings of the carapace and above all on the claws are nevertheless orange in colour and thus enliven the overall impression to some degree. An even more extreme form, reduced to a single

Procambarus clarkii, red variant.

Egg-bearing female of *P. clarkii*.

American species: genus *Procambarus*

A red-blue wild form of *P. clarkii.*

P. clarkii, white cultivated form

P. clarkii, white cultivated form

P. clarkii, white cultivated form

P. clarkii, light blue cultivated form

Procambarus clarkii, blue and orange cultivated form.

P. clarkii, orange cultivated form

P. clarkii, orange cultivated form

P. clarkii, pink cultivated form

P. clarkii, blue cultivated form

colour, can be anywhere from pink to orange in hue, with the intensity of the coloration increasing with age. Older specimens become bold red -orange with time and then are real eye-catchers! Another variant which can at least be termed striking is a pure white form, which is not, however, an albino, as can easily be seen from its black eyes.

Unfortunately, despite their attractive colours these crays cannot be recommended without reservation. Specifically, they not only grow to more than 20 cm long, but also devour and destroy any plants present. In addition they require large territories, such that juveniles are better reared separate from one another. If several individuals are kept together in a single aquarium, usually one grows larger and over time kills all the rest so that only that one cray remains alive. On the other hand it is generally possible to keep adult *P. clarkii* in spacious aquaria in the company of larger fishes

Procambarus geodytes

(cichlids) provided enough hiding-places are supplied. The species is undemanding and adaptable and will tolerate cold (15 °C) as well as rather warm water (28 °C) for short periods. In the summer it should be maintained at 23 - 24 °C, but cooler in winter. The water should not, however, be too soft and in addition a certain amount of salt should be added. The reproductive biology of this species is largely similar to that of *P. cubensis*.

From C. Lukhaup I obtained some *Procambarus geodytes* Hobbs, 1942, a species that is currently assigned to the subgenus Hagenides (the name is an honorific), whose members have very broad and heavy claws, almost triangular in shape. The specific name geodytes signifies "earth-dweller", referring to the fact that during dry periods or when the water level drops these crays like to burrow their way into soft soil. The species lives in the southern United States in Florida, along the St. John's River and in its tributaries in the area from Putnam County and Orange County and/or Seminole County.

Like *P. alleni* (see below), *P. geodytes* is not primarily an inhabitant of running water but prefers swampy regions where water accumulates in depressions when it rains. During dry periods these crays excavate underground burrows in which it remains cool and damp; these can be single tunnels or extensively branched. The various entrances/exits can be recognised by their raised funnel-shaped openings, termed "chimneys", which can be between 5 and 10 cm high. Copulation and egg-laying also take place underground. Large females can carry around 100 eggs. When the rain comes after a dry period the crays emerge from their tunnels and migrate cross-country to find water, where the young leave their mother and go their own way. A striking feature of these rather short-bodied crays is the round, balloon-like cephalothorax posterior to the head, terminating in a rather slender telson. In juveniles the body is an orange or brownish colour, later more grey-blue to black-blue. These crays are then rather dusky in appearance. With a body length of around 6 cm they also remain rather small and do not do any harm to one another in aquaria of suitably large size provided with plenty of caves. Because of their small size they are also unlikely to be a danger to healthy fishes. *Procambarus geodytes* are undemanding crayfishes that can be maintained in a small group in aquaria of 50 to 150 litres capacity (offering as large a bottom area as possible). They like to hide and

Procambarus leonensis, female

exhibit an extraordinarily strong tendency to dig. Reproduction takes place in the aquarium without the need to simulate the dry and rainy periods described above, and follows a similar course to that of other American species.

Procambarus leonensis Hobbs, 1942 also originates from Florida, where the species inhabits slow-flowing and still waters in the drainages of the rivers Apalachicola and Suwannee. In its habitus the species resembles *P. clarkii* and has a similar attractive coloration. As regards aquarium maintenance, it seems that this *Procambarus* species at least will not tolerate long-term high temperatures (around 30 °C).

Not all *Procambarus alleni* are such a bright blue colour as this male.

The specific name of *Procambarus alleni* (Faxon, 1884) is once again an honorific. It is popularly known as the Blue Florida Cray and can be recognised by its spotted, "warty" armour. It grows to at least 12 cm body length and can be extremely variable in coloration: it is mostly vivid blue or bluish-violet specimens that are imported, but there are also inconspicuous bluish and brown individuals. The species is distributed east of the St. John's River and throughout the Florida peninsula south of Levy and Marion counties, and inhabits slow-flowing brooks, quiet shallow waters, and swampy regions, which means that, just like *P. geodytes*, it lives a semi-terrestrial life, i.e. sometimes out of water.

In the aquarium these crays tolerate temperatures between 15 and 28 °C, but the optimal temperature range is

Procambarus alleni, brown variant Photo: F. Teigler

Mating in *Procambarus alleni*.

Procambarus alleni in defensive mode.

Procambarus milleri, the Tangerine Cray, is troglodytic and hence has reduced eyes. Photo: Sch. Nakano

supposedly 20 –27 °C. The pH of the water should be alkaline and lie between 7.5 and 8. On the other hand the hardness of the water plays only an insignificant role. It is, nevertheless, important that the water is free of copper, nitrates, and other organic toxins, adequately circulated or aerated, and subject to regular partial changes.

Procambarus milleri Hobbs, 1971, the Tangerine Cray, is named in honour of George Miller, who made this species, discovered by Bill Drummond, available to Dr. Horton Hobbs for description. The species again originates from Florida, but is troglodytic, i.e. the species lives in underground streams and aggregations of water in the apparently rather thin upper layer of limestone in Dade County, Florida, which is also the location of the natural springs mentioned earlier. The surface of the rock is much fractured, full of cracks and crevices, so that surface water can readily flow in and accumulate in the eroded tunnels and caverns below. The influx of water also carries plant material, small organisms, and animal remains beneath the ground and these undemanding crays use this material as food.

The Tangerine Cray can easily be recognised by its intense orange coloration, exhibited even by juveniles. From a scientific viewpoint the coloration is actually regarded as albino. The eyes are not in fact red or white, but the dark eye pigment is reduced to a tiny little black dot. But it has apparently been established that the species is not light-sensitive and can be kept in normally illuminated aquaria without concern on this point. This also means that these crays by no means spend their time hidden away in dark corners in the aquarium, but are also to be seen out and about, looking for food, by day.

The Tangerine Cray attains a body length of only 8 cm, in exceptional cases maybe 10, and is particularly well suited for aquarium maintenance. Although it consumes plant detritus it by and large leaves higher plants alone. In addition the species is extraordinarily peaceful in its behaviour towards fishes and above all conspecifics. These crays do not fight among themselves and do not harm their young.

The species, in which both sexes develop claws of about the same size, is said to be easy to breed. The breeding season is purportedly not limited to specific times of the year and reproduction may take place year-round. The eggs, which the female carries around with her between her swimmerets, are large and black. A single brood can supposedly number around 100 young, which are easy to rear using animal and vegetable food. At the same time they are not as markedly cannibalistic as in other species, which means that broods can be raised virtually without losses.

In addition these crays are again undemanding – they do

Procambarus ranei

Procambarus natchitochae Photo: K. Crandall

well in any harder water with a pH value above the neutral point and are best kept at temperatures varying between 20 and 30 °C depending on the time of year.

Procambarus raneyi HOBBS, 1973 - the specific name is an honorific - was first brought back by Arne NOLTE in the 1990s. It belongs to the subgenus *Pennides*, members of which have asymmetrically formed first pleopods in males, which means that the two gonopods are of different lengths. The species occurs in the south-east of the United States, from Oconee County to Aiken County in South Carolina, in tributaries of the Savannah River, and in Georgia from Stephens County to Screven County. In addition it is found in large and small affluents of the upper Ocmulgee River in the area comprising the counties of De Kalb, Gwinnett, Newton, and Walton.

P. raneyi inhabits fast-flowing streams and rivers, but the species has also been found in subterranean passages in the hard loamy soil of their banks. It is, however, not certain whether the crays actually dig these tunnels themselves. It may be that they use existing passages in order to remain in a moist environment out of the water.

These slender, generally elegant looking crayfishes have long narrow claws with small wart-like growths or spines of a different colour. The fingers of the claws are overall dark, but with orange tips. The base coloration of the body is a "cold" brown. The edges of the head and thorax are patterned with dark brown. In addition a broad brown band extends from behind the eye along the middle of the dorsal carapace to the join with the abdomen, after which it continues between vertical stripes bordering the individual segments and running downwards in a wedge-shape, creating a sort of zigzag pattern. A brown band again runs along the middle of the telson. The upper surfaces of the head and tail-fan are decorated with fine brown speckling.

Because of its coloration the species is easy to confuse with *Procambarus natchitochae* PENN, 1953, a species in which the thorax is unspeckled and traversed by a clearly delineated brown stripe with wedge-shaped indentations, and which is noticeably bolder than the corresponding pattern element in P. raneyi. Moreover there is a dark band along the sides of the telson, which does in fact have a slightly crenellated lower edge but does not look like a zigzag band.

These crayfishes, with a maximum body length of 8 cm, can again be described as small. It is thus generally possible to keep them together with small healthy fishes. Plants are apparently another matter – these crays don't eat them but will sooner of later nip them off. In other respects they are once again undemanding and have no special requirements; a few individuals can be maintained in an aquarium with a bottom area of 80 x 50 cm. These crays hide only rarely and exhibit no particularly strong tendency to dig. Because of their preference for running-water habitats the aquarium water should be clean and well aerated. By contrast water parameters appear to play no special role in their well-being.

The provenance and identity of the Marbled Cray, a common aquarium occupant, remain uncertain, but

Egg-bearing female of the Marbled Cray.

Female Marbled Cray with eggs .....

...and with already-hatched young crays between her pleopods.

If Marbled Crays are kept in soft water they become an attractive blue within a few weeks.

because it possesses an annulus ventralis it must be a cambarid, perhaps even a *Procambarus* species. Its base coloration is usually brownish, but can change to blue within a few weeks if it is kept in soft water. The species grows to about 7 centimetres and is said to be rather aggressive. In addition, it eats plants or chops them off. As already mentioned, New World crayfishes are as a rule determined by means of the first pleopods in males, which are transformed into gonopods, or by the hooks on their peraeopods. But in the Marbled Cray all individuals look like females. Nevertheless they reproduce without problem and are extremely prolific. They start laying eggs at a carapace length of 3.5 to 4 centimetres upwards, carrying them about as thick packets attached to the abdomen. Large females can lay up to 200 eggs! During their development bluish-white spots appear on these eggs. At 27 °C the larvae hatch after about 12 days. After a further 6 to 7 days the youngsters clamber down from their mother to begin independent life.

It is probable that these crays reproduce via parthenogenesis, that is, "virgin birth". In such cases there are as a rule only females, though exceptionally males may occur as well. Reproduction occurs via the fusion of two (haploid or diploid) egg cells within the same individual. It has also occasionally been suggested that these crays may be hermaphroditic, i.e. that they possess the gonads of both sexes; but against this is the fact that copulation has never been observed. Nevertheless hermaphroditic crays (with gonopores in both sexes) do in fact exist. They have for a long time been known from southern South America. They are members of the family Parastacidae (southern-hemisphere crayfishes), and of the genera *Samastacus, Virilastacus,* and *Parastacus*, which sometimes live in caves. Adult individuals of these species that assume the role of females develop a broader abdomen.

American crayfishes of the genus *Cambarus* Erichson, 1846

The genus *Cambarus* is regarded as particularly specialised, and not only in its morphology but also in its behaviour. In sexually active males the first pleopods are blade- or sickle-shaped, particularly powerful, and in almost all species (there are two exceptions) the two sharp tips are directed backwards at an angle of almost 90°. The inner "sickle" is extremely rigid. Ischial hooks are invariably found on only the third pair of peraeopods in males.

The Latin name of the genus *Cambarus* means "surrounded with a bony skin", presumably referring to the external skeleton of the crayfish. The genus is at present divided into 10 different subgenera and contains a total of around 60 (!) species and subspecies. Although *Cambarus* are encountered in large parts of eastern and central North America, to date only a small number of species have been imported for maintenance in the aquarium.

American species: genus *Cambarus*

Cambarus friaufi

The species *Cambarus friaufi* Hobbs, 1953 - again the specific name is an honorific - was first imported in 2002 by Bitter Exotics. It is assigned to the subgenus Jugicambarus, whose members can be recognised by their particularly broad antennal scale, which is more than twice as broad as long.

This cray, which attains a total length of 4 to 5 cm, is found in Tennessee in the south-east of the USA, in fast-flowing, stony watercourses in the drainage of the Cumberland River at the so-called Eastern Highland Rim. According to other reports the species is supposedly also found somewhat further north-east in Kentucky. *Cambarus friaufi* is a small but at the same time broad-built species, with a short, plump body. Nevertheless these crays are rather active, and enjoy climbing and digging, though they hardly ever plants, so the latter can be included in the aquarium. The base coloration is yellow-brown, and the sides of the head and/or those of the carapace may also exhibit a greenish or bluish sheen. The abdomen, the claws, and the upper surface of the head, along with the tail-fan, are lighter than the central part of the carapace, whose upper central region exhibits a few dark spots, termed areola. The first pleopods have a distinct projection on their posterior lateral base.

Because of their small size these crays can readily be kept even in relatively small aquaria of length 40 cm upwards, including in the company of smaller fishes. They won't even harm small fishes that are awkward swimmers, for example fancy guppies. The depth of the container is unimportant, but the aquarium for these crays should be provided with numerous caves as they will develop an order of rank and fight for the best hiding-places. Unpolluted water with strong circulation is important for their maintenance, but by contrast water chemistry plays no special role in the well-being of these crays. The temperature can vary between 18 and 25 °C, and it is essential to allow these crays an annual period of cooler maintenance lasting two to three months.

The American crayfishes include several species in different genera that live underground all or at least some of the

When *Cambarus rusticiformis* feels threatened it raises its tail.

time, spending their lives in the half-dark or total darkness as they wander through subterranean watercourses. These species include a number of *Cambarus*, which in line with their lifestyle are assigned to the subgenus *Erebicambarus* (the Latin Erebus is a name for the classical underworld.) One of these is *Cambarus rusticiformis* RHOADES, 1944, whose Latin specific name means "simple in form".

This species, first imported around 2000 by BITTER, is distributed in the south-eastern United States in the drainages of the Cumberland River and the Green River in Kentucky and Tennessee and in the Ohio River in southern Illinois. It inhabits rocky, fast-flowing rivers and streams, apparently including those that disappear underground into the limestone.

With a body length of up to 9 cm this is a relatively small and – as is the case in the majority of *Cambarus* - relatively plumply built crayfish, whose rostrum normally has slightly concave lateral edges. The claws, carapace, and telson are exceptionally wide. In addition, in this species both sexes are particularly colourful, although the coloration of these crays can vary from individual to individual.

I have found these crays to be robust but nevertheless very mobile and active creatures, which like to move around the aquarium and are unusually fond of climbing, so that it is absolutely essential to make sure they cannot escape from the aquarium. I can guarantee that they will make use of filter hoses, cables, irregularities in the silicone sealant, and electrical equipment to clamber up and squeeze through the tiniest gap in the cover-glasses. If they can find a firm enough foothold they can demonstrate immense strength and even lift the glasses! It is essential to have a totally escape-proof cover and not too high a water level, especially during the early days when the crays haven't yet settled in.

Because of their small size and their heavy claws these crays again represent virtually no threat even to smaller fishes, though if they do manage to seize anything as prey it stands no chance of escaping again. When danger threatens or they are actually attacked they react immediately by lowering the head and raising the abdomen, at the same time spreading the tail-fan. They probably do this to make themselves appear larger and more dangerous. Although these attractive crays are not particularly aggressive among themselves, it is, of course, important to provide them with sufficient hiding-places. Aquaria of around 80 cm upwards in length are adequate for maintenance; frequent water changes and strong circulation are important to simulate the living conditions they enjoy in the wild.

Cambarus rusticiformis

American species: genus *Cambarus*

Cambarus speciosus

Cambarus speciosus is very similar to *C. rusticiformis* in its appearance, behaviour, and maintenance requirements in the aquarium.

American species: genus *Cambarellus*

American crayfishes of the genus *Cambarellus* Ortmann, 1905

The smallest American crays, also known as dwarf river crays, belong to the small subfamily Cambarellinae. In *Cambarellus* the first pleopods in males always end in three short points, albeit not always clearly discernible, with that nearest the centre of the body being hardened. There are ischial hooks on the second and third pairs of peraeopods.

The genus name *Cambarellus* is the diminutive of the crayfish genus name *Cambarus* (= little *Cambarus*) and itself refers to their small size. Cambarellus species purportedly attain 2 to 4 cm or slightly more and are found from Mexico along the coast of the Gulf of Mexico to northern Florida. Mexico is home to nine species of the subgenus *Cambarellus*, while further north we find *Cambarellus (Digiricambarus) shufeldtii*, the only member of its subgenus (which is thus monotypic) and seven American species of the subgenus *Pandicambarus*. There are thus species that tolerate lower temperatures and sometimes even require them.

They can be kept and bred in small aquaria, are hardy, and reach sexual maturity at the age of about three months, so that a succession of generations are produced rapidly. Egg numbers vary from 5 to 70 depending on the species and the size and condition of the female, so that these crays may initially appear not very productive, but a female can produce young around three times in a single year.
Cambarellus shufeldtii (Faxon, 1884) is a tiny species that grows to only two or three centimetres. If it is kept in a very

Cambarellus shufeldtii, striped form

small tank, it is essential to ensure that the small amount of water is kept as free of nitrate as possible. These crays have no special requirements, but females often remain hidden during the daytime – in general only the bolder males are to be seen. At night (or during the twilight periods) both sexes (which can be determined as in *Procambarus* species) seem to be more active.

These small crays are not aggressive towards their own kind, and are found at rather high population densities in nature. In the aquarium too they can be kept without problem in a group of several conspecifics, as cannibalism is comparatively rare.

There are two forms of this species, one with four stripes and another with an irregular pattern of spots. In the wild both forms can be found syntopic (in the same place). Intermediate forms are unknown, even though striped parents may, for example, produce spotted young.

Because these crays are rather short-lived – life expectancy is supposedly between one and a half and two and a half years - they become sexually mature at an early age. According to Nadal & Bitter (2006) female *C. shufeldtii* can often be seen carrying eggs in their third month of life,

Cambarellus puer Photo: C. Lukhaup

when they are still far from full-grown.

The aquarium hobby has F. Bitter to thank for the availability of *Cambarellus puer* Hobbs, 1941, a small species of 18 to 33 mm body length, in which males are always smaller than females of the same age. This may explain the Latin specific name, which means "boy" or "youth". Depending on their size and condition females produce clutches of between 40 and 110 comparatively large eggs, so that the species is easy to breed.

This dwarf cray is distributed from southern Missouri and Illinois southwards along the Mississippi to Louisiana and into western Texas and south-eastern Oklahoma. Its habitat is shallow areas in the often muddy bank zone, where marginal vegetation and marsh plants provide shade and hiding-places and the water is full of dead wood. In this part of the USA the daytime temperature range is around 0 to 10 °C in January and 20 to 32 °C in August. From this it can be seen that wide fluctuations in the water temperature take place on both a daily and annual basis. It thus makes no sense to keep these crays – and this applies equally to practically all American species – at constant high temperatures.

Like *Cambarellus shufeldtii, C. puer* also occurs in both a striped and a spotted form. The base colour is red-brown, dark red, pale orange, or grey. The claws are coloured to match, and are always smooth, without any "warts".

Cambarellus are probably descended from northern ancestors that subsequently spread further south to regions where the temperature doesn't fluctuate so dramatically. There are a number of *Cambarellus* in Mexico, but nowadays they are found only between the 8th and 22nd parallels of latitude. The main species involved are *Cambarellus montezumae* (Saussure, 1857) and its subspecies - which some authors now regard as valid species - and closely allied forms such as *C. alvarezi* and *C. chapalanus.*

Cambarellus montezumae was originally described as a *Cambarus*. The specific name honours Montezuma II. This Aztec ruler, who was killed in 1520, lived in Tenochtitlán, which once stood where Mexico City stands today. And because this little cray is to be found around Mexico City, in the "Mexico Basin" or "Valley of Mexico", it has borne Montezuma's name since 1857. Its subspecies are distributed further east and south-east. Because they differ

Camabrellus chapalanus, female with eggs

from each other only in small details, it is difficult to distinguish them, at least in live specimens.

Cambarellus chapalanus (Faxon, 1898) from the Lago Chapala (the species has been recorded from the Mexican states of Jalisco and Michoacán) are yellowish or brownish, with two dark double bands (not necessarily always clearly visible) running along the sides of the cephalothorax and abdomen.

These crays can be kept even in a decoratively planted aquarium: *Cambarellus* neither eat plants nor do they chop them off. But they do eagerly use them to leave the bottom, climbing about on their leaves and stalks. They are very active in contrast to many of their larger relatives, which in general move rather sedately and spend a lot of time in their hiding-places. They seem to be neither crepuscular nor sedentary, and are visible throughout the day.

Females are a little larger than males and their abdomens are broader, while the smooth claws are longer in males. The annulus ventralis of the females takes the form of an inverted U. Females lay between 30 and 40 eggs, about 1.5 mm in diameter, which under favourable circumstances develop within two weeks. A uniformly high temperature (around 25 °C), clean water, and strong aeration will encourage rapid development, without losses.

A very similar species, the Orange Cray, which may be coloured brownish or bright orange, has appeared in the aquarium literature variously as *C. patzcuarensis* Villalobos, 1943 and *C. zempoalensis* Villalobos, 1943. Both names relate to the origin of the two species in question, the Lago de Patzcuaro in the state of Michoacán in Mexico and the Lagunas de Zempoala in the state of Morelos, again in Mexico. On this basis, assuming the little Orange Cray is in fact one of these two taxa, its requirements are similar to those of *Cambarellus montezumae* and other Mexican species.

It should be noted, however, that these crays are more delicate than other types of dwarf crayfishes. There have been regular reports of sudden lethargy, problems with moulting, and premature death. In yet other cases females have lost their clutches for no apparent reason. Nadal & Bitter (2006) are of the opinion that the moulting problems at least may be attributable to too rich a diet, specifically too much protein, as these crays require large amounts of protein only when young, i.e. when they are moulting frequently. Later on a predominantly vegetarian diet is more beneficial. But they also advise against keeping these crays in too small an aquarium, and recommend filtering and/or aerating the water, performing regular water changes, and not keeping them at too high, and above all constant, a temperature, instead alternating cooler and warmer periods. I myself have found that the males can be rather aggressive among themselves, so it makes sense to keep only one male – if appropriate, with several females.

The identity of the popular bright orange dwarf crayfish has not yet been unequivocally determined. It may be either *Cambarellus patzcuarensis* or *C. zempoalensis*.

Crayfishes from the Indo-Australian area

The rivers, lakes, and swamps of Australia, New Zealand, and New Guinea are home to some 110 different endemic crayfish species, which have been assigned to various genera. *Cherax, Engaeus*, and *Euastacus* are the largest, each comprising some 30, 40 or more species, while the numbers in *Astacopsis, Engaewa, Geocharax, Gramastacus, Paranephrops, Parastacoides*, and *Tenuibranchiurus* are considerably smaller.

Many of these crays inhabit clearly defined ranges, which are often rather small. According to their type and provenance, they are called by a number of different names. There are crawchies (= small crayfishes), jilgies (*C. quinquecarinatus; C. crassimanus*), koonacs (*C. plebejus; C. glaber*), lobbies (= lobsters), marrons (*C. tenuimanus*), and yabbies (*C. destructor; C. albidus*). Some of them are real giants, and the biggest crayfish in the world lives in Australia. It attains a body length of 60 cm and weighs up to four kilos. But there are also small species with a body length of 20 mm upwards, and which are - at least in some cases – exceptionally attractively coloured, so we can hope for further interesting imports.

And it would be a good thing if more of these species were to be imported, as, except for the large species, many of these crays appear to be better suited to aquarium maintenance in terms of their requirements than are the species from North America. In the first place, they don't need to be kept cool for some of the time and will also tolerate high temperatures in the long term. In addition they are less aggressive and their often bulky, heavy claws mean they are far less capable of catching fast-moving prey such as healthy fishes, and less likely to climb out of the aquarium. A further plus point is that almost all species are eye-catchingly decorative in their coloration.

To date, however, only species of the genus *Cherax* have been imported. The genus name dates back to ERICHSON, 1864 and is sometimes cited by older authors as *Cheraps* or *Chaeraps*. It means "engraved" or chiselled".

Cherax are parastacids with 21 gills on each side and membranes on the telson and uropods, and in which the telson is not divided centrally. The abdomen is always smooth or at most covered in tiny excrescences but never with longitudinal rows of spines or other outgrowths. The rostrum is strongly developed and has two cephalic ridges extending posteriorly. Members of the genus may exhibit a total of up to five cephalic ridges: as well as those on the rostrum, sometimes known as carinae, there are also postorbital (= behind the eye) and medial (= central, ie situated between the rostral) cephalic ridges. As far as is known at present, *Cherax* species from New Guinea, which will be discussed later, never have medial cephalic ridges. The basal, i.e. the lowest, segment of the antennae is always the longest, the anteriormost the shortest. Some species have stout, forward-directed spines beneath the eye. The mouthparts are strongly developed and serrated. The first peraeopods are particularly strongly developed and bear the claws; both the right and left claws are the same large size but vary considerably in form depending on the species. Practically all *Cherax* are strikingly coloured, adaptable in their requirements, and hardy and easy to maintain. In the wild they are found in both running and still waters. Negative points include their relatively large size and their tendency to dig enthusiastically, plus they are more active in the twilight or even at night than in the day.

Cherax males lack the striking gonopods (they are present but inconspicuous) that make it so easy to determine the sexes in American crayfishes.

Australian species of the genus *Cherax* Erichson, 1846

The type species of the genus *Cherax* is *Astacus (Cheraps) Preissii* Erichson, 1846. The species now known as *Cherax preissii* Erichson, 1846 - the specific name is an honorific – is only rather rarely imported. In Australia members of this species, which exhibits four cephalic ridges, are popularly known as Koonacs.

The rostrum exhibits no or only very weakly developed serrae. The carapace is smooth, i.e. it lacks any "warts" or humps, and there are no hairs of any kind on the inner faces of the powerful, relatively broad claws. The species can attain a total length around the 20 cm mark and is rather variable, albeit always fairly dark, in its coloration: it can be brown, brownish-green, or brown-black to black. It is

In *Cherax* females the sexual openings are clearly visible at the base of the third pair of legs.

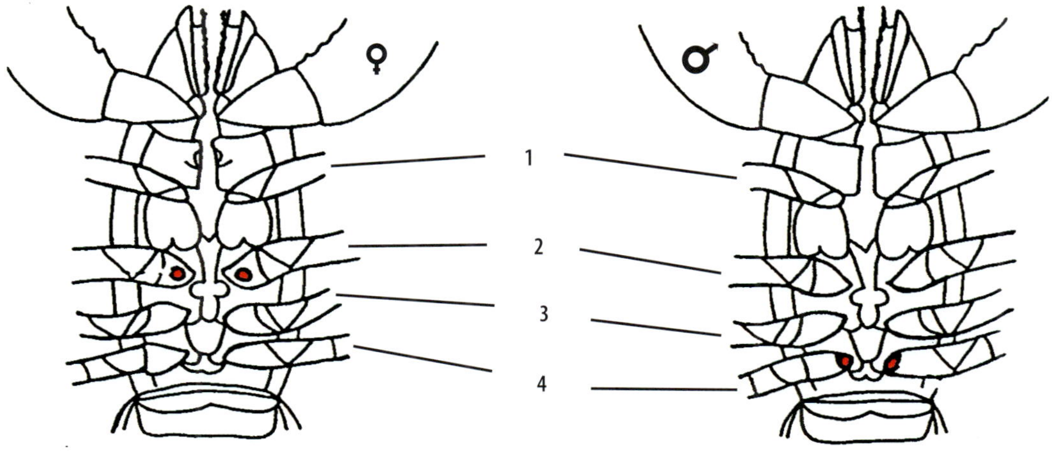

The sexes are most reliably determined in *Cherax* species by examining the crayfish from below. In females the openings to the oviducts (shown in red) are visible at the base of the second peraeopods, while in males the openings to the sperm ducts (again shown in red) are situated at the base of the fourth peraeopods. Individuals sometimes occur with both female and male sexual openings. These are males and the female openings are not functional. Diagram after Merrik & Lambert, 1991

Australian species of the genus *Cherax*

Cherax preissii Photo: F. Teigler

distributed in Western Australia in the area around Perth and further south to Albany. The species is found in both running water (streams, rivers) and also in still (lakes, swamps), and also inhabits waters that sometimes dry up. This means that the species is a powerful digger that buries itself in the damp bottom when the water of its habitat disappears. These crays can then survive unharmed in their damp burrows until the rains begin again.

W. ILG (2003), who has bred this species successfully in the aquarium, reports that imported specimens are very sensitive to temperatures above 22 °C. He gives the optimal maintenance temperature as 15 to 18 °C. Captive-bred individuals, however, seem to be appreciably more adaptable and will tolerate temperatures of up to 25 °C without problem.

Cherax destructor CLARKE, 1936 is the best-known member of the genus; in the past it has been the Australian cray most frequently kept in the aquarium, and this probably still applies today. It has four cephalic ridges and a practically smooth, at most weakly serrated rostrum and a smooth carapace. Unlike the morphologically similar *C. preissii* it has fine hairs on the inner faces of its powerful claws.

This cray, known as the Yabby in its native land, where it is protected, is bred on special farms for the delicatessen trade and for export. There is no need to be put off by its specific name, which translates as "destroyer", and which it received because it likes to dig – tunnels up to five metres in length have been found - and its activities destroy the dams of ponds. It attains a body length of around 14 cm, in exceptional cases as much as 16, so that it measures around 20 cm including the claws. But it is appreciably less aggressive towards conspecifics than *Procambarus clarkii* and hardly ever predates on fishes. These rather clumsy crays stand little chance of capturing fast-moving prey. On the negative side they do also like to dig in the aquarium, so any rockwork must be well founded.

Cherax destructor is a very successful and adaptable crayfish that has conquered large parts of eastern and southern Australia (Victoria, New South Wales, Queensland, Northern Territory) as its natural habitat and which is also particularly common. These crayfishes are said to be most abundant in the western districts of Buronga, Menindee, Balranald, Bourke, and Condobolin.

The Yabby lives in gently-flowing and overgrown waters in the cool wet regions of Victoria, in the southern coastal areas, and in the snow-covered mountains, as well as in the hot and arid areas of central Australia. This says a lot for its adaptability as regards water temperature, with a setting within the range 20 to 28 °C being optimal. But it will also tolerate significantly cooler or somewhat warmer water for short periods. In addition it is more often found in murky than in clear water. It is said to bury itself in the mud in dry years, in order to survive until the next rains.

Photos of *Cherax destructor* almost always show a brilliant sky-blue cray in which the claws in both sexes (!) are broad and smooth, roundish in shape, and usually have a pattern of light spots on their upper surface. The joints of the claws and legs are red. But the species is by no means uniform in its coloration: there are black, olive-blue, and greenish Yabbies and others that are dark and pale blue in colour. Yet others are almost brown on the back and abdomen; their claws are dark blue with heavy patterning on the upper part. And in all forms the coloration may also change when they moult.

Cherax destructor

A light, white-grey form has been described as a subspecies, *Cherax destructor albidus* CLARKE, 1936, with the subspecific name *albidus* meaning "white". But because both forms are found together practically throughout the species' entire range it would appear to be only a matter of time before *C. destructor albidus* is declared a synonym and regarded as simply a colour form of *C. destructor*.

Unfortunately it is usually only possible to buy specimens damaged during transport (unless you know someone who is breeding the species in the aquarium), and these are often in poor condition and often also missing legs, claws, or antennae. These will, of course, be replaced at the next moult, but first the crays must survive the move to a new home and settle in. Provided all goes well at this stage, they will subsequently prove be easy to keep. The pH should be fairly high (7-10) rather than low and the hardness of the water should likewise not be too low. It is sometimes recommended that a little salt should be added to the aquarium water, but this is not actually necessary. These crays are sensitive to fertilisers containing iron and medications that contain copper. Fungal diseases can supposedly be avoided by feeding with dry oak leaves.

Female *Cherax* - and this includes *Cherax destructor* females – usually remain slight smaller than males.

Cherax destructor received its specific name (= "the destroyer") because its digging activities can damage dams built by Man.

Sexual maturity is attained before the first year of life is over. Yabby females lay 300 to 350 eggs two or three times per year, in the wild usually between mid-spring and mid-autumn. The eggs are orange in colour but with a greenish or bluish sheen, and slightly oval, with the large diameter measuring barely 2.5 mm. After a week has passed they assume a blackish coloration, while unfertilised or dead eggs retain their original colour. The larvae hatch after somewhat more than three weeks, and are then carried around by the female for a further two to three weeks; even after they have "alighted" she continues to guard them for a few days more. During this period the female doesn't feed.

A second Australian crayfish, *Cherax quadricarinatus* Martens, 1868, is nowadays as good as always available in the aquarium trade. The species is more slender than *C. destructor* and has appreciably longer and narrower claws. In addition it has two or three pairs of spines on the rostrum, absent from *C. destructor*. Meanwhile *C. destructor* has a kind of "pectoral keel" between the third and fourth pairs of peraeopods, lacking in *C. quadricarinatus*. The scientific specific name quadricarinatus (= "with four keels or ridges") refers to the four cephalic ridges in this species; those on the rostrum are particularly long and extend to well behind the eyes. The carapace is smooth and in adult specimens there is a kind of longitudinal "brush", formed of tiny hairs, on the inner surfaces of each claw.

Cherax quadricarinatus lives on the northeast coast of Australia in eastern Arnhemland, a region whose rivers drain into the Van Diemen Gulf and thus the Timor Sea, and also in rivers further east that flow into the Gulf of Carpentaria. Except for a small area in the east, the entire Cape York peninsula is also included in the natural distribution of this cray. In addition, it has been released in recent years into waters in southern Queensland and north-eastern New South Wales.

In their natural habitat these crays are found in both clear and murky rivers and streams, lakes, and pools (so-called billabongs), and adult specimens will tolerate various degrees of water quality and pH values between 6.0 and 8.5. This hardiness also applies to temperature. If the oxygen supply becomes too low in warm water – these crays can withstand up to 42 °C for short periods – they extend their abdomens as far as possible and paddle vigorously with their swimmerets, and their respiratory activity is thereby reinforced. As a next stage the abdomen is also raised and the tail-fan spread as wide as possible. If the oxygen supply becomes even poorer these crays will climb above the surface or even leave the water completely. At low temperatures their activity levels are reduced and at less than 20 °C they virtually stop growing. Laboratory experiments suggest that the species can, however, survive short periods of cooling to 9 or even 5 °C. But most authors cite a temperature of between 24 and 32 °C as optimal for maintenance and breeding.

Pair of *Cherax quadricarinatus*, male right.

A newly-hatched young cray on the abdomen of a *Cherax quadricarinatus* female.

Cherax quadricarinatus youngster with residual egg-yolk on its back.

Australian species of the genus *Cherax*

Male *Cherax quadricarinatus* can be recognised by the half-moon-shaped spots on the claws.

This female *Cherax quadricarinatus* is carrying a clutch of eggs.

The bluish base coloration may vary from blue-green to brown, but can also be a brilliant light blue in places. The back and tail are spotted with yellow or brown, above all in females. In sexually mature males the outer edge of each claw exhibits a striking, elongate, brilliant red blotch, which why this cray is also popularly known in its native land as the Red Claw. In exceptional cases the species can attain more than 20 cm in body length, but is not very aggressive towards conspecifics. It can generally be kept with fishes as long as they aren't too small.

In suitably warm water *Cherax quadricarinatus* are exceptionally fast-growing and will reach sexual maturity as early as their fourth month. Male *Cherax* lack the stirrup-like gonopods that make sex determination in American crays so easy. But if they are viewed from below then it is possible to see the paired genital openings at the base of the fourth (last) pair of peraeopods. They are noticeably smaller than those of the female, in which they are found at the base of the second pair of peraeopods. It should be added that there are specimens with both male and female genital openings! But the latter are without function so all these crays are simply males.

These *Cherax* are also easy to breed. Copulation is, however, different to that in most crayfish species as the male doesn't throw the female onto her back but simply touches the female and keeps jerking his claws in her direction. Eventually he allows himself to fall backwards and then pushes himself beneath the female, whereupon the two crays grip one another with their legs. In this position the male releases his sperm, which can be seen as a "packet" between the last pair of peraeopods of the female. The female then cleans the underside of her tail and releases a slimy secretion which dissolves the sperm packet and allows it to spread all over the underside of the telson. The next stage is for her to lay her eggs there, which she does with her tail-fan rolled up (Gottschalk, 2002).

The 100 to 300 eggs are initially dark grey or greenish and measure around two mm in diameter. Later on they swell up a little and become lighter: yellowish, then brownish, and eventually orange, so that the development of the young crays in the eggs can be monitored. The development period takes around 21 days at 25 °C. The larvae, once hatched, continue to be carried around and don't leave their mother until a further two to three weeks have elapsed. They will immediately and eagerly take any food offered, but also decimate their own numbers through cannibalism. Under favourable conditions (as regards water quality, aeration, temperature, and food supply) they will grow on to 8 to 9 cm total length within nine months.

Maintenance and breeding in ponds has revealed that eggs and larvae tolerate old water and low oxygen levels badly, if at all. Oxygen-rich water with a pH value of 7.0 - 7.5 appears to suit both adults and broods the best. Fungal infections are supposedly commoner in acid water, leading to the death of eggs and larvae. But under normal circumstances it seems that chlorinated water, fresh from the tap, doesn't harm either adult crays or eggs and larvae.

Another Australian species, *Cherax tenuimanus* Smith, 1912, is apparently also imported occasionally. Its Latin specific name refers to the slender claws in this species: tenuis means slender, manus hand. And these crays do in fact have much slimmer claws than, for example, the Yabby or the *Euastacus* species (not yet imported), but they are only slightly more slender than those of *Cherax quadricarinatus*.

It is difficult to differentiate this species from a form that has been described as *Cherax cainii* Austin, 2002 (the specific name is again an honorific). Whether its specific status is justified or it should be seen as simply a form of *C. tenuimanus*, only the future will tell.

In Australia both these forms are popularly known as Marrons, referring to their chestnut-brown coloration. They can be recognised by several characters: firstly they have five longitudinal protrusions termed cephalic ridges on the upper surface of the head (the central ridge of the five is supposedly a different length in the two species); secondly there are three pairs of short spines on the rostrum; and thirdly they have two small spines on the centre of the tail-fan. Fourthly the carapace of these crays is not always smooth but may exhibit small protuberances laterally. In addition the claws are particularly slender and never exhibit "pads" of fine hairs.

This crayfish was imported from Australia as *Cherax tenuimanus*.
Photo: F. Teigler

Cherax tenuimanus can be ochre to chestnut brown in colour. But there are also brown-violet, blue, and black *Cherax tenuimanus*.

Cherax tenuimanus

Both forms occur in the same range of colour variants: as a rule these crays are brownish, but they can also tend towards dark violet as well as completely black, and there are also red-brown and even bright sky blue or blue specimens. The Marron is the largest known *Cherax* species, attaining a total length of up to 38.5 cm, though individuals are classed as adult at a carapace length of 7 to 8 cm.

Cherax tenuimanus is found in the south-west of Australia in the Margaret River. Its natural distribution comprises only the area from south of Perth via Harvey and Pemberton to Albany. But nowadays Marrons of the form designated *C. cainii* are also to be found in the coastal region further north and further east in the interior. Some of them have been introduced, some have spread via irrigation channels, and yet others are maintained in large breeding ponds from which they repeatedly escape into natural waters. The success of these introductions as well as pond culture has, however, been rather limited by the fact that Marrons have a very high oxygen requirement!

It is also for this reason that they aren't to be found in every billabong, but live in the deep and fast-flowing water of larger rivers, where they occur primarily over sandy bottoms in places where detritus has accumulated. Unlike other *Cherax* they don't construct long tunnels but spend the day in the shelter of rocks and aggregations of dead wood, mainly to avoid predation by cormorants. Of course they may enlarge their hiding-places if necessary, moving sand and gravel outside. At sunset they leave their retreats and search for food. Their population density appears to depend on the number of hiding-places available.

These crays are rather aggressive among themselves and for this reason their aquarium should be spacious. Of course it is also possible to rear them separately and then, when they become sexually mature, put them together under supervision. But it is more important to provide good aeration and efficient filtration in order to guarantee stable water quality. In addition the Marron tolerates only temperatures in the range 15 to 20 °C, with the optimum being 17 °C. In fact adult specimens will survive up to 25 °C on a short-term basis, but juveniles will die in water that warm. The pH should lie between 7.0 and 8.0.

This *Cherax* species has to date been imported only once, from Australia at the end of the 1990s. They were despatched under the name *C. pallidus*. *Cherax pallidus* HOLTHUIS, 1949 is a valid species (the specific name means "pale"), but *C. pallidus* is endemic to New Guinea, so that the identity of these crays from Australia remains unclear. Photo: F. Teigler

The Zebra Cray, imported from New Guinea, was initially incorrectly identified as the already described species *Cherax misolicus* and *C. papuanus*. But it is now clear that this species is as yet undescribed scientifically.

Cherax species from New Guinea

Cherax species have also been scientifically described from New Guinea, the majority of them by Holthuis in 1949. There are also a small number of older descriptions. But apart from two species, none of these crays are at present available for aquarium maintenance. On the other hand, additional species discovered in recent years are generally available, but because these are undescribed they are known by popular names, mainly relating to their appearance or origin, and these are not always used consistently. For this reason it is good to know that the descriptions of at least a few of these species is now in progress.

The first species imported from New Guinea was the Tiger or Zebra Cray, which was initially identified as *Cherax misolicus*, later as *Cherax papuanus*, as it was assumed that it must be an already described species. But more recent study suggests that it is in fact an undescribed species, for which to the best of my knowledge a scientific name will soon be available.

The Zebra Cray originates from the central part of southern New Guinea and is definitely known to be distributed in the swamps and rivers around Merauke, and probably northwards from there to Kiunga. But the precise boundaries of its range are unknown.

In this species the outer surfaces of the claws are usually white or cream in colour, bluish towards the inside and marbled with spots on the upper surface, similar to in *C. destructor*. The brown, blue, or blue-green carapace always exhibits a light lateral zone, while the dark abdomen has light stripes on the posterior edges of its individual segments, creating the zebra-like striping from which the popular name derives. Specimens with reddish claws are found in a stream in the vicinity of Kiunga that empties into the Fly River. According to the Dutch importers the majority of Zebra Crays currently sold for aquarium maintenance are no longer imported direct but originate from European and above all Asian (!) breeders.

All populations attain a body length of 10 to 12 cm and have proved to be fairly robust and hardy in the aquarium. However, they do like to dig enthusiastically and are extraordinarily secretive in their habits, so that they are only rarely to be seen, usually only at feeding time. In particular females carrying eggs and larvae remain hidden to such an extent that on occasion the first hint of successful breeding has been when their owner has come across youngsters when turning over rocks or cleaning the internal filter.

Cherax-species from New Guinea

The Zebra Cray has become established in the aquarium hobby and is available in the trade mainly as captive-bred specimens.

At the time of this book going to press the Zebra Cray was in the process of being described scientifically. Photo: F. Schäfer

It is also without doubt important to be aware that the males can indulge in serious fights, so it is best to keep only one male together with several females. The species tolerates a pH range between 7 and 8, does well in moderately warm water at between 21 and 25 °C, and likes to eat twigs and leaves, which, along with food tablets and frozen food, should always form part of the diet.

Cherax papuanus HOLTHUIS, 1949 is a good species from Lake Marguerite (also known as Lake Kutubu), which lies 850 m above sea level in Papua and is connected via the rivers Samaka and Mobi to the River Kikori, which in turn empties into the Gulf of Papua. The type specimens used for the description were 90 and 84 mm long, but the species may grow at least slightly larger. The sexes can supposedly be distinguished by the size of the claws: they appear particularly broad and heavy in males. The species has not been imported to date.

Cherax misolicus HOLTHUIS, 1949 is a small species (the only known material has a body length of 60 mm) and is particularly noteworthy in that the species inhabits an offshore island named Misool (the specific name thus relates to its origin) to the north of the Vogelkop Peninsula, where it lives in small, gently flowing streams that dry up before they reach the coast and in the Waitama River (near Fakal). The light outer edges of the claws in larger males are not calcified (i.e. they are soft), a feature otherwise seen only in *C. lorentzi*. *C. misolicus* has again not yet been imported for the aquarium hobby.

Cherax lorentzi (ROUX, 1911) was catalogued by LORENTZ back in 1905 under the scientifically inadequate designation kreeft (= crayfish) and was subsequently described as *Cheraps lorentzi* in his honour. The species attains just 16 cm body length and lives in western and north-western New Guinea, in the Upper Lorentz River west of Geelvink Bay, in the Etna Bay area at the foot of the Charles Louis Mountains, in the Mimika River, and on Regen and Bivak islands. The

Cherax lorentzi is rather similar to *C. quadricarinatus*. The photo shows a male, recognisable as such by the red markings on the claws. Photo: F. Schäfer

species is highly reminiscent of *Cherax quadricarinatus*, but differs from it in some details. Thus, for example, the claws are more angular in form and the colours are more clearly demarcated from one another. One very important difference is that in adult males of *C. lorentzi*, as in *C. misolicus*, the outer edges of the claws are soft and not protected by calcareous armour. The species, which is occasionally imported, should no be kept too warm. The optimum temperature appears to be around 25 °C. *C. lorentzi* has already been bred in the aquarium, and it turns out that this Cherax is nothing like as productive as the Australian species: 40 to 60 youngsters can be regarded as a good result.

A subspecies of *Cherax lorentzi, Cherax lorentzi aruanus* (Roux, 1911), has been described, and inhabits the Aroe Islands (Trangan and Kobroor) to the south-west of New Guinea. The subspecific name thus relates to the provenance (Aroe) of the taxon. The morphological differences from the nominate form are very slight: for example the rostrum is somewhat more slender and the claws are slightly wider.

In addition to the species already mentioned a further taxon, *Cherax albertisii* (Nobili, 1899) (the name is an honorific), has been described from the northern Katau River (not far from the mouth of the Fly) in the south-west of

Cherax lorentzi, female Photo: F. Schäfer

Cherax albertisii Photo: F. Schäfer

Papua New Guinea. The species again appears to be very closely related to *Cherax quadricarinatus*. At any rate the coloration is rather similar, including that of the claws, but the latter are particularly long and slender. The species grows to at least 14 cm long.

Cherax pallidus (HOLTHUIS, 1949) - the specific name means "pale", though this refers to preserved material and doesn't necessarily reflect the live coloration – again grows to around 14 cm long and appears to be endemic to Lake Paniai, which lies at an altitude of 1,742 m in New Guinea. The altitude alone indicates that these crays should not be kept too warm in the aquarium. A temperature between 21 and 25 °C would appear appropriate, and the same applies to the other species, discussed below, from the same mountain region. It is unclear whether this species has been imported yet - see also the caption to the photo on page 114.

Cherax murido (HOLTHUIS, 1949) – the name derives from the native term moerido (pronounced "mooreedo") is again found only in Lake Paniai. It has large eyes and grows to around 13 cm long. According to a description of the coloration dating from 1939 the species is supposedly pale red with blue legs. The upper surface of the body is described as pale brick red to pale red-violet. According to the details provided the claws are blue with red-violet to carmine red tips. The species has probably not yet been imported.

Cherax buitendijkae (HOLTHUIS, 1949) (the specific name is another honorific) again originates from Lake Paniai; it grows to more than 17 cm long and is mainly blue in colour, at least as far as the legs and claws are concerned. The fingers of the claws exhibit a light stripe. This species too so far remains unknown in the aquarium hobby.

The Apricot Cray has been scientifically described as *Cherax holthuisi.*

Cherax-species from New Guinea

Cherax holthuisi can be very variable in its coloration: there are not only orange but also grey or pink individuals.

The same applies to the next species, *Cherax longipes* (Holthuis, 1949), which originates from Lake Tigi (1,650 m above sea level) to the south of Lake Paniai. It grows to at least 13.5 cm long and, as far as can be ascertained from preserved material, has a bluish to yellowish-brown body, blue claws, and brownish legs. The specific name signifies "long foot" and refers to the long slender peraeopods.

Cherax communis (Holthuis, 1949) occurs in lakes Paniai and Tigi, and the specific name apparently relates to this "shared" origin. The species has also been recorded from the Elegeboe River, where it remains smaller. These up to 18 cm crayfishes are supposedly grey-blue with bluish claws and peraeopods, but can also be dark violet, sometimes mixed with pink shades, or greenish to brown, with the brown coloration predominating. Unfortunately this species has again not been imported yet.

Cherax boschmai (Holthuis, 1949) was again described from Lake Paniai. The largest specimen known measures 134 mm. According to Professor Boschma, who collected the material and in whose honour the species was named, these crays are vivid brick red. The claws in this species are supposedly particularly long and slender, as in *C. pallidus*. The species is not yet available in the aquarium hobby.

Cherax paniaicus (Holthuis, 1949) received its specific name from its occurrence in Lake Paniai and attains a body length of around 13 cm. It is supposedly dark grey, almost black, dorsally, while the claws are blue-grey to azure blue and the legs bluish to grey-green. There have not yet been any importations for the aquarium hobby.

Cherax solus (Holthuis, 1949) originates from Lake Tigi. Apparently only a single specimen measuring 11.5 cm was available for the description, and this is the reason for the specific name (= "alone"). The live coloration of this crayfish can only be surmised, but it is probably a predominantly blue species. This is yet another species that is at present known only from preserved museum material.

A species hitherto popularly known as *Cherax* sp. "Apricot" or *Cherax* sp. "Orange" has now been described by Lukhaup and Pekny and named in honour of L. B. Holthuis of the National Museum in Leiden, who described the majority of the New Guinea *Cherax*, and hence this crayfish is now correctly known as *Cherax holthuisi* Lukhaup & Pekny, 2006. Its most striking characters are the smooth, wedge-shaped rostrum, the small eyes, and the form of the claws. In addition the coloration is eye-catching.

The species originates from the Vogelkop Peninsula in the extreme west of New Guinea, where it occurs in Lake Ajtinjo at least. This lake is essentially a widening in the course of a river, more than 4 km long and up to 350 m wide, and probably ending in a subterranean connection with the Kais

The "Orange Tip" is currently regarded as a colour variant of *Cherax holthuisi*. Photo: F. Schäfer

River. The river itself contains rapids and small waterfall, as well as having steep banks as well as swampy areas. The clear water has a pH of around 6.5 (in the aquarium this can be increased to slightly above the neutral mark) and there is lush vegetation where the current is less and the bottom not quite as rocky and stony.

Cherax holthuisi is not, however, a plant-eater – in fact the same applies to all known *Cherax* species. But this species does live a secretive, retiring existence. The describers even suggest the possibility that individuals of the orange form may actually spend most of their lives underground. As well as the orange variant there are also light grey to bluish, yellowish, or even whitish forms. At the same time there are colour variants that are largely identical genetically but in which the body is a relatively dark green to olive colour, with yellow stripes (similar to those in the Zebra Cray) running across the abdomen. The tail-fan and the outer edges and tips of the claws are bright yellow or even orange-red. These forms are usually sold as *Cherax* sp. "Orange Tip" or *Cherax* sp. "Green Orange Tip".

All these Apricot Crays attain a body length of just 10 to 12 cm and are extraordinarily peaceful among themselves. Their mating in no way resembles a wrestling match. Before they set about producing offspring, potential partners often share one and the same cave, touch each another, and apparently get to know one another "personally". The actual mating usually takes place in darkness and is again a secretive affair. Egg- and larvae-bearing females also conceal themselves so well that their owner is usually quite unaware there are young crays on the way. In addition the female lays significantly fewer eggs than the majority of other *Cherax* species bred in the aquarium to date. They usually number only 40 to 80, and take a period of 7 to 9 weeks to develop at 24 to 25 °C - the optimal maintenance temperature range is 20 to 25 °C. The youngsters grow very slowly and often at very different rates, so that they need to be sorted by size in order to avoid cannibalism.

Hardly anything at all is known about a species imported from New Guinea and sold as *Cherax* sp. "Blue Moon". These up to 12 cm long crays are generally dark blue to blue-black or dark brown, including the peraeopods. The upper surface of the carapace is always dark, but the sides can generally also be light - olive, yellowish, or brownish. There are narrow light cross-bands on the abdomen and the lower edges of the abdominal armour are light. The outer parts of the tail-fan are an eye-catching yellow. The inner edges of the fingers of the claws and the basal part of the dactylus are also light – specifically white to yellowish. In males the outer edges of the claws exhibit a wide yellowish-white stripe.

Cherax-species from New Guinea

Cherax sp. "Blue Moon" is one of several *Cherax* species from New Guinea that are available in the hobby but not yet determined.

Cherax sp. "Irian Jaya/Hoa Creek" is the trade name of an as yet scientifically undescribed species with a body length of around 13 cm and which is particularly brightly coloured. Its most striking characters are the violet coloration of the carapace and abdomen, while the claws and legs are bright blue. The outer edges of the claws and joints of the claws and legs are brilliant white. The tail-fan is bluish to yellow.

Cherax sp. "Blue Moon"

These crays owe their popular name to their provenance. Hoa Creek lies on the Vogelkop Peninsula in Irian Jaya, i.e. in the extreme west, and crosses the road to Ayamura some 8 to 9 km east of Teminabuan. The river is 3 to 5 m wide at this point, barely 2 m deep, and crystal clear with a stony to rocky bottom. The crays are usually to be found in areas with little water movement. They should be maintained at a temperature between 20 and 25 °C in the aquarium as they won't tolerate too cool or too warm a temperature, at least not in the long term.

Cherax sp. "Blue Moon"

Even cooler water (specifically a temperature between 19 and 21 °C) is said to be required by the species sold in the trade as *Cherax* sp. "Red Brick" or *Cherax* sp. "Blue Brick". The unusual popular names relate to the broad heavy claws and the coloration of the individual cray. In the "Red Brick" the carapace is red with a blue cast, while the merus and ischium, along with the peraeopods, are dark blue to violet, and the carpus light violet

Cherax sp. "Hoa Creek" is one of the most colourful crayfish species.

Cherax sp. "Red Brick" is also very strikingly coloured.

Cherax-species from New Guinea

As in many species from New Guinea, in males of *Cherax* sp. "Red Brick" the outer fingers of the claws are swollen and balloon-like.

In *Cherax* sp. "Red Brick" the contrasting colour of the inner edges of the claws is particularly attractive.

Cherax-species from New Guinea

Cherax sp. "Blue Brick", another new crayfish from New Guinea.

Cherax sp. "Blue Brick" and *Cherax* sp. „Red Brick" (see previous page) are probably only colour variants of a single species.

Cherax sp. "Violet Blue", male Photo: F. Schäfer

Cherax sp. "Violet Blue", female Photo: F. Schäfer

with white edges; the claws are red but with blue on their outer parts and blue-black tips to the fingers, while their inner edges are adorned with a whitish zigzag band. This last feature is also present in the "Blue Brick", but the surface of the claws is blue, the hinge of the fingers and the merus are yellowish, the carapace greenish, and the abdomen or reddish dorsally and greenish laterally. The tail-fan is also greenish. In both forms males can be recognised by a yellow stripe or yellowish-white balloon-like spot on the outer edges of the claws.

These crays grow larger that the majority of the species found in New Guinea and can attain a body length of up to 25 cm, so that a larger aquarium of at least 200 litres capacity is required for their maintenance. It is not known how widely they are distributed in New Guinea and whether the colour variants are geographically separated local forms. The only information on its provenance is than it comes from an unnamed lake near Djidmaoe.

Cherax sp. "Violet-Blue" is the latest import from the group. The yellow edge to the telson appears to be typical for the form.

Cherax sp. "Violet-Blue", which looks very similar to C. sp. "Hoa Creek", again originates from New Guinea. Photo: F. Schäfer

Anomuran freshwater crabs of the genus *Aegla*

In 1989 S. BERGLEITER in wrote in the German aquarium periodical DATZ about some small South American crustaceans which he termed Krabbenkrebse (= "crab-crays") because of the way their pleon was folded beneath the belly. Purportedly he tried to bring back a few of these unusual creatures alive to Germany, and his article awakened the interest of aquarists. Nowadays these crustaceans are imported commercially.

They are members of the genus *Aegla*, which belongs to a monotypic family, the Aeglidae (superfamily Galatheoidea). From a scientific viewpoint they are regarded as unique freshwater members of the infraorder Anomura, which also includes the mole crabs, hermit crabs, and porcelain crabs, while the crayfishes and the crabs, both of which they resemble in part, are assigned to other infraorders. The crayfishes are "long-tailed crustaceans" of the infraorder Astacidea, the crabs "short-tailed crustaceans" of the infraorder Brachyura.

LITZ & PRIETO (2003) estimate that the Aeglidae at present include around 60 different recent species of the genus *Aegla* and one fossil species of the genus *Haumuriaegla* FELDMANN, 1984. According to their data three species, all described by SCHMITT in 1942, occur in Uruguay. *Aegla platensis*, with a body length of 38 mm (not including the claws) is supposedly the largest species of the genus (the specific name refers to its distribution in the La Plata basin), while *A. prado* (named for the type locality), at 25 mm, is the smallest. *Aegla uruguayana* (named after the country of Uruguay) is intermediate in size to the other two.

The Aeglidae are residents of the southern part of the South American continent, that is southern Brazil, Bolivia, Uruguay, Argentina, Paraguay, and Chile. Because many inhabit small, fast-flowing mountain streamsthey require cool water, though it is difficult to give precise temperature data as the optimal maintenance temperature will differ depending on the species and its origin. In the Argentinian Andes, for example, *Aegla* are found at an altitude of up to 4,500 metres! The majority of species probably live in running-water biotopes, so that a certain amount of current is indicated in the aquarium as well. There are, however, also species that occur in calmer water, and this applies to, for example, the troglodytic populations such as are known from the Gruta da Tapagem and the Grutas des Areias in the vicinity of São Paulo in Brazil. In Chile *Aegla* live in a lake where they have been recorded at 320 metres of depth!

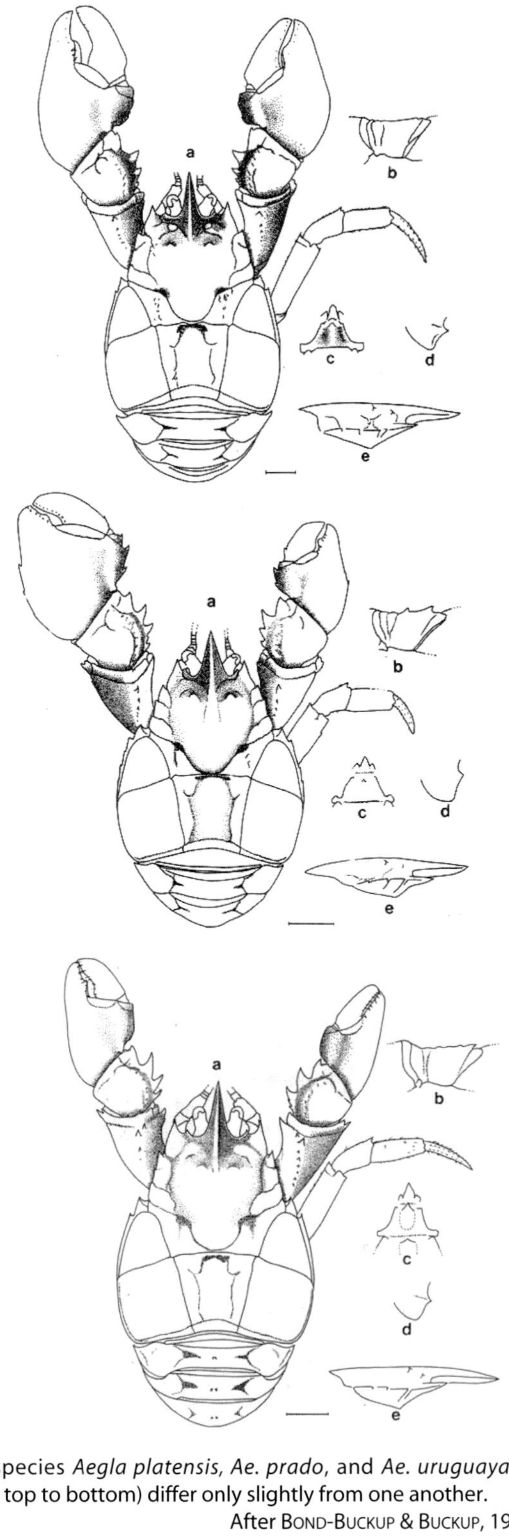

The species *Aegla platensis*, *Ae. prado*, and *Ae. uruguayana* (from top to bottom) differ only slightly from one another.
After BOND-BUCKUP & BUCKUP, 1994

LITZ & PRIETO, who adduce these examples, also provide ecological data for two species from Uruguay, *Aegla platensis* and *Aegla uruguayana*. They cite data from MARTIN & ABELE, 1988, who found both species syntopic in April at 22 °C in the Arroyo San Antonio, which flows into the Río Cebollatí. The population density was between 6 and 48 individuals per square metre.

Anomuran freshwater crabs of the genus *Aegla*

Although *Aegla* appear to lack a pair of peraeopods, they are nevertheless decapods. The fifth pair of peraeopods are greatly shortened and concealed in the gill chamber!

LITZ & PRIETO also caught *Aegla* themselves but were reluctant to assign them to any particular taxa as the species differ only slightly. Their own observations showed that these crustaceans live in streams and rivers with a stony, but sometimes also a sandy, bottom. In the latter case there are accumulations of leaf litter and sometimes even muddy zones, but the water is probably always clear and cool. In March (i.e. at the beginning of autumn) they caught Aegla in the Arroyo Tropa Vieja around 25 km east of Montevideo at 25 °C, pH 6.8, and a conductivity of 110 µS; and in August (in winter) at 20 °C, pH 6.5, and 220 µS. In the Río Negro near Paso de los Toros they recorded 11 °C, pH 6.5, and 110 µS in mid-August.

In the wild *Aegla* are found almost exclusively in the densely vegetated marginal zones of streams or rivers. Sometimes they are also found buried in the sand beneath stones. They appear to be Nature's attempt to evolve heavily armoured crab-like forms, poor swimmers but well able to walk and climb, from long-tailed crustaceans that are strong swimmers, by dint of folding the pleon beneath the body. The ability to walk and climb – perhaps also out of water – may be very useful in the type of biotopes for which these "crab-crays" are designed. Mountain streams sometimes change direction and may dry up seasonally or in places. Crustaceans that are able to move around out of water can then make their way to deeper water or any water available.

Aegla are in fact extraordinary in form, namely shallow and broad, so that – seen from above – the body looks like an oval plate. The abdomen looks rounded, while the head is somewhat more pointed. The rostrum is short and pointed, the black eyes are globular and the large antennae only as long as the carapace. The impression that the latter extends further back than in the crayfishes is an illusion, as the pleon is folded beneath the abdomen which hence looks extremely short. Viewed from the side, in its normal body position the crab-cray raises its head in such a way that the line of the dorsum forms an angle of 20 to 30° with the ground. Posteriorly it "sits" with its folded telson on the ground, while the rest of the body rests on the peraeopods and the claws.

Anyone who has read this book, and looks at a specimen from above or below, will initially be puzzled. Because in addition to the chelipeds, which count as the first pair of walking legs or peraeopods (and, as in the crabs, are enlarged and above all much broadened anteriorly, ending in powerful claws) there are only three further pairs of peraeopods visible. But *Aegla* too are decapods and must therefore have five pairs of peraeopods! The fact is, the fifth pair simply aren't visible, but are greatly shortened and concealed in the gill chamber. It is thought that they perform some sort of cleaning function.

Anomuran freshwater crabs of the genus *Aegla*

The bizarre *Aegla platensis* has gained an astonishingly large circle of fans within a very short time.

This individual is eating a piece of (frozen) fish.

The first peraeopods or chelipeds are, as in the crabs, greatly enlarged and widened anteriorly, ending in powerful claws that appear even heavier in males than in females. Otherwise the sexes can be recognised by the gonopods in males and the sexual openings in females; these are concealed beneath the pleon which are must be carefully unfolded to find them. The pleon, like the entire abdomen, is symmetric and ends in a broad tail-fan, which the crab-cray can jerk forwards – as crayfishes and shrimps do - to catapult itself backwards in lightning-fast leaps. Essentially, however, they are poor swimmers, as already mentioned.

The female also carries her eggs beneath her abdomen, i.e. between the underside of the body and the folded pleon. In *Aegla*, as in the crayfishes, the eggs hatch into fully-formed juveniles, but this is not the case in all crustaceans. There are, for example, a very large number of shrimps, whose – usually very small – eggs hatch into larvae that then have to pass through several developmental stages and may also be washed from fresh water into brackish regions or even into the sea, where they live pelagic (in open water) for a while before migrating back into fresh water. But their direct development means that breeding *Aegla* species in the aquarium, albeit not always easy, should be possible without major problems, as the juveniles are released and become independent at an already rather large size and can take the same food as their parents.

Litz & Prieo cite a paper by Verdi (1978), according to which *Aegla prado* at least is not seasonal, but breeds year-round; its eggs are orange and their development until the young hatch supposedly takes around a month, though the actual period may depend heavily on the water temperature and oxygen content of the water.

Anomuran freshwater crabs of the genus *Aegla*

In Aegla platensis, as in so many crustaceans, the base coloration of the armour can be very variable.

The *Aegla* currently available in the aquarium trade probably all originate from Paraguay. SEIDEL (2005) terms them *Aegla platensis* and in so doing is probably following SCHÄFER (2005), who reported the first importation. The identification was undertaken by Sandra KALSCHEID of Dirk BRANDIS's work-group. I haven't seen the original description of this species myself.

Anyone buying crab-crays should transport them not in water, but more or less "dry" in wadding sprayed with water or between damp plants or leaves. It would perhaps make sense to keep crab-crays in a long aquarium, in which an element of current can be created with the aid of a very small submersible pump. But I declined to do this and instead rely on the adaptability of these crustaceans, of which LITZ & PRIETO write that during water changes the tank can be refilled with cold mains water without prior treatment of any kind. In addition water parameters supposedly play a subordinate role in successful maintenance as long as the pH is around 7. My crab-crays lived in rather hard water (11 °KH and 19 °dGH) with a pH of 7.5.

As regards temperature, SEIDEL recommends a temperature of 23 to 25 °C, while LITZ & PRIETO suggest using an unheated aquarium in an unheated room with the window open so that the temperature fluctuates in a day-night rhythm and the temperature in winter drops to around 10 °C, while rising to more than 25 °C in summer. In my view these crustaceans are more likely to remain healthy if kept in cool water (up to 20 °C) rather than warm. If they are kept at high temperatures for too long they will die. All my specimens perished at a stroke during my summer holiday in 2006, which I attribute to the continuous heat during the month of July, which caused the temperature in the *Aegla* aquarium to rise to 28 °C.

When *Aegla* are introduced to an aquarium they immediately look for a solid surface, such as is provided by the side of a rock, and begin, using this surface to protect their rear, to dig themselves in – tail-first. As a result the sand flies only upwards and forwards. At the same time they display astonishing strength, moving pieces or wood and lifting pebbles of around their own body size. The distance from conspecifics appears to play no special role in the choice of a redoubt, or at least they don't seem worried if the adjacent crab-cray constructs its own shelter nearby. Sometimes they even encroach on one another and dig away back to back while facing in opposite directions. To the best of my knowledge quarrels, let alone fights to the death, never occur.

Anomuran freshwater crabs of the genus *Aegla*

Aegla-species should never be released into the wild!

Their peaceful behaviour, even sociability, is a great advantage for their aquarium maintenance as a large number of crab-crays can be kept together without problem, and without any worries that they will decimate one another as is very often the case with crabs and crayfishes. But the negatives should also be mentioned. At night they climb around on the aquarium décor and thus appear to be more or less nocturnally active, making them difficult to study. And their ability to climb is also a disadvantage – or at least they require a tight-fitting cover to their aquarium and constant vigilance to ensure that not so much as the tiniest gap remains open. They are far too ready to take the least opportunity to escape from the aquarium, and in most cases this results in losses.

Aegla are not specialists when it comes to feeding, but will eat a huge variety of different types of frozen, flake, and tablet foods, and even (Malayan burrowing) snails. They do not eat higher plants (I used only the harder-leaved types), at least not to the extent of causing damage. It must, however, be taken into consideration that they will prey on small fishes, at least those that are poor swimmers, or may overpower them at night. In my aquarium a number of small cyprinids disappeared, and when I offered the crab-crays small pieces of fish (such as I feed to my cichlids) I was not a little surprised at the way they eagerly seized even larger chunks and the short space of time in which they devoured them.

At feeding time they come out of their hiding-places and gather up the food, grasping it in their claws and – in my experience – usually eating it immediately on the spot. They are thus not particularly shy and do not drag their food back to a safe place before eating it, as many shrimps and crayfishes do. This makes removing uneaten food a lot easier. It is best to siphon it off and then top up the aquarium with fresh water, which at the same time confers an additional benefit as regards water quality. Because these crustaceans originate from unpolluted waters and react adversely to nitrate and other forms of pollution, such measures appear just as important as regular partial water changes.

Aegla have only recently been available for the aquarium hobby for the first time, and hence our knowledge of them grows day by day, so to speak. This new information includes the observation that *Aegla* die after eating *Anubias* (a popular aquarium plant from Africa). It is possible that *Anubias*, which is normally left unmolested even by confirmed herbivores among fishes, contains a toxin that is dangerous to crab-crays. For this reason the use of this plant in an *Aegla* aquarium is not advised.

Professor Ludwig Buckup of the Universidade Federal do Rio Grande do Sul in Brazil, who, along with his wife and colleague Dr. Georgina Bond Buckup, has worked extensively on *Aegla*, has written to us with the following interesting advice. He feels that it is perhaps very important to advise our readers never to release living *Aegla* into our native European freshwaters. It is true that *Aegla* come from the cold rivers, lakes, and streams of the southern Neotropics and would do very well in European waters. He says we are probably aware that in Argentinian and Chilean Patagonia *Aegla* are now probably the most important source of food for native and in particular introduced trout. For this reason Argentinian rainbow trout attain a much greater length and weight (up to 15 kg!) than in North America. Some years ago some Americans took a Chilean *Aegla* species back to California in the hope that this might encourage better growth in the trout. But the outcome was instead catastrophic as the *Aegla* began to eat the eggs of the trout and attempts are still being made even today to eradicate the crabs. So what would happen in German and other European rivers and streams in the event that any *Aegla* species established stable populations there? So beware!

We are very grateful for this warning and would like to take this opportunity to reiterate once again that aquarium livestock, no matter what type, must never, under any circumstances, be released into the wild!

Anomura
Hermit crabs

Hermit crabs – general

The Anomura at present comprise a total of around 1,700 species. However, in addition to the Aeglidae, already discussed above, we are concerned here only with the family Coenobitidae (terrestrial hermit crabs) with the two genera *Birgus* and *Coenobita* that will be presented in detail below, as well as two members of the genus *Clibanarius*, the only hermit crab species imported to date that are inhabitants of brackish water. Although this book is intended primarily for freshwater aquarists, we have decided to include these latter hermit crabs as well, as they are regularly available in the pet trade.

General shot of a *Coenobita compressus* male without shell, dorsal view. Photo:F. Schäfer

Hermit crabs can easily be recognised by the fact that they usually protect the posterior part of their body by concealing it in an empty gastropod shell. Some species also use the empty homes of other creatures, for example tubeworms, and there are also specialised species that live in symbiosis with stinging coelenterates or sponges that grow around the posterior body of these hermit crabs. But all these specialists are exclusively marine species that won't be discussed further here.

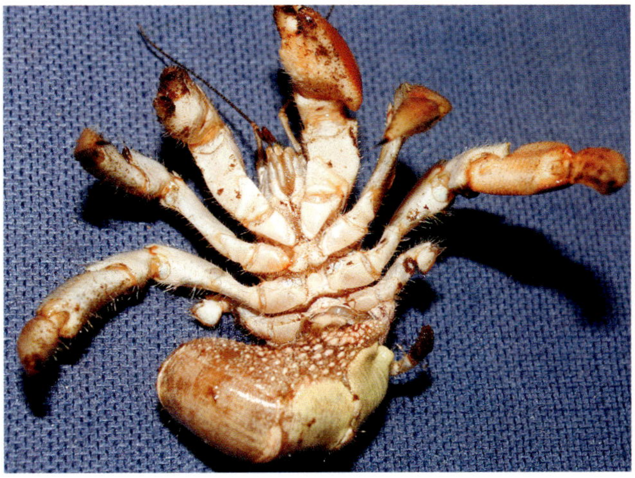

General shot of a *Coenobita compressus* male without shell, ventral view. Photo:F. Schäfer

But this is not the case with the Palm Thief, *Birgus latro*, which is discussed immediately below.

Of the five pairs of peraeopods - the hermit crabs are again decapods (Decapoda) – only three are readily visible. The powerful pair of claws constitutes the first pair of peraeopods. A typical feature of all Anomura is that one of the two claws is larger than the other. The claws are used to block the opening of the shell the hermit crab has chosen as its residence and make it impregnable. Next there are two large, well-developed pairs of peraeopods. The fourth pair of peraeopods are much abbreviated and located inside the shell; they are used to move the crab backwards and forwards within the shell. The fifth pair of peraeopods are even more specialised; the tips are modified and brush-like and are used to clean the complex structure of the respiratory apparatus and expel excrement. The pleon is soft and curved. The females have pleopods (these are lacking in males), which they use to hold the eggs securely in place. At the end of the pleon we find the uropods, which are used to anchor the crab securely in the shell. In females the sexual openings (gonopores, lacking in males) are located at the base of the third pair of peraeopods.

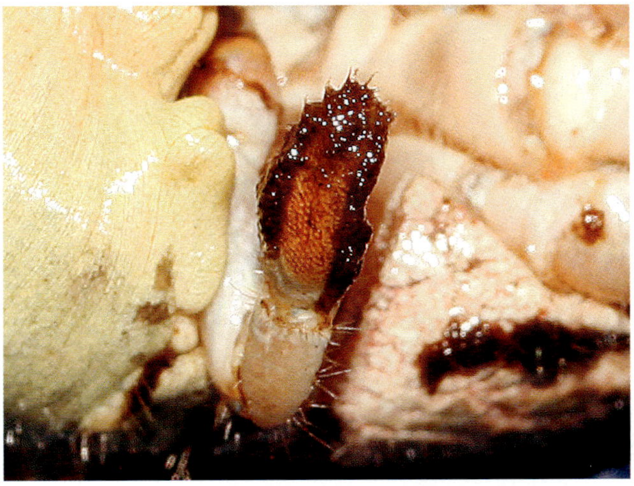

The fifth pair of peraeopods are modified into special cleaning tools, used to clean the "lungs" and keep them moist. Photo:F. Schäfer

There are no sexual differences visible in hermit crabs that are ensconced in their shells. The only way of differentiating the sexes reliably is to examine the underside of the pleon and the base of the third pair of peraeopods. But this is not possible in the pet store as a hermit crab cannot be persuaded to leave its shell without resorting to measures that constitute cruelty to animals. Under no circumstances whatsoever should such an

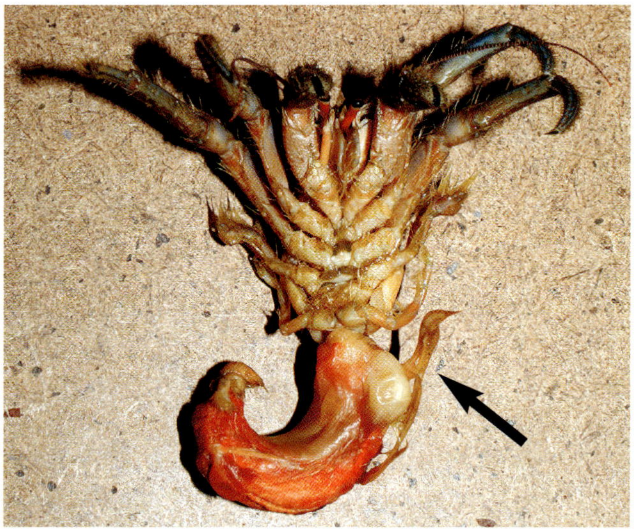

Habitus shot of a dissected female *Clibanarius longitarsus*. The pleopods (arrowed), which are found only in females, are readily visible at the sides of the pleon (in hermit crabs often also termed the abdomen). Photo: F. Schäfer

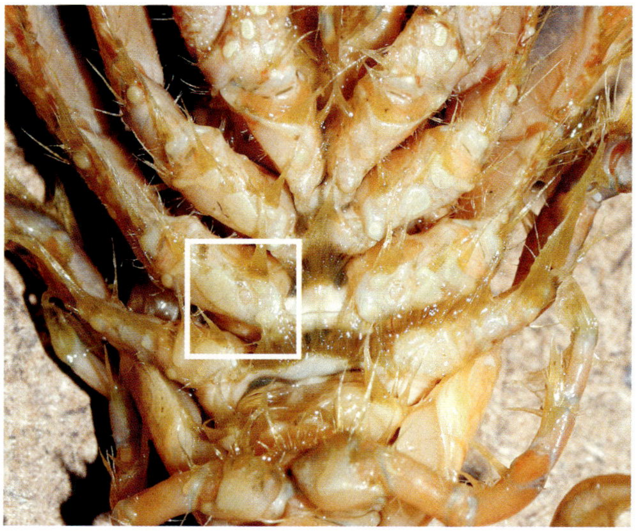

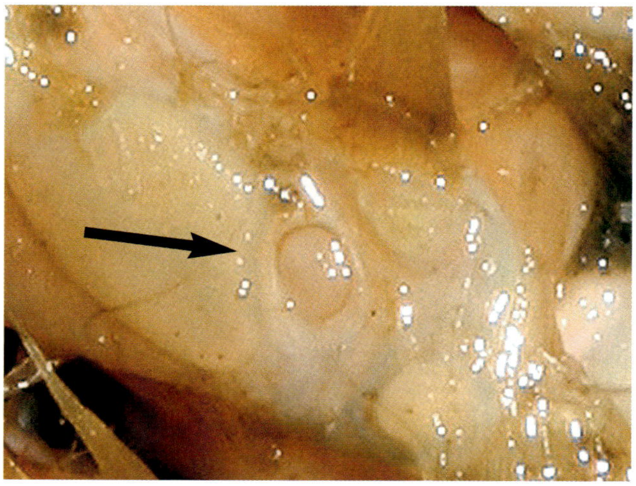

The gonopores at the base of the third pair of peraeopods can often be recognised only with practice and under strong magnification. The lower photo is an enlargement of the area marked in white in the upper photo. Photo: F. Schäfer

attempt be made! The only possible exception – and this requires both patience and skill – involves exploiting the fact that many hermit crabs are rather "impatient" members of their kind. If the shell is picked up and held so that the opening is directed upwards then they will relatively quickly endeavour to turn the shell back into the correct position, ie with the opening downwards. In the process they come a long way out of their "house" and in relatively large specimens the practised observer can then see whether or not there are gonopores present at the base of the third pair of peraeopods. And it is also often possible in such situations to see the pleopods in females. Sometimes, however, the attempt will be thwarted by the hermit crab remaining obdurately in its shell for hours……

Terrestrial hermit crabs (*Coenobita*) don't nip very often, but when they do it really hurts, even with small specimens. So if you allow one to clamber over your hand, make sure that the latter is fully outspread, as if the crab decides to grab hold of a fold of skin with its claws then it may well deliver a powerful nip!

In the final analysis males grow larger than females, but, as all hermit crabs available in the trade are wild-caught specimens of indeterminate age, this fact is only rarely of practical help. So there is often nothing for it but to buy a large number of hermit crabs and hope thereby to obtain both sexes. But this is a good idea anyway, as terrestrial hermit crabs are sociable creatures that should not be kept singly (see below).

As far as is known all hermit crabs belong to the primitive reproductive type and must thus return to the sea in order to breed. The larvae pass through several zoëa stages, then a megalopa stage, before adopting the lifestyle of their parents. To date there have been no reports of the breeding of terrestrial hermit crabs or *Clibanarius* by private individuals, but it is nevertheless essentially possible, as *Coenobita compressus*, for example, has already been reared successfully under laboratory conditions (Brodie & Harvey, 2001) and marine aquarists have already reported success in rearing some small marine species. The rearing of the zoëae takes place in full-strength sea water using Artemia nauplii as food. The zoëae are positively phototactic, in other words they will swim towards a light source. This means they can be attracted using "light-traps". And because *Artemia* nauplii are also positively phototactic it is in addition readily possible to concentrate the zoëae and the food organisms with the aid of a localised light source.

The number of zoëa stages varies, even within a single species. In *Coenobita compressus*, for example, 88% of the larvae undergo five zoëa stages and 12 % four such stages, before metamorphosing into megalopae after 21

Palm Thieves are only occasionally imported, as they become very big and are protected in many countries due to over-collecting for food purposes. The big picture shows a female, the smaller a male, the inlay a cheliped of the Palm Thief. The animals were imported by Aquaristik Service Reuter in the beginning of 2008.

Photos: F. Schäfer

The Palm Thief is the largest terrestrial arthropod in the world. This one was photographed on the Tuamotu Islands (Makatea).
Photo: O. Gargominy

to 33 days at 26°C. The megalopae leave the water after seven days and bury themselves in damp sand for 29 days. A further one to five days later their metamorphosis into fully-formed little terrestrial hermit crabs is complete.

The rearing of hermit crabs is undoubtedly time-consuming and of no economic interest, but it is extremely interesting to work with the offspring of these crabs. On the one hand details of the reproductive behaviour of many species are still completely unknown, while on the other hand some, for example the Palm Thief (Birgus latro), are serious endangered in parts of their natural distribution. Thus it may one day prove expedient to stabilise some populations by planned breeding programmes - and that will be possible only if the appropriate knowledge is available.

Hermit crabs mate in a belly-to-belly position and come a long way out of their shells to do so. The male transfers spermatophores (sperm packets) into the gonopores of the female.

Terrestrial hermit crabs – Coenobitidae

The family Coenobitidae Dana, 1851 contains two genera and 17 species, 16 of which belong to the genus *Coenobita* Latreille, 1829 - the name is derived from the Latin coenobium, which actually means "monastery", but also signifies life in a religious community. The genus name perhaps relates to the fact that the lifestyle of human hermits is usually religiously motivated, but perhaps the original describer was aware that *Coenobita* species live in colonies).

And then there is the Palm Thief, the only species of the genus *Birgus* Leach, 1816 (the name *Birgus* is supposedly a personal name, but whose is unknown). Its full scientific name is *B. latro* (Linné, 1767) and the Latin word latro signifies a robber or bandit. Palm Thieves are highly specialised animals that when adult are exclusively terrestrial, and the species constitutes a good example of some of the special features of the terrestrial hermit crabs. The Palm Thief is the largest terrestrial arthropod in the world. They can attain a body length of around 40 cmwith a side-to-side span of easily a metre and a weight of about 4 kg. The males grow larger than the females and sexual maturity is first attained between the third and seventh years of life. Different sources cite a potential lifespan of 30 - 60 years for the species! But it is only as a small juvenile that the Palm Thief carries a snail shell around with it. Later on it develops a strong layering of calcium carbonate and chitin on the back and carries its posterior abdomen folded beneath its body, like the true crabs do.

The adaptation of these terrestrial hermit crabs to a life on land is extensive and above all affects the respiratory system. While hermit crabs that live in water breathe via gills, these terrestrial hermits utilise chambers located in the posterior part of the cephalothorax; these are equipped with an extensive blood supply and a much-folded lining of skin. In principle these branchiostegites function in much the same way as our lungs. But they can perform their role in the uptake of oxygen only if they are kept moist. In addition they appear to be very sensitive to dirt and to "gumming up", for which reason the fifth pair of peraeopods are specially adapted for cleaning these respiratory organs. Perhaps this is why terrestrial hermit crabs are primarily nocturnal creatures, as during the day the danger of dehydration of the delicate respiratory organs is too high. But after prolonged heavy rainfall these crabs, which otherwise shun the light, are also to be encountered by day.

Both the Latin and English names of the Palm Thief relate to its purportedly scaling palm trees in order to steal coconuts. But despite their name, Palm Thieves are, like all hermit crabs, omnivorous; and coconuts do not by any means form part of their normal fare, as despite the immense power of their claws (beware of being nipped by one of these crabs, they can easily break a finger!) they are hardly capable of cracking open the hard shell of a coconut.

These crabs are relatively tolerant of conspecifics, but in contrast to other terrestrial hermits they are rather unsociable. Unfortunately the Palm Thief has become uncommon in some parts of its distribution as too many are collected for human consumption. And this despite the fact that the Palm Thief is potentially poisonous: after it has consumed certain plants it can produce similar symptoms of toxicity in humans as those caused by eating puffers!

Palm Thieves turn up only in very occasional ones and twos in the pet trade and command a high price. There is no doubt that the trade in live specimens for the purpose of private ownership has no influence at all on populations living in the wild.

The Palm Thief is really quite unsuitable for maintenance by the private owner as these huge creatures require a vast amount of space. However, in principle their maintenance parallels that of the terrestrial hermit crabs described below, except that they require terraria of correspondingly larger size. It is advisable to keep them singly even though group maintenance may be possible temporarily (for a few months). But these crabs do not require the company of conspecifics and the likelihood of successful breeding is undoubtedly greater if they are kept separate and put together only for a planned breeding attempt, as high stress levels - and there is no doubt that being housed with conspecifics will stress a Palm Thief – are actually likely to be an impediment to successful breeding.

In the wild the mating season of the Palm Thief occurs in the months from May to September, with the peak of mating being in the months of July and August. At this time Palm Thieves migrate close to the shore. As in the long-tailed crabs, the males are said to throw the females onto their backs for copulation as the climax to ritualised mating battles. The mating act itself lasts for only around 15 minutes, and egg deposition takes place only a short time thereafter. The eggs are then for a while carried around by the female beneath her pleon. The precise time required for the eggs to develop is unknown, but the few observations available suggest a period of some 20 - 25 days. Ripe eggs rupture immediately on contact with sea water, as described below for *Coenobita*. This gives the female the ability to trigger a synchronous mass hatching of the zoëa larvae. The eggs are taken into the sea by the female during the new moon period.

The zoëae of the Palm Thief have already been reared under laboratory conditions (Reese & Kinzie, 1968). Over a period of 17 - 28 days they pass through four to five zoëa stages. Zoëa larvae can be fed using freshly-hatched *Artemia* nauplii. The subsequent, amphibious larval stage is termed the glaucothoë and lasts for a further 21 - 28 days. The glaucothoë can leave the water only after it has occupied an empty snail shell. The youngsters carry such a shell until they attain a total length of around 15 mm, and then they adopt the lifestyle of the adult crabs.

The smallest egg-carrying female recorded to date had a total length of only 25 mm. These crabs thus become sexually mature very early and at a small body size.

Further interesting information on the Palm Thief can be found in Amesbury (1980).

Of the 16 known species of the genus *Coenobita* two are regularly seen in the trade, with further species available occasionally. But it isn't always clear which species are involved as they are very similar to one another. The easiest way of identifying the two species most often available is by their origin, as both come from the New

Terrestrial hermit crabs – Coenobitidae

*Coenobita clypeatus*is the more colourful of the two species that occur in the New World, with shades of red predominating, unlike in the rather grey-brown *C. compressus*. The individual in the photo was found among *C. compressus* from Ecuador, so perhaps this species – originally found only on the Atlantic side of the Americas – has now found its way through the Panama Canal.

Photo: F. Schäfer

World: *C. compressus* H. MILNE EDWARDS, 1837 (the specific name means compressed) is the only species imported from the west (Pacific) coast of the New World, while from the east coast (Florida, Caribbean and parts of the Atlantic coast) we have *C. clypeatus* (FABRICIUS, 1787) (the name signifies "shield-bearing", from the round shield known as a clypeus carried by Roman legionaries).

Additional *Coenobita* species are exported – albeit only occasionally - from south-east Asia, mainly via Singapore and Thailand. The following names have been applied to them: *C. brevimanus, C. cavipes, C. perlatus, C. purpureus, C. rugosus, C. variabilis,* and *C. violescens*. All these species are valid, and all are widespread in the western Indo-Pacific area, but in general it is doubtful whether the imported species are correctly identified.

Until recently *C. clypeatus* was the species most frequently sold in the U.S.A., while this species turns up only comparatively rarely in the European pet trade. These crabs appear to be exceptionally popular and are frequently sold as domestic pets, particularly for children. But obviously terrestrial hermit crabs are no more suitable than any other wild animal as domestic pets in the accepted sense. In particular invertebrates are totally unsuitable for children to keep as pets, as their interest is solely as study objects with no possibility of forming any sort of relationship. They cannot – and should not – be picked up, stroked, or played with. And so it is likely that a very high percentage of those "misused" as pets are under sentence of death, not surviving the first six months after purchase.

By contrast *C. clypeatus* maintained correctly in a terrarium can attain an age of more than 30 years. These crabs grow astonishingly large and can supposedly achieve basketball size, though I personally have never yet seen such a giant. In fact specimens the size of a good-sized fist are generally considered large.

These hermit crabs appear to follow a seasonal cycle as mating and egg-laying have been achieved only under outdoor maintenance in Florida. Here in Europe a winter rest period at lower temperatures (16-18° C), and above all a reduced photoperiod, may be a prerequisite for successful breeding. It has been established that in three of the larger (Asian) *Coenobita* species (*C. brevimanus, C. cavipes*, and *C. perlatus*), just as in the Palm Thief, females by preference cast their young adrift at new moon. The lunar cycle thus appears to be equally important in the breeding of *Coenobita* species. The eggs are very numerous and visible when the gravid female emerges from her shell. In *C. clypeatus* the eggs attached to the pleopods change colour

Terrestrial hermit crabs – Coenobitidae

Coenobita compressus, from the Pacific side of the New World, is the most commonly imported species of terrestrial hermit crab. It is collected mainly in Ecuador. The species-typical dark stripe on the merus of the second pair of peraeopods is clearly visible. Photo: F. Schäfer

The base coloration can also vary in *Coenobita compressus*. The photo shows a grey and a reddish specimen. With a maximum cephalothorax length of 12 mm *C. compressus* is the smallest known species of terrestrial hermit crab. Photo: F. Schäfer

from brick red to dark grey during the development period. The initial coloration derives from the colour of the yolk and changes as the embryos develop.

When the eggs are ready to hatch they develop a mechanism that allows them to rupture very quickly when they come into contact with sea water. This adaptation clearly makes sense as the female could easily drown if she had to remain in the water for too long.

In captivity, as soon as the eggs are ready to hatch the female will make for the water if a suitably large dish filled with sea water is available. As in the case of other crustaceans discussed in this book whose larval development takes place in the sea, full-strength sea water is necessary for rearing. The zoëae can be fed with *Artemia* nauplii. Under laboratory conditions – to date there have been no published reports of successful rearing by private individuals – the zoëae were reared either individually in 20 ml containers or in groups of five in 75 ml containers.

It is also worth mentioning that *Coenobita clypeatus* has a very interesting nomenclatural history. As a rule Herbst, 1794 is incorrectly cited as the author (fide McLaughlin & Holthuis, 2002). In addition McLaughlin & Holthuis established, on re-investigating the two type specimens of *Pagurus clypeatus* (the species was originally described under this name by Fabricius), that these represented not only two different species, but two Indo-Pacific species that are known today as *Coenobita rugosus* Milne Edwards, 1837 and *C. violascens* Heller, 1862. In order to avoid immense taxonomic confusion they placed a proposal before the International Commission for Zoological Nomenclature (ICZN) that the type material of *C. clypeatus* should be declared invalid and a neotype selected from the Caribbean, in order to maintain the existing usage of the three specific names. The ICZN decided in favour of this sensible proposal and hence in favour of the stability of zoological nomenclature!

The species *Coenobita clypeatus* is very similar to its Pacific coast counterpart, *C. compressus*, although the latter appears to remain considerably smaller. As far as aquarists are concerned the best way to distinguish them is by differences in the coloration. It is the case that all decapods are very variable in their coloration, and this applies equally to *Coenobita* species, but essentially *C. clypeatus* has a reddish or red-brown base coloration verging on violet, while *C. compressus* tends more towards grey and brown shades, and is often also striped. Because strikingly red coloured specimens are sometimes to be found among *Coenobita compressus* imported from Ecuador, it cannot be ruled out that *Coenobita clypeatus* has made use of the Panama Canal and now also occurs on the Pacific side of the Americas. A relatively reliable distinguishing characteristic between the two species is the coloration of the merus (i.e. the third element of the leg counting from the tip of the foot) of the second pair of peraeopods. In *C. compressus* the upper surface of this leg element always exhibits a dark stripe, absent in *C. clypeatus*. If these two *Coenobita* species are compared in anatomical terms, then it is noticeable that *C. clypeatus* is "hairier" and has more "pimples" on the upper surfaces of the peraeopods.

Coenobita variabilis, photographed in the field, Northern Territory, Australia. Photo: V. Pike-Russell

Egg-bearing females of *C. compressus* have been observed in Panama from March to May.

In Australia there are two species of terrestrial hermit crabs: *Coenobita variabilis* McCulloch, 1909 and *C. perlatus* Milne Edwards, 1837. But of these two species only *C. variabilis* (the specific name means "variable") is endemic to Australia. This species is not available in the international pet trade, however, as since the 1980s the commercial exportation from Australia of live animals or plants, collected in the wild, has not been allowed. This is a pity, as *C. variabilis* is to date the only *Coenobita* species in which abbreviated larval development has been recorded, which would seem to offer the possibility of breeding the species under vivarium conditions. According to Harvey (1992) it takes only six days at 30 °C for the larvae to pass through two (non-feeding) zoëa stages to the (feeding) megalopa stage, which - as described for *C. compressus* above – metamorphose further only on land.

The second species mentioned above, *C. perlatus*, occurs in Australia only on offshore coral islands and is regarded as uncommon there. The meaning of the scientific name is unclear. It is perhaps a latterday Latinisation of the Italian word for "pearl" (the actual Latin for pearl is margarita, but the Italian is perla) and thus signifies "pearly", in allusion to the striking white granulae (i.e. the "pimples" on the surface of the armour) in this species.

Terrestrial hermit crabs – Coenobitidae

Coenobita perlatus is a very attractive species; this is a specimen from Tuamotu Moruroa Atoll. Photo: J. Poupin

Juvenile *C. perlatus* are initially white, then striped, but always have red antennae. Photo: J. Poupin

Excessive collection for the pet trade has been blamed for the rarity of the species in Australia, but it is difficult to ascertain whether this is based on fact or simply propaganda by opponents of keeping animals in captivity, who constitute a powerful lobby in Australia. There are confirmed reports of *C. perlatus* fromPolynesia (Gambier Archipelago, the Marquesas, the Society Islands, and Tuamotu) and other South Sea islands. The species is also said to occur from the Seychelles to Madagascar, as well as on islands offshore of the latter and the East African coast opposite. Japan is cited as the most easterly point in the distribution. In addition the species has purportedly been introduced elsewhere by Man as a food resource, such that nowadays there are even reports of it breeding in the U.S.A. (e.g. at Cape Cod, Massachusetts). But in many cases the identification of the species appears suspect.

C. perlatus is a very attractive species, popularly known in the hobby as the Strawberry Hermit, which is a very apt description of its coloration. Fully grown individuals are bright red and the numerous granulae (the little "pimples") on the claws and legs are whitish. Juveniles are white initially and later become beige with brown bands. At all ages the antennae are red, which is an important character for identification of this hermit and supposedly distinguishes it from other similar species. The remaining species are also distributed in the western

Terrestrial hermit crabs – Coenobitidae

Indo-Pacific. Dealers' lists mention the names *Coenobita brevimanus* DANA, 1852 (the specific name means "with a short hand"), *C. cavipes* STIMPSON, 1858 (the specific name means "hollow foot"), and *C. rugosus* H. MILNE EDWARDS, 1837 (the specific name means "wrinkled"), and occasional specimens of *C. purpureus* STIMPSON, 1858 (the specific name means"purple") and *C. violascens* HELLER, 1862 (the specific name means "with a violet shimmer") are also offered for sale. The last two species originate from Japan. But in view of the considerable variability in coloration in all these hermit species it is highly questionable whether they are in fact always correctly identified in the pet trade.

For this reason the general principles for successful maintenance of all terrestrial hermits will be summarised again here. All terrestrial hermit crabs are essentially nocturnal creatures, which are active by day only if the atmospheric humidity is suitably high. This means, in terms of maintenance, the terrarium should be sprayed several times in the course of the day so that a relative humidity of 70 to 80% is achieved for several hours daily (or during the night if appropriate). Failure to do this will lead to the terrestrial hermits reacting initially with lethargy and eventually dying.

Because terrestrial hermit crabs have evolved to breathe via "lungs" rather than gills, they will drown in water after only a few hours! And for this reason they must be kept only in a terrarium. But they do nevertheless require water - both for drinking and for keeping the respiratory cavity moist - to be permanently available in a shallow dish into and out of which they can clamber with ease. There are species or populations fro which fresh water will suffice for this purpose, while others require full-strength sea water. But because there is no way to predict which is the case, the terrarium for terrestrial hermits should also contain a bowl of clear fresh, and another of clean sea. Only top quality salt mixes, such as are manufactured for coral-reef aquaria, should be used for the preparation of the sea water. Domestic salt intended for human consumption is unsuitable and can even prove fatal to the crabs, as it contains additives such as iodine or fluoride. This also applies to so-called "sea salt" from the health food shop. The best method is to prepare a supply of sea water (33 grams of salt per litre) in advance and store it in a container made of food-grade plastic; this will make the daily replacement of the water much less effort.

A third essential prerequisite for the successful maintenance of terrestrial hermit crabs is an adequate depth of substrate, which should always be kept moist (but not wet!). "Adequate depth" means at least three times as deep as the hermit is long, but in any case at least 15 cm. The substrate should consist of a mixture of three to five parts sand and one part garden soil. The garden soil acts as a binding agent to keep the tunnels and burrows excavated by the hermits from collapsing. At the same time it will introduce a bacterial and fungal flora that will prevent the substrate from starting to putrefy.

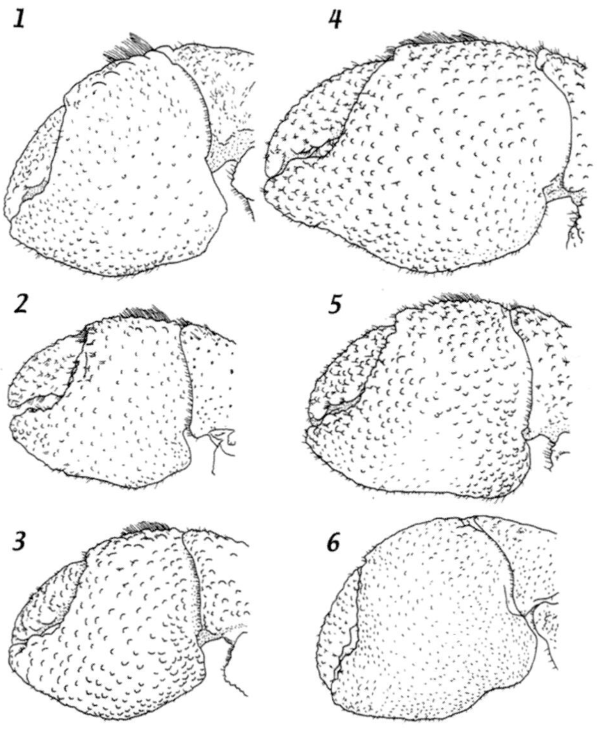

As can be seen from comparison of the claws of the six taxa found on the Ryukyu Islands (Japan), the species-diagnostic characters of *Coenobita* species are not very distinct. 1 - *C. rugosus*; 2 - *C. purpureus*; 3 - *C. perlatus*; 4 - *C. cavipes*; 5 - *C. violascens*; 6 - *C. brevimanus*. After NAKASONE, 1988

Terrestrial hermit crabs need to be able to bury themselves to moult. Moulting is by the most dangerous phase for a terrestrial hermit in the terrarium. Many owners do not realise that it is only in darkness that the hormone required for moulting is produced in adequate quantities. And essentially this is why terrestrial hermit crabs bury themselves to moult. The corollary of this is that an inadequate depth of substrate is the commonest cause of death among terrestrial hermit crabs in captivity. Of course, Nature is flexible and terrestrial hermit crabs can, if absolutely unavoidable, also moult above ground, but this is accompanied by enormous stress to the animals; this applies especially if they are maintained in groups, and does them no good at all in the long term (i.e. over several years). In addition terrestrial hermits remain underground for some time after moulting, regenerating and the allowing their new armour to harden. The younger the hermit crab, the more frequently it will moult each year and hence the shorter the periods required for each moult and regeneration. It can thus happen – especially in the case of individuals kept in isolation – that they survive for a few years even without an adequate depth of substrate

Terrestrial hermit crabs – Coenobitidae

Coenobita purpureus - this is a specimen from the island of Okinawa – are not necessarily purple. Photo: F. Schäfer

being available. But such cases are rare exceptions and should not be regarded as generally applicable.

In principle it can be said that a young *Coenobita* will moult several times per year and disappear into the substrate for around two weeks for the purpose, while fully grown specimens moult only once every 12 to 18 months and then bury themselves in the substrate for up to three months (!).

There are various advance signs that a hermit is about to moult. Firstly, it will, naturally, tend to dig more than usual, but because terrestrial hermit crabs are nocturnal animals this may go unnoticed. Secondly, before moulting terrestrial hermits will visit the seawater bowl more frequently than normally, as they need salt in order to build up sufficient pressure to rupture their old armour. Thirdly, they will eat more than usual as they need to be in good condition to survive the post-moulting period, during which they consume only their old skin. Supplies of food and water are stored in a bladder-like structure on the pleon; if this is full to bursting that is often a sign that moulting is imminent. Finally, it can often be observed that immediately prior to moulting a hermit will change its shell for a smaller one. This may sound paradoxical, as the hermit effectively grows during its moult, but this behaviour may be linked to the necessary burrowing. While as large a shell as possible may be advantageous above ground, as the crab can retreat well out of the way of any potential predator, a large shell with a correspondingly large opening may prove an impediment when burrowing.

When it comes to feeding, terrestrial hermits are easy to satisfy. They are carrion-eaters that will take any sort of organic material or animal or plant origin. There are also special foods that have been developed for terrestrial hermit crabs and which are available at specialist pet stores offering a wide range of goods. Surprisingly these crabs often consume only small amounts of food. A *Sepia* (cuttlefish) bone, such as can be purchased in pet stores as a source of

Coenobita brevimanus is notable for its particularly powerful claws. This is a specimen from Guam. Photo: G. Paulay

calcium for cage birds, should be placed in the terrarium as a dietary supplement. In practice there are some hermits that will simply ignore such a source of additional minerals, but there are many others that will utilise it enthusiastically. The actual food can simply be dropped onto the substrate, there is no point in offering the food in a dish. Uneaten food should be removed if it starts to go mouldy or dry out, even though terrestrial hermits, being carrion eaters, are not particularly fastidious about their food.

A phenomenon often observed is that these crabs spontaneously change their shell. But if they abandon it and run "naked" around the terrarium that is a sign of enormous stress! Although they live in large colonies in the wild, these crabs are often very quarrelsome among themselves and may fight violently over a particular shell, while another lying close by, and equally good by human standards, is completely ignored. These quarrels can even have fatal consequences. It frequently happens that a hermit crab is evicted from its shell by a conspecific and then goes around without a "house". For this reason a reasonable selection of shells of different sizes should always be available so they have a choice. Obtaining suitable shells can be a problem, but the specialist pet trade can as a rule provide something appropriate.

The various *Coenobita* species also have different preferences as regards their shells. Thus, for example, *C. perlatus* prefers the shells of *Tonna* spp. and *Turbo* spp., which have relatively circular entrances. But because the identification of tropical marine gastropods is not easy there seems little point, given the usually uncertain identification of the hermits discussed here, in listing the various gastropod genera involved. It makes more sense to lay in a supply of additional suitable shells at the time of buying the hermits themselves. Because of the curvature of the pleon terrestrial hermit crabs can occupy only right-handed shells. The direction of the spiral of a gastropod shell can be determined by holding it with the opening directed towards the observer and the tip of the shell pointing upwards. If the shell spirals clockwise then it is right-handed, if it spirals counter-clockwise then it is left-handed. In the U.S.A. at least, where terrestrial hermits are particularly popular, there are companies that produce artificial shells specially designed for these crabs. I do not know if these products are available elsewhere in the world or whether they are actually any good.

It may seem hard to believe, but terrestrial hermit crabs are accomplished and enthusiastic climbers, and so it strongly advised that a few branches should be placed in the terrarium for this activity. The most suitable are those of fruit trees (apple, pear, cherry) as they not only look attractive but are guaranteed non-toxic and rot relatively slowly. But it is important not to use wood from trees that have been treated with pesticides as even slight traces of such chemicals are lethal to *Coenobita*. It is best to collect such branches from old, neglected gardens.

Coenobita rugosus is a further Indo-Pacific species that occasionally turns up in the pet trade. Given its variability of coloration (both the specimens pictured originated from the island of Moorea) the species is most reliably identifiable by the ridge-like swellings on the upper edges of the claws. Photos: P. Bacchet

With regard to additional décor, it is essential that any rockwork, if desired, must be firmly based on the bottom glass of the terrarium. Otherwise it is bound to be undermined, cave in, and become a death trap for the hermits. Heaps of dead leaves are much better. Here too the leaves of fruit trees are again very good, but it is also possible to use oak (*Quercus* spp.) or beech (*Fagus* spp.). (For the use of leaves please see the chapter on true crabs!). Pieces of concave bark lying on the sand are eminently suitable daytime retreats for the hermits.

The terrarium itself should be deep rather than long – as can be seen from the suggestions on décor (deep substrate, branches to climb). There is much debate over the necessary terrarium size. Limited space is often a relatively minor problem when it comes to keeping wild animals in captivity,

Terrestrial hermit crabs – Coenobitidae

This species has been imported recently from Indonesia. In all probability it is *Coenobita pseudorugosus*. Photo: F. Schäfer

Most of the *Coenobita* cf. *pseudorugosus* are red, but some of them are blue. Photo: F. Schäfer

Coenobita cavipes - this is a specimen from Guam – is an impressive creature. Photo: G. Paulay

Coenobita brevimanus from Indonesia. Photo: F. Schäfer

and this applies in the case of *Coenobita*. But even so the crabs must, of course, be given sufficient space to move around freely. A bottom area of 50 to 80 x 40-50 cm with a depth of around 80 cm is adequate for a group (6 to 15 individuals) of small hermits 3 to 5 cm in length. If the container is too large then it will be all too easy to lose track of these secretive and nocturnal animals. If it is too small then there is the possibility of deaths during group maintenance, through stress from population pressure. Larger hermits thus require correspondingly more space. However, it is not necessary to enter into a detailed discussion on terrarium size here because – as can be seen from all the above - terrestrial hermit crabs are in fact only suitable for maintenance by enthusiasts with a special interest, because they are nocturnal, secretive in their habits, and require a relatively time-consuming amount of attention every day.

Another topic subject to much debate is the question of whether it is better to keep terrestrial hermits singly or in groups. Only in the case of the Palm Thief can this question be answered relatively unequivocally: the maintenance of single individuals is greatly to be preferred to group maintenance, as already explained above during the discussion of the species. But the species of the genus *Coenobita* live in colonies in the wild. We know that these crabs have even evolved a highly-developed mode of communication among themselves, which includes the production of sounds. These noises sound like a gentle chirruping and are produced by special stridulation organs. Stridulation signifies the production of sound by scraping, unlike, for example, in us humans, where vocal chords are set vibrating by air pressure. *Coenobita* are thus essentially social creatures. But from this it can nevertheless be deduced that assertions that *Coenobita* kept singly don't live as long as those maintained in groups belong to the realm of legend. On the contrary, it can be deduced that terrestrial

Coenobita spinosus is fairly similar to *C. cavipes*. The specimen in the photo originated from the island of Tubuai (Austral Islands).
Photo: O. Gargominy

hermits kept singly will have a higher individual life expectancy because of the removal of social stress. As already mentioned, *Coenobita* have lived to more 30 years old in the terrarium! The interpretation of the fact that terrestrial hermit crabs kept singly are less active as meaning that they are enjoying life less is nothing more than anthropomorphic. Nobody knows how and what an animal feels , especially not a creature so remote from us in evolutionary terms as a terrestrial hermit crab. The reduced activity levels in a *Coenobita* kept singly as opposed to in a group can equally well be interpreted as denoting inner peace and relaxation.

Even so group maintenance is greatly to be preferred, as the object of keeping wild animals can - and should - only be to study their behavioural repertoire in full. And this also includes aspects of their social interplay, for example mating, battles to establish order of rank, etc. The maintenance of single individuals should be the method of choice only in the case of species that are strictly solitary or exhibit only a very small degree of social tolerance of conspecifics, as is the case with the Palm Thief. But even then it is obviously preferable to maintain several individuals – albeit in separate accommodation – in order to be able to observe the complete life cycle of the species in question under vivarium conditions. However for completely practical reasons it may be better to keep particularly expensive, difficult to obtain, species singly in the first instance. Once they have settled in then group maintenance can be tried. This procedure in any case increases the chances of successful acclimatisation of imported specimens to captivity.

Finally, it is important to obtain an adequate number of specimens from the same population of species right from the very start. It is often not possible to buy additional specimens to "match" at a later date. In *Coenobita* species in particular then anyone with a serious interest should start by buying 6 to 15 individuals right at the very beginning.

Hermit crabs for the brackish-water aquarium - *Clibanarius*

Brackish-water hermit crabs of the genus *Clibanarius*

The genus *Clibanarius* DANA, 1852, which comprises some 37 species, derives its name from the Greek klibanophoros, which turn derives from the Persian criba-pana-bara. Clibanarius is the word for a man very heavily armoured cavalryman (kataphraktes) with full body armour for rider and horse. Members of this genus are imported as "freshwater" or "terrestrial" hermit crabs, although there is only one truly freshwater species among the hermit crabs! Specifically, *Clibanarius fonticola* MCLAUGHLIN & MURRAY, 1990, from the South Sea Island nation of Vanuatu (the specific name signifies "spring-dweller"). But this species has not yet been imported for maintenance in the aquarium. All the other species are coastal in their range and breathe via gills, so they cannot be kept in completely fresh water for any length of time or survive for long on land!

Clibanarius africanus are essentially peaceful among themselves.
Photo: F. Schäfer

A small species (around three cm in length when full grown) has been imported from Nigeria, more precisely from the Majidun River close to Ikorodu, and subsequently identified as *Clibanarius africanus* AURIVILLIUS, 1898 thanks to Steven DUNBAR and Chris TUDGE. The specific name means "from Africa". The majority of individuals carry shells belonging to the species Tympanotus fuscatus, a typical mangrove gastropod that lives on muddy bottoms. Thus neither the original owners of the shells nor the crabs are inhabitants of fresh water, though they may live in brackish water of very variable salt content. Or at any rate *C. africanus* can be maintained for several months in relatively weakly brackish water (around 5 grams of salt per litre) without the crabs showing any signs of ill effects. They are very peaceful among themselves and towards fishes, but are also very greedy feeders. They cannot capture a healthy fish but will eat dead ones, and possibly also prey on those that are unwell or not good swimmers. They will also consume freshly moulted conspecifics.

Clibanarius africanus cannot survive long-term in completely fresh water. They belong in a brackish-water aquarium, which they will greatly enrich.
Photo: F. Schäfer

Hermit crabs for the brackish-water aquarium - *Clibanarius*

Clibanarius africanus Photo: F. Schäfer

A second species that can be kept in the same way, namely *C. cooki* RATHBUN, 1900, is again of Atlantic coast provenance. The specific name is an honorific. It is very similar to *C. africanus* in its appearance and its ecological requirements, but its legs are not striped and are more densely covered in hairs. It is not known for certain to have been imported but it is not unlikely that it has now and then arrived in consignments of *C. africanus*.

In 2006 "terrestrial hermit crabs" were brought in from Thailand by several importers, but proved unable to survive out of water. They turned out to be brackish-water hermits of the species *Clibanarius longitarsus* (DE HAAN, 1849). The specific name means "with a long foot". This is one of the species than are widely distributed in the mangrove regions of the western Indo-Pacific, supposedly occurring from the Red Sea to Japan and northern Australia (OSAWA & FUJITA, 2005). At around eight cm total length they are significantly larger than *C. africanus* and also carry appreciably larger "houses" around with them. An unmistakeable characteristic of this species is the brilliant blue stripes on the legs, giving it a very attractive appearance. There are often barnacles on the shell, a clear indication that these hermits like it salty, although they can also be maintained very successfully in relatively weakly brackish water (10 grams of salt per litre). These hermit crabs are again peaceful among themselves and towards fishes, at least as far as can be ascertained from experiences so far. It was probably thought that they were terrestrial hermit crabs because they are often left high and dry at low tide, but like all *Clibanarius* they breathe via gills and hence are unable to survive on land for any length of time.

Nothing is known about breeding in the aquarium, but it ought to be quite possible. It is known that a number of *Clibanarius* species can breed all year round, while some require a reproductive at certain times of the years (VARADARAJAN & SUBRAMONIAM, 1982). The development of the larvae probably takes place in pure sea water in every case. Like all hermit crabs known to date members of this genus belong to the primitive reproductive type and need to pass through several zoëa stages (which can be fed with *Artemia* nauplii) in order to develop into megalopae, which then make the transition to bottom-living.

A number of small marine hermit species have already been bred successfully in the aquarium and the survival rate of the larvae was around 10% (BÖNIG, DEUSS & REITH, 2005).

There are a whole series of additional Pacific *Clibanarius* species that occur in brackish-water regions but which have not so far been imported and hence won't be discussed here even, especially as good photographic material is lacking. The interested reader is referred to the overview of Pacific *Clibanarius* species and their habitat preferences in OSAWA & FUJITA, 2005, which is well worth reading.

Hermit crabs for the brackish-water aquarium - *Clibanarius*

Clibanarius longitarsus has been erroneously regarded as a terrestrial hermit crab, but it breathes via gills and can survive for only a few hours, or at most a few days, out of water. Photo: F. Schäfer

The attractive blue stripes on the legs are a reliable character of the species. As in all *Clibanarius* species both claws are almost the same size, an exception among the Anomura. Photo: F. Schäfer

General; River crabs – Potamoidea

Crabs

The suborder Brachyura, the true crabs, which without doubt represent the most highly developed crustaceans of all, comprises a large number of marine species, but also a few that are to a greater or lesser extent adapted to brackish or fresh water. Of these, the most interesting for the freshwater aquarist are a number of members of the families Potamonidae (river crabs), Grapsidae (mangrove crabs), Ocypodidae (fiddler crabs), and Gecarcinidae (land crabs).

In all crabs the sexes are easy to distinguish (see page 12). Mating takes place in a belly-to-belly position, with the male inserting his copulatory organs (specially adapted pleopods) into the sexual openings of the female and thus delivering his sperm. The female is equipped with so-called spermathecae, which in many species can be used to store sperm and keep it viable for several years.

River crabs – Potamoidea

The crabs of the super-family Potamoidea – the name means "river crabs", although nowadays it includes species to which the epithet does not strictly apply – are the only major group of Old World crabs that comprises only freshwater forms which spend their entire life cycle in fresh water. That is to say, unlike the mangrove and land crabs they do not migrate back into brackish or sea water to release their brood. Their counterparts in the New World, the Pseudothelphusoidea and Trichodactylidae, have a comparable life cycle but to date have played no role in the vivarium hobby.

There are a whole series of forms, ranging from strictly fluviatile crabs to amphibious species and true land crabs which no longer enter water at all. They are found in dry forests and tropical lakes and rice fields, and some species aestivate, sometimes "baked" into the ground. Unfortunately, they are seldom found in the pet trade, perhaps due to the fact that they do not live in colonies but are solitary, so that they cannot be caught in large numbers. They live not only in the tropics, but also in the countries of the northern Mediterranean. Most are well camouflaged, as many of their enemies, e.g. birds and mammals, attack from above. There are, however, a number of colourful species in Southeast Asia, for example the members of the genus *Phricothelphusa* and the land-dwelling species Demanietta sirikit.

The maintenance of crabs in the freshwater aquarium can in general be described as easy, and possible even for novice aquarists. Even so a number of special points should be noted. Firstly, as a rule it is not possible to grow plants for any length of time as all aquatic plants are likely to be uprooted, eaten, or otherwise destroyed by the crabs. Maintaining fishes and crabs together is likewise problematical. Small fishes may be eaten (and usually are), while larger fishes can represent a danger to the crabs, especially after the latter have moulted and their armour is still soft. Even though several crabs can often be captured together in the wild, maintaining them in groups in the aquarium is generally inadvisable, and it is much more sensible to keep them singly except when putting them together for breeding purposes – and then they must be constantly supervised. Experience has shown that even in large aquaria with copious hiding-places often only one individual survives for an extended period of time (several years). Unlike many of the colonial-living mangrove and land crabs, the river crabs seem not to have evolved any significant degree of social behaviour among themselves and can safely be classed as asocial creatures. The optimum scenario – from a vivarium viewpoint – is that they will tolerate one another, the worst that they will finish one another off in short order. For this reason, if in doubt it is best to set up a number of small aquaria, each housing just a single individual, rather than risk losing expensive specimens through letting them loose together.

When purchasing an unknown river crab species it should first of all be housed in an experimental aqua-terrarium, which in the first instance should contain shallow water (5 to 10 cm deep) and a number of "land areas" onto which the crab can climb out. These can be large stones, cork bark laid on the water, pieces of styrofoam, or even piles of sand. If the crab spends a lot of time on the "land area" then it is probably unsuitable for permanent maintenance in water and should be housed in an aqua-terrarium (= paludarium) for further observation. At the same time it should be borne in mind that the vast majority of crabs that live in or close to fresh water are crepuscular and/or nocturnal. It is sometimes the case that during the day even a completely terrestrial crab will seek refuge in the water or, on the other

European river crabs of the genus *Potamon* are frequently brought back from Mediterranean holidays. They are highly intolerant of one another. Photo: B. Migge

River crabs – Potamoidea

Demanietta sirikit, the Queen Crab, may belong to the river crabs from a systematic viewpoint, but is actually a terrestrial crab that will drown in an aquarium.

hand, a river crab will look for a hiding-place on land, perhaps because there is insufficient cover to its liking in the water.

It is also important always to monitor the water parameters. The nitrate content should not exceed 70 mg/l, and nitrite should remain below the minimum level detectable using normal aquarium test kits. It is also important to ensure good aeration. If nothing is known about the natural habitat of the species, then moderately hard water (up to 15 °dGH) with a pH around neutral (6.5 to 7.5) is a good starting point. If the water parameters are not to their liking many crabs will react by leaving the water.

A relatively good indication of the behaviour of the crab species under study can be obtained by observing it at night by the light of a low-powered infra-red lamp. This will hardly disturb the crab(s) at all and their owner can learn a lot about the requirements of the species in question by this close observation of its behaviour.

The aquarium size required varies from species to species. But as a rule you won't go far wrong by providing each crab with a tank length of four to six times its total breadth (i.e. including the out-spread legs) and a tank depth of two to four times its total breadth. The crabs include both very sedate and very active individuals and their owner must decide for himself what tank size is most appropriate for each specimen in the long term. The depth of water in industrially manufactured aquaria is governed by their design, but in home-made set-ups it is essential to avoid filling the tank too near to the brim as otherwise the gas exchange above the water's surface may be inadequate, and in the event of any failure in the filter and aeration systems this can very quickly result in death by asphyxiation. Essentially, when it comes to maintaining river crabs it is always preferable to provide a large surface area in relation to the depth of the water, in view of the water quality desired. As far as the crabs are concerned it makes little difference whether the water is 15 or 50 cm deep.

The accommodation for crabs must always be tightly covered as they will use the tiniest crack to escape and even lift covers that aren't firmly secured in place. Any crabs that do escape must be promptly recaptured as otherwise they will die of dehydration. The best way to trap them is to place a damp sponge on the floor. Because they prefer moist places, as a rule they will be found hiding beneath the sponge next morning.

With regard to water temperature, crabs are essentially more susceptible to higher temperatures than lower. Almost all river crabs are crepuscular or nocturnal and in the wild spend the day in cool dark hiding-places. The majority of tropical species can thus also be readily maintained at room temperature (18-22 °C) without additional heating. If the aquarium is illuminated then the temperature will rise slightly during the day and drop slightly at night. This will do no harm and is even desirable for the health of many species. If additional electrical heating is installed then it should be set for a maximum temperature range of 24 to 26 °C. In an aquarium for crabs it is preferable to use systems that are installed outside the aquarium (i.e. heating mats or systems integrated in the filter) and thus out of reach of destruction by the occupants, rather than internal heaters (standard immersion heaters, heater cables, etc). Larger crabs can be astonishingly destructive. In all cases the mains supply should always be fitted with a circuit breaker whenever any electric cables are actually within reach of the crabs.

In all other respects the installation of equipment for a crab aquarium is just the same as that used for the maintenance of fishes, except for the need to be crab-proof. In this regard, notable weak spots are any suckers used to secure filter inlet and outlet pipes and airlines, for example. These will quickly destroyed or pulled free by crabs, and this can easily lead to catastrophic flooding of the living-room carpet. In addition filter guards (for inlet pipes) are particularly vulnerable and must be firmly secured. Any filter with exposed or accessible media, for example air-driven sponge filters, is quite unsuitable for a crab aquarium as the occupants will shred it. Bottom filter mats can be used only if they are protected with a superimposed perforated plastic plate (see also pp. 159 ff.). Air-driven bubble-up filters, filled with gravel with a grain size of 3 to 6 mm, have proved very effective in practice. These can be made from a plastic container of the preferred shape and size or even a simple soup bowl. A plastic kitchen funnel, pre-drilled with a hole for an airline, is inverted on the

Attractive though *Demanietta sirikit* may be, its strictly nocturnal and secretive way of life means that it is suitable only for specialists.
Photo: Sch. Nakano

bottom of the container which is then filled up with gravel – and the filter is ready. The water level needs to be at least as deep as the filter is high, so that the surface of the water is vigorously agitated by the rising bubbles of air. The device may not look very attractive and is also relatively noisy, but it works.

Otherwise the maintenance of river crabs is similar to that of aquarium fishes of corresponding size, that is regular partial water changes (weekly to fortnightly, 25 to 50 %, in both cases depending on the metabolic-waste output of the crabs) should be performed. The replacement water should match that removed in terms of its hardness, pH, and temperature. The nitrate level is a good indication of the degree of pollution of the water with metabolic by-products potentially harmful to the occupants of the aquarium. The target should be to keep the nitrate pollution below 50 mg/l. Because, as already mentioned, it is normally impracticable to grow plants in a crab aquarium, a denitrifying filter system should be installed if necessary.

In the wild many river crabs bury themselves in muddy bottoms. However, mud is not suitable décor for an aquarium as it would result in constant clouding of the water. That wouldn't harm the crabs, of course, but it would make observing them impossible. For this reason fine sand is an alternative medium when it comes to choosing substrate. A layer of sand 3-5 cm deep should be used. More is not required, while less would make it difficult for the crabs to bury themselves. If rockwork is to be used it is very important to put this in place before adding the sand (which should, by the way, be well washed first), placing the foundation rocks directly on the bottom of the aquarium. To avoid scratching or even cracking the bottom glass it is best to cover it with a thin sheet of styrofoam before adding rocks. Styrofoam does not release any harmful substances into the water but the crabs will dig down to it and shred it to pieces. The result will be unsightly pieces of styrofoam constantly littering the aquarium. For this reason, once the rockwork is in place, the exposed styrofoam should be trimmed away as close as possible to the edges of the rocks using a sharp knife, so that only the pieces protecting the bottom glass remain. If the rockwork were to be erected on the sand then the crabs would undermine it sooner or later. The result is either squashed (and dead) crab or the complete collapse of at least one area of rockwork, which can in turn easily lead to a broken aquarium glass. In general it is best to avoid over-complicated rockwork. Crabs are very powerful in relation to their size and can move astonishingly large stones. It is better to use wood instead of rocks to decorate the crab aquarium and create hiding-places. Another tried and tested décor item is PVC tubing;

this is easy to clean and monitor, cheap to buy, and happily accepted by the crabs. But it looks horrid.

The feeding of river crabs in the aquarium is extremely easy, as these creatures are out-and-out opportunists. They will eat any type of food, whether of plant or animal origin – in short, anything that is normally offered to small or medium-sized aquarium fishes as food. They also have the additional characteristic of eating a lot of detritus, that is the decomposing remains of animals and plants. Dead leaves have a special role to play in this regard. The previous year's leaves of fruit trees, beech, alder, and/or oak should always be available in the aquarium for the crabs to eat as and when they wish. The leaves should be collected in the autumn and stored in a dry, well-aired place. The leaves of some trees (e.g. beech, *Fagus* spp.) should be boiled before use as they have a waxy coating. This won't harm the crabs, but it will produce an oily film on the surface of the water, and this may impede gas exchange. Generally speaking the leaves, if not eaten, will last a few weeks before disintegrating and needing to be replaced. It is important to ensure that the leaves do not accumulate in several layers as this can lead to putrefaction, noticeable by the unpleasant, bad-eggs smell of hydrogen sulphide, which is poisonous and hence undesirable in the aquarium.

To date there have been no descriptions published in the literature regarding the breeding of river crabs in the aquarium. The main problem is undoubtedly that the two sexes can be put together safely only when they are ready to mate. But how to know when it is the right time? Unfortunately the only answer in most cases is to experiment. However the fact that the reproductive cycles of numerous tropical river crabs are linked to the rainy seasons can be used as an indication. Appropriate climatic charts for every part of the world are nowadays easy to find on the Internet. The more precisely the provenance of the crabs is known, the easier it is to imitate their annual cycle. It is undoubtedly best if you have caught your crabs

Demanietta sp. from Laos. Photo: F. Schäfer

yourself, but it is important always to comply with the laws on the collecting, exporting, and importing of live animals. Wild-caught, sexually mature females will have in most cases already been inseminated. Because they have the ability to store sperm, the chances of breeding with just a single female are thus quite good. But because of this possibility of their already being fertilised it is also advisable to keep river crabs separately for a while immediately after purchase to avoid stress, as only completely healthy, unstressed females will produce eggs and carry them. Because all river crabs reproduce via direct development, i.e. the eggs hatch into fully-formed little crabs, rearing should be no great problem. Further information will be found below on the maintenance of those river crabs that are amphibious or live on land.

The only more or less regularly imported species of so-called river crab is *Demanietta sirikit* Yeo, Nayanetr & Ng, 1999. Both species and genus names are honorifics, the latter in honour of Queen Sirikit of Thailand, hence its popular name of Queen Crab. "So-called" as this species is entirely terrestrial and cannot survive in an aquarium. The species digs burrows up to a metre deep and ending in the ground water. These crabs leave their burrows only at night, to search for food and to mate. The development of the eggs is direct, i.e. they hatch into fully-formed miniature crabs.

These crabs occur in two colour morphs, one with a white and one with a reddish base coloration. Unfortunately it is very rare indeed to find them maintained correctly. The species is known only from a small distribution region in Thailand and hence should be purchased only by specialists.

A second *Demanietta* species is sometimes imported from Laos and Thailand but has not yet been identified. It may be an as yet scientifically undescribed species. In the short term its maintenance has proved problem-free, but unfortunately no longer-term reports have as yet been published.

Thaipotamon chulabhorn Nayanetr, 1996, is again a land-and/or swamp-dwelling species, and occurs in a red and a blue colour variant. It too is a burrowing species. The genus name *Thaipotamon* is an amalgamation of "Thai" (= of Thailand) and potamon. Potamon is ancient Greek and actually means "river", but is at the same time the genus name of the European river crabs (see below). Thus *Thaipotamon* signifies "Thai river crab". The specific name *chulabhorn* is again the name of a member of the Thai royal family. These crabs can be maintained in the same way as *Demanietta sirikit*, but fortunately they are not quite as secretive in their habits.

A pair of the red morph of *Thaipotamon chulabhorn*. These attractive crabs belong in an aqua-terrarium and cannot be kept long-term under water. It is advisable to keep them singly. Photo: F. Schäfer

Thaipotamon chulabhorn, blue morph. Photo: F. Schäfer

In comparison to these species the above-mentioned members of the genus *Potamon* are colourless but comparatively diurnal in their behaviour and hence good subjects for study. They are not imported commercially but are regularly brought back by hobbyists from Mediterranean holidays. They like to lurk among stones at the edges of streams. Even though they are often found together in large numbers in the wild, it is advisable to keep them strictly singly as they are extremely quarrelsome among themselves.

Two species of river crabs with direct development are

Potamon sp. Photo: B. Migge

regularly imported from the island of Sri Lanka, and despite their unremarkable coloration they are well suited to aquarium maintenance. They are only slightly amphibious and spend a lot of time in the water. The first of these species is *Ceylonthelphusa kandambyi* Bahir, 1999, the second *Oziothelphusa ceylonensis* (Fernando, 1960). Neither belongs to the family of the true river crabs (Potamidae), but instead both are members of the family Parathelphusidae, which again comprises totally

Ceylonthelphusa kandambyi Photo: F. Schäfer

Oziothelphusa ceylonensis Photo: F. Schäfer

freshwater species with direct development of the young.

Ceylonthelphusa kandambyi (the genus name is a combination of the old name for Sri Lanka, i.e. Ceylon, and Telphusa, the name of a naiad (water nymph) from ancient Greek mythology, while the specific name is an honorific) is one of 51 species of freshwater crabs found in Sri Lanka. Many of these species are nowadays regarded as endangered due to biotope destruction in Sri Lanka. They are above all very sensitive to environmental pollution of all types. This crab remains relatively small (around 4 cm carapace breadth) and has proven to be an outstanding aquarium occupant.

Practically the same applies to *Oziothelphusa ceylonensis* (0zio means "worthless" or "idle" in Italian, I know of no other etymology), another freshwater crab from the island, which is now regularly exported. According to the exporter the species lives in the aquatic plant nursery on his fish farm, where it occurs in such abundance that this population alone is able to satisfy the demand from Europe.

Another member of the same family, *Heterothelphusa insolita* Ng & Lim, 1986, is imported from Thailand. (Hetero means "different", insolita means "unusual"). It is uncertain whether the crabs imported do actually belong to this species, as it is supposedly endemic to Malaysia.
A striking feature of these crabs is the greatly enlarged chelipeds of the males. *Heterothelphusa* species are generally regarded as predominantly aquatic.

River crabs are also imported more or less regularly from India. These species too practise direct development. The species most commonly seen here is undoubtedly *Sartoriana spinigera* Bott, 1969, which is widely distributed from the plains to the Himalayas and can attain a carapace breadth of around 10 cm. *Sartoriana* derives from sartor = "tailor", but it is likely that in this case not "tailor" is meant,

This species has been imported from Thailand as *Heterothelphusa insolita*. The photo shows a male. Photo: F. Schäfer

but a place named Sartor, while *spinigera* signifies "bearing a spine or spines". The specific name refers to the striking spine-like "tooth" (spinus = spine, thorn) on the outer anterior edge of the carapace.

In the wild the species supposedly sometimes burrows into holes in the bank, purportedly in order to withstand the rather cold winter in the higher parts of its distribution region. In the aquarium it is largely aquatic. The genus Sartoriana is at present assigned to the family Potamonidae.

In the aquarium *Sartoriana spinigera* are skilful climbers and fond of eating plants.

The dorsal pattern of *Sartoriana spinigera* is rather characteristic. The tooth on the outer edge of the carapace, from which the species takes its name, is clearly visible. Photo: F. Schäfer

Another Indian species that is sometimes imported is the very attractively coloured member of the genus *Parathelphusa* H. MILNE EDWARDS, 1853. The genus name

Parathelphusa sp. Photo: F. Schäfer

means "sister group to Thelphusa" and the genus itself is assigned to the family Parathelphusidae. The species in question inhabits a river at the edge of the Himalayas but has not yet been identified to species level.

To date the Yellow Moon Crab has been imported only once. It may be *Geothelphusa albogilva* SHY, NG & YU, 1994,

Geothelphusa albogilva Photo: F. Schäfer

a species of the family Potamidae that is endemic to Taiwan and practises direct development of the young. Geo means "soil" and by extension "land", albo = "white", and gilva = " pale yellow", so the name signifies white-yellow land-dwelling Thelphusa. It is a predominantly terrestrial and very secretive species that attains a carapace breadth of around 35 mm.

Sayamia bangkokensis (NAIYANETR, 1982), a member of the family Parathelphusidae, is an impressive species that is often sold for human consumption in Bangkok. The genus name is an honorific and the specific name means "from Bangkok", although the species is actually fairly widespread in Thailand. The males of this species develop one enormous claw. These crabs live almost exclusively in water and practise direct development of the young.

Larnaudia beusekomae is one of the numerous species of river crabs from Thailand. Photo: F. Schäfer

There are a very large number of species of river crabs. In principle they can all be maintained and bred in the aquarium and/or terrarium. But the identification of the species is virtually impossible for the layman (even if he or she is a trained biologist!). Because numerous species are carriers of paragoniasis, a serious disease that affects more than 22 million people, many countries in the tropics have initiated research programmes to evaluate the number of species of freshwater crabs that exist. Paragoniasis is caused by parasitic leeches in the lungs of humans, inter alia, and can take a severe, sometimes fatal course. Humans become infected by eating raw or inadequately cooked crabs, but in rare cases infection is also thought to have occurred where crabs have been crushed and their remains have found their way into drinking-water supplies. But there is no risk of the aquarist becoming infected.

Examination of the lists of species that exist for various regions (for example the Checklist of the freshwater crabs of Malaysia by NG & YEO, 2007) reveals that this increased research activity has led to the number of known species being almost doubled over the last 20 years, and very many are now known but as yet undescribed and awaiting scientific consideration. For this reason only specialists are able to identify the species correctly, as only they are cognisant of the copious but widely scattered literature and attend conferences where they obtain information on the current research projects of their colleagues. For this reason we will refrain from cataloguing possible candidates for importation here.

River crabs – Potamoidea

Sayamia bangkokensis is a gorgeous but large (around 10 cm carapace breadth) species of river crab. It comes from Thailand where it is in great demand for human consumption. Its maintenance in the aquarium is problem-free. Photo: F. Schäfer

The female *Sayamia bangkokensis* can easily be distinguished from the male. Even so it is advisable to take a discrete peek at the underside as claws can be lost and initially grow back smaller! Photo: F. Schäfer

River crabs – Potamoidea

However, this discussion of the river crabs relevant to the aquarium hobby would be incomplete without a mention of the species that occur in lakes Malawi and Tanganyika in the African Rift valley.
The species *Platythelphusa armata* A. Milne Edwards, 1887 is imported relatively regularly. The genus *Platythelphusa* (the name means "broad Thelphusa") is endemic to Lake Tanganyika and comprises nine species, eight of which have not yet been imported. The specific name *armata* signifies "armed". The strength of this species is not to be underestimated, for example they enjoy eating snails and can crack open fairly thick shells! Their maintenance is essentially problem-free, but, as for the majority of river crab species, it is again advisable to keep them singly. This species is again an omnivore and hence will destroy any vegetation, and sleeping fish will provide easy prey.
In addition to the nine river crabs of the genus *Platythelphusa* (family Platythelphusidae), Lake Tanganyika is also home to the likewise endemic species *Potamonautes platynotus* (Cunnington, 1907), which is probably been exported occasionally but I have not yet maintained myself. *Potamonautes* means "river sailor", *platynotus* "with a broad back". The genus is assigned to the family Potamonautidae. While *Platythelphusa* species are completely aquatic and die relatively rapidly on land, *Potamonautes platynotus* is somewhat more flexible and has even been observed out of water feeding on Aufwuchs growing on wet rocks along the shore of Lake Tanganyika.
Additional *Potamonautes* species occur in affluents of Lake Tanganyika but not in the lake itself. They include the only freshwater crab species to occur in Lake Malawi, namely *Potamonautes lirrangensis* (Rathbun, 1904). The specific name derives from the type locality, Lirranga in the Democratic Republic of Congo. In the trade the species is usually known as the Blue Malawi Crab or identified as *P. orbitospinus* Cunnington, 1907 (= with a spiny edge), but this name is currently regarded as a synonym of *P. lirrangensis*. Unlike Lake Tanganyika, Lake Malawi is not home to any endemic crab species. *P. lirrangensis* is widely distributed in East and Central Africa. It is so common in Lake Malawi that it is even the object of a small fishery. With a carapace breadth of easily 8.5 cm it represents quite a good-sized morsel. It is easy to maintain in the aquarium, but these crabs are predatory little villains that should be kept by themselves to avoid endangering the lives of tankmates. They are also highly intolerant of one another.

Potamonautes lirrangensis is usually seen under the synonym *P. orbitospinus* in the trade. Photo: F. Schäfer

Platythelphusa armata is one of the 10 river crab species endemic to Lake Tanganyika. Photo: E. Schraml

Brachyura

The brackish-water aquarium for crabs

To a large degree the same applies to the maintenance of crabs from brackish water as has been described above for the river crabs. By far the majority of crabs from brackish-water zones that are regularly imported for the aquarium hobby belong in a paludarium, hence again see above. But because in addition to the mangrove crabs covered in the next section, the attractive horseshoe crabs (see p. 177 ff.) and the dainty *Clibanarius* hermit crabs (see p. 144 ff.) require brackish water, the special features of brackish-water biotopes will be discussed separately in somewhat greater detail here in order to avoid unnecessary repetition elsewhere.

In the wild, brackish-water zones are characterised by two very important factors: firstly an enormous food supply, and secondly, constant extreme fluctuations as regards the salt content of the water. The copious food supply results from numerous marine animals and plants that die off on entering the fresh water issuing into the sea in the vicinity of river estuaries. The same applies in reverse, i.e. to the freshwater animals and plants that find their way into the sea. This is to the benefit of the animals and plants that are capable of tolerating the extreme conditions in these variable habitats. Species with this capability occur in vast numbers in brackish-water zones, which are among the most productive habitats on planet Earth.

A crab that lives in the estuary region of a river needs to be euryhaline. In other words, it must be capable of tolerating, without any special problems, any level of salinity that occurs in the water of its natural habitat, from an almost zero salt content (there is no absolute zero) to full-strength sea water. There is virtually no time available in which to adapt. A heavy thunderstorm may require a switch to completely fresh water fresh in a matter of seconds, and even in sections of river further upstream, where the tides rarely have any effect, a spring tide can require a crab to change from fresh to sea water almost instantaneously. But regardless of the huge adaptability vis-a-vis salinity that crabs have to possess to survive, the salt concentration in the aquarium should nevertheless be maintained as constant as possible. This is because the bacteria and fungi that live in the filter, and which are required to convert biologically "dead" water into living aquarium water, can be rather intolerant of major fluctuations in salinity. In addition, experience has shown that a brackish-water aquarium requires an appreciably longer "running-in" period before any livestock can be introduced. It can be six to eight weeks between setting-up and the nitrite level dropping back to safe, that is, three to four times as long as in the freshwater aquarium. But because of their adaptability, once a brackish-water tank has been matured there is no need to worry about the salinity of the water in which the crabs have been living at the dealer's and it is not necessary to acclimatise them gradually.

Practically all crustaceans that live in brackish water can be kept in completely fresh water for a short - sometimes a long – time, but they all then exhibit an increased sensitivity to nitrite and nitrate in the water. Sodium chloride, the main component of marine salt, reduces the toxic effect of these compounds on the organism, and perhaps this is the reason for the greater sensitivity to nitrate seen in brackish-water creatures when maintained in fresh water.

From a practical viewpoint, it is often the case that the aquarist unexpectedly comes across a long-sought specimen in an aquarium store. If this is an inhabitant of brackish water then it is rare to have a suitable mature tank available back home. But it is possible to get by if a well-matured freshwater tank is available (the only exceptions are aquaria containing very soft water). A good dessertspoonful of salt per l0 litres of water can in such cases be added to the freshwater tank (if necessary pure sodium chloride, but it is always better to use a marine salt as sold in the trade for reef aquaria; domestic salt containing added fluorine and/or iodine compounds are totally unsuitable for aquatic use and can lead to the death of both fishes and crustaceans). This won't do the filter bacteria much good (or the majority of plants, as well as almost all fishes, which in any case won't have much chance of survival in the company of crabs and should be removed first). The new acquisition(s) can then be provisionally housed in the salt-treated freshwater aquarium. Because experience has shown that nothing created by mankind lasts as long as a good temporary measure, there will be a tremendous temptation to leave matters thus. But don't even think about it! You should immediately set up a separate brackish-water tank and allow it to mature. The salinity should be around half that of sea water, i.e. 15‰ or in other words around 15 grams of salt per litre of water, though it doesn't have to be absolutely precise. But it is once again very important to use only proper aquarium marine salt! No "sea salt" from the health-food store or similar, and no domestic salt from the supermarket. These are quite unsuitable for the purpose in hand.

Otherwise the technical side of the set-up can be as for a freshwater aquarium. Only one additional piece of equipment is required, a so-called hydrometer to measure the salinity. These are available in a wide range of models at different prices. The cheapest will be quite adequate for the purpose in hand, as no great degree of precision is required. But because when water evaporates the salt remains behind, the salinity of a brackish-water tank can rise quite astonishingly in the course of time. Hence it should be monitored by measuring from time to time. With regard to the "hard décor", there is only one difference between the brackish-water and the freshwater aquarium: wood decays very rapidly in brackish water and will pollute the water, and hence should be used only very sparingly.

Mangrove crabs - Sesarmidae

Mangrove crabs - Sesarmidae

The so-called mangrove crabs, formerly all assigned to the catch-all genus *Sesarma* SAY, 1817, are fairly frequently imported. The origin of the scientific genus name is supposedly the local name for one of the contained species. Current systematics distinguishes three families in the superfamily Grapsoidea: the Sesarmidae - Mangrove crabs, the Grapsidae – rock crabs, and the Varunidae.

In places where these crabs occur they do so in large numbers and can easily be collected in bulk. They can leap five to ten times their own body width and usually inhabit rocky habitats close to the sea. They have colonised the entire tropical and sub-tropical regions of the world, living in tidal coastal regions and the brackish water of river estuaries and mangrove swamps. They are apparently currently in the process of migrating into fresh water. Some are extremely adept at climbing: *Metopaulias depressus* lives almost exclusively on the roots of trees and uses the water that collects in the centre of bromeliads for breeding. The so-called *Nepentes* crabs live on trees with a heavy growth of epiphytes and use the water collected in pitcher-plants (*Nepentes* spp.).

Current estimates are that the so-called red mangrove crabs comprise around 150 species, all very similar and all remaining small, with a carapace diameter of barely more than four cm. In the past the species most commonly seen in the trade was sold as *Sesarma bidens* DE HAAN, 1835 but is thought to actually be *Pseudosesarma moeschi* (DE MAN, 1892). The name *bidens* means "with two teeth", *Pseudosesarma* signifies "false Sesarma", and *moeschi* is an honorific. The natural distribution of this group is said to be Japan, Hong Kong, Sulawesi (Celebes), the Philippines, the Nicobar and Andaman islands, and Sri Lanka (Ceylon).

A common feature of the species of this group of *Sesarma* (in the widest sense) imported to date is that they are fairly tolerant of one another, and often even exceptionally social. But it is nevertheless very important that each individual should be able to find a hiding-place of its own. Moreover it is often life-threatening for new specimens to be introduced to an existing population with an established order of rank. If this is necessary then it is better to remove all the crabs from the tank, re-arrange the décor, and thus destroy the existing social hierarchy. In this way all the crabs start off on an equal footing and increasing the size of the group is more likely to be successful. But in this regard it should be noted that several weeks of quarantine is essential for new purchases before they come into contact with the established population. There is still no medication known that will treat the majority of the infectious

The Red Mangrove Crab, *Pseudosesarma moeschi*, is regularly available in the aquarium trade.

diseases that can lead to plague-like mass die-offs in crab populations. It is only rarely possible to tell if a crab is sick or healthy from external signs. One of the few exceptions is the dreaded "Brandflecken-Krankheit" (= gangrene disease), which is characterised by red-brown dots that become larger and darker with time and is caused by thread fungus (*Ascomycetes*). If this disease is diagnosed then the affected crab should be isolated immediately, and sometimes it will heal spontaneously. But it is unknown whether or not individuals that heal in this way remain infected and long-term carriers of the pathogen.

With a very few exceptions, mangrove crabs do not actually live in fresh water, although in the wild they do migrate via brackish water to fresh, so that adults do not generally come to any harm if kept in freshwater aquaria in the short term. If you want to do keep them healthy, just add some common salt (sodium chloride) to the water, change a percentage of the water regularly, and provide an adequate oxygen supply via aeration or filtration (see above). As they lead an amphibious life, the aquarium should be only half filled, and wood (with care in brackish-water tanks as they will rot very quickly there) and stones should be arranged so as to not only create numerous hiding-places, but also provide spacious "perches" out of the water. It is also important that their home is tightly-covered so that they cannot escape and the air space remains warm (to avoid chilling) and humid. Ideally the water should be heated to 24 -25°C and circulated using a small filter or aeration. At the same time the lighting will ensure an air temperature of 28 - 30°C and the necessary high degree of humidity.

All the mangrove crabs imported to date (the few exceptions in the *Sesarma* assemblage can be ignored here as these species have not yet been seen in the vivarium hobby) breed by means of very small eggs that hatch into zoëa larvae which require at least brackish, but usually full-strength sea water to thrive. These zoëa larvae are free-swimming, globular creatures somewhat smaller than a pin-head in size. They are predatory and can be fed on Artemia nauplii. If the latter prove too large initially then the rotifer Brachionus plicatilis has proved viable as a first food, but when used alone will provide an adequate diet for only the first few days, after which Artemia nauplii should be given as well.

Rearing the zoëae is very time-consuming and may involve numerous setbacks. Basically there are two different methods. In the first very small groups of zoëae are reared in very small aquaria, in the second they are placed en masse in a single large aquarium. In both cases only a fraction of the thousands of zoëae

Red Mangrove Crabs breed readily enough, but rearing the young is time-consuming. Photo: F. Schäfer

larvae that hatch should be reared. As a rule any attempt to rear them in bulk will simply result in the loss of the entire brood. There are several zoëa stages (usually 4-6) followed by the megalopa stage. While the zoëa looks roughly like a water flea, the megalopa already resembles the adult crab but still carries its pleon extended backwards as in the shrimps and river crayfishes. At this stage the megalopae should be provided with places to rest as otherwise they will literally swim themselves to death. After the next moult their development will be complete and the fully-formed young crabs will emerge. The length of the development period depends greatly on various external factors but normally takes place within four weeks.

The filtration of an aqua-terrarium poses special problems. Because of the low water level many filters designed for use outside the aquarium cannot be used, and many internal filter systems won't work properly either, as they are forever sucking in air. As well as the evergreen bubble-up filter, which can readily be modified for use with a low water level, there is also a more aesthetically pleasing solution in the form of a special bottom filter for aqua-terraria of this type. But in order to crab-proof such bottom filters the crabs must be prevented from getting into the filter-bed. The inlet of the bottom filter is a narrow gap between the bottom glass of the tank and a pane of glass, siliconed in place and separating the filter from the water area. This gap should never be wider than the carapace depth of the smallest crab to be maintained. The filter medium itself is a suitably-sized piece of foam matting such as is available in the trade in a wide variety of thicknesses and pore sizes. This filter mat is topped by a cloth of suitable size which will prevent the sand that in many cases forms the substrate of the land area in the aqua-terrarium from being sucked into the filter mat and clogging the medium. The cloth should in turn be covered with a perforated plastic plate, and the perforations must be so small that even the smallest crab to be maintained cannot get through them. One rear corner of the bottom filter should be left free as a clean-water chamber fitted with a pump or an airlift. This chamber can be constructed using perforated plastic so that the crabs cannot get into it. The water drawn through the filter by the pump or airlift can be returned directly to the water area over wood or stones, or part of the land area can be used as a trickle filter. The disadvantage of this type of filter is the difficulty of cleaning the foam mat that forms the heart of the system, which may be necessary if the matting becomes so clogged with fine particles that the pump in the clean-water chamber runs dry. But with a normal population of, let us say, ten Red Mangrove Crabs in a 60-cm aquarium this should not be the case until after several years of running time.

It looks very attractive when aquaria-terraria of this type are run as tidal set-ups. The construction of such a set-up is described at length in the book Aqualog Minis: Freshwater Crabs, which also provides copious additional information on the biology, maintenance, and breeding of crabs, which simply cannot be included here for reasons of space.

Pseudosesarma bocourti (MILNE EDWARDS, 1869) is another mangrove crab that is nowadays regularly encountered in the pet trade. The name *bocourti* is an honorific. This species grows significantly larger than *P. moeschi* and can easily attain a carapace breadth of 6 cm. It is often found as a by-catch among *P. moeschi* from Thailand, but is also intentionally exported from Vietnam as the Blue Vietnam Crab. Its maintenance is easy, but a tank at least a metre long is required to keep a group.

The vivid blue *Pseudosesarma bocourti* is regularly imported from Vietnam. Photo: F. Schäfer

By contrast *P. edwardsi* (DE MAN, 1887) remains as small as *Pseudosesarma moeschi*. It is commercially exported from India and has a more yellowish-beige colour than *P. moeschi*. *P. edwardsi* (the specific name is again an honorific) is a very peaceful species that is easy to maintain.

Pseudosesarma edwardsi from India. Photo: F. Schäfer

The giant of the *Sesarma* assemblage is *Perisesarma huzardi* (DESMAREST, 1825), which is at present being regularly imported. The Greek peri- signifies "around, close to" and *Perisesarma* indicates that the genus is a closely related sister group to *Sesarma*; *huzardi* is another honorific. Specimens of this species with a carapace a good 8 cm wide have been imported via Nigeria. These crabs are not only drab in appearance but they are also significantly more aggressive among themselves than are their smaller relatives. For this reason plenty of space and hiding-places should be provided, and each individual is best quarantined singly.

Perisesarma huzardi is a rather large, drab-coloured species. Photo: F. Schäfer

Mangrove crabs – Sesarmidae

Pseudosesarma crassimanum Photo: F. Schäfer

Chiromantes angolense Photo: F. Schäfer

Another member of this genus group that is sometimes imported is *Pseudosesarma crassimanum* (DE MAN, 1887) from south-east Asia. It grows somewhat larger than *P. moeschi* but is similarly peaceful and easy to maintain. The specific name means "with thick hands".

Sesarmops intermedium Photo: F. Schäfer

By contrast the very attractive *Sesarmops intermedium* (DE HAAN, 1835), which is sometimes imported from Singapore, is very quarrelsome. It is very common in the wild. Perhaps therein lies the reason for its high aggression potential, as bright coloration in association with a high population density are often typical of animals with a belligerent lifestyle. *Sesarmops* means, loosely, "related to *Sesarma*" and the Latin word *intermedius* means "intermediate".

The dainty *Chiromantes angolense* (BRITO CAPELLO, 1864) has been imported several times from Nigeria. Many specimens have a cream-coloured stripe between the eyes, which gives them a very pleasing appearance. This is a small, peaceful species, whose maintenance largely corresponds to that of *Pseudosesarma moeschi*. The etymology of *Chiromantes* is not entirely clear: the prefix Chiro comes from the Greek cheir, which means hand, and mantes is possibly cognate with mantis, meaning seer or prophet. On this basis the genus name signifies "hand prophet", but why escapes me! The specific name angolense means "from Angola".

Neosarmatium meinerti (DE MAN, 1887) is a very pretty but rather large species (around 7 cm carapace breadth). The genus name means "new *Sarmatium*" (another genus of crabs), while the specific name is an honorific. The species is widespread along the of Africa. When it comes to feeding this species it is important to ensure that they always have sufficient leaves available. In the wild these crabs feed mainly on the leaves of the trees growing in mangrove swamps and play an important role in the mangrove ecosystem. The species has only recently become available in the hobby. On the basis of experience in its maintenance so far, this is a peaceful crab despite its size.

Neosarmatium meinerti Photo: F. Schäfer

Mangrove crabs – Sesarmidae

Vampire crabs are very colourful and each specimen can be recognised by its own individual coloration. Their popular name is not because they drink blood but because they have bright red eyes. Photo: F. Schäfer

A special group of jumping crabs has recently created a furore as they not only look incredibly attractive but can also be bred without complications in the aqua-terrarium. These are the so-called vampire crabs of the genus *Geosesarma*, three species of which have so far been imported from the island of Sulawesi (formerly Celebes) in Indonesia. Their precise scientific classification is not yet known. These species are exclusively inhabitants of fresh water, and are in fact amphibious with a tendency to live predominantly on land; for this reason they should be housed in an aqua-terrarium with a large land area (ideally a sand-earth-clay mixture, see below) and small water component. The larvae of these species undergo direct development. Gravid females conceal themselves in tunnels they excavate themselves and to date it has not been possible to observe the release of the 20-80 young produced per brood. Vampire crabs can readily be maintained in groups of around a dozen individuals in a

Mandarin crabs are also members of the genus *Geosesarma* and should be maintained in the same way as vampire crabs. Photo: F. Schäfer

The same applies to the *Geosesarma* species imported as purple crabs. Photo: F. Schäfer

60-cm tank. The adults rarely predate on the young, but there may be cannibalism when rearing the youngsters if the population density is too high.

This seems a good point at which to mention that even many of the social crab species will not shrink from killing members of other crab species and/or eating them. For this reason maintaining several crab species together in the same container carries an incalculable risk and should be avoided at all costs.

Unfortunately the beautiful vampire crabs are chiefly nocturnal and crepuscular, and very secretive in their habits.

The latest stars in this crab family are the members of the genus *Metasesarma* H. Milne Edwards, 1853. The word meta comes from the Greek and literally means "after" or "behind". It is popular in zoological names where the author wishes to indicate the similarity of the new genus to an existing one, in this case *Sesarma*.

Metasesarma aubryi A. Milne Edwards, 1869 is an attractive, small (around 3 cm carapace breadth) species from the islands of the western Pacific. It often lives far from the sea and has largely adopted the lifestyle of a terrestrial crab. It is nevertheless very susceptible to dehydration, so

The male (above) and female (below) of the forest-dwelling *Metasesarma aubryi* are differently coloured. Photos: F. Schäfer

Metasesarma obesum often lives on islands with no permanent fresh water. Photo: C. Lukhaup

it is important to ensure a fairly high relative humidity and provide a deep substrate (around 10 cm), which should always be kept slightly moist. Males and females are very differently coloured.

Metasesarma obesum (DANA, 1851) has a very wide distribution in the Pacific and is found from Tahiti and Guam to Malaysia via Australia and the Sunda Islands. It may well also occur in East Africa. It is a specialised species that is often found on islands with large expanses of shingle and sand beach and no fresh water. The Latin obesus means "fat". It has only recently been discovered that *M. obesum* is a senior synonym of the well-known species *Metasesarma rousseauxi* H. MILNE EDWARDS, 1853. This is mentioned here only because there is a relatively large amount of scientific literature on the species under these now synonymous names.

Both the above species have only recently appeared in the hobby for the first time. For this reason not much more can be said about them here, and we do not yet know how their larval development takes place, although the vast distribution region suggests that we are dealing with species with primitive reproductive behaviour (planktonic zoëae). Either way it is advisable, particularly in the case of *M. obesum*, to provide not only a bowl containing fresh water, but also one filled with sea water in the terrarium.

Armases elegans Photo: F. Schäfer

Armases elegans, a small tree-dwelling species recently imported for the first time from Nigeria, is very interesting. It can apparently be readily maintained in groups. Once again I do not know the derivation of the genus name, but elegans means "elegant" or "fine".

The only member of the Grapsidae to be imported commercially to date is the fabulous *Goniopsis pelii* (HERKLOTS, 1851). I do not know the meaning of the genus name, but the specific name is an honorific. These large and aggressive crabs are best kept singly and the sexes placed together only for breeding. This Atlantic species has also been imported from Nigeria.

Goniopsis pelii is a fast-moving and aggressive species that is best kept singly. Photo: F. Schäfer

Members of other crab families found in fresh water

A number of species of the primarily marine family Varunidae have only very recently been imported for the aquarium hobby. As far as is known all species belong to the primitive reproductive type.

This magnificent male of the Chinese Mitten Crab originates from the Elbe river near Kiel, Germany. Photo: F. Schäfer

The best-known of all the varunids is undoubtedly the Chinese Mitten Crab, *Eriocheir sinensis* (Milne Edwards, 1853). The genus name signifies "wool hand", the specific name relates to the provenance of these crabs "from China". Around 1912, in bilge water containing zoëae of this species was discharged in the mouth of the Weser in Germany and since then these crabs, which are completely euryhaline and hence just as much at home in totally fresh water as in full-strength sea water, have spread relentlessly across central Europe, so that nowadays millions of them inhabit European rivers, in particular the lower reaches. In order to breed – after which they normally die – these crabs must return to the sea, as the zoëae require full-strength sea water in order to develop. Their spawning migrations take place en masse and are influenced by temperature and the phases of the moon. *Eriocheir sinensis* is an omnivore. These crabs are best kept singly in the aquarium as they are quarrelsome and cannibalistic.

The Pom-Pom Crab is a member of the genus *Ptychognathus*. The females do not have "tufts" on their claws. Photo: F. Schäfer

A dainty little varunid with a similar way of life has been imported from Singapore for the hobby. It is a member of the genus *Ptychognathus* Stimpson, 1858, which contains around 20 species, but has not yet been determined to species level; the genus name is a combination of the Greek words for "fold" and "jaw". These miniature crabs attain a carapace breadth of only around 1 cm. In this species the males do not have "hands" completely covered in "hair", just "tufts".

For a long time swimming crabs were known only from the sea. But recently a member of the genus *Varuna* has been imported that thrives in brackish water and can also live readily in completely fresh water. This species is *Varuna litterata* (Fabricius, 1798), which is widespread in the western Indo-Pacific. *Varuna* is a deity in the Vedic religion; whether or not the genus name relates to this or to something else I know not. The specific name derives from the Latin littera meaning letter. It is very interesting to watch these crabs swimming elegantly through the water by beating their swimming legs (modified last peraeopods) up and down. With a carapace breadth of around 6 cm, these crabs are not particularly small and they are also exceptionally rapacious. Nothing – be it animal or plant – is safe from them. When I acquired some they started to munch away at the *Ludwigia* within seconds of being placed in the photographic aquarium. After they had been photographed they were transferred to a large brackish-water aquarium with various hermit crabs, horseshoe crabs, and fishes, where during the first night the pair of them devoured an adult *Clibanarius longitarsus*, which they pulled out of its shell, and the next day they successfully hunted down an adult sailfin molly (*Poecilia velifera*). So care is required when it comes to keeping them with other livestock! *Varuna litterata* is completely euryhaline and – like *Eriocheir sinensis* – occurs predominantly in fresh water in the wild.

This section concludes with the dwarf crabs of the family Camptandriidae, which are exported for the hobby from Calcutta, where they live in the middle of the city, in ditches that only occasionally contain an element of salt. Their generic and specific status is unknown; the genus *Camptandrium* Stimpson, 1858, to which they were initially thought to belong, has only recently been revised (Tan & Ng, 1999) and none of the species now regarded as valid originates from India. Be that as it may, they are very dainty little crabs and comparatively peaceful among themselves, and make interesting objects of study. They probably belong to the primitive reproductive type, but without knowing their precise identity there is not much else that can be said about them at present.

The interesting crab *Varuna litterata* is a wonderful subject for study, albeit rather destructive by nature and hence requiring caution when decorating the aquarium and selecting tank-mates. Photo: F. Schäfer

This tiny crab from the family Camptandriidae is an ideal subject for study for the aquarist with limited space. It lives in association with human civilisation, in the middle of the metropolis of Calcutta. Photo: F. Schäfer

Ocypodoidea: Fiddler crabs – Ocypodidae

Fiddler crabs

From time to time members of the running and fiddler crab family (Ocypodidae) are also imported. Of these, the so-called running-crabs of the genus *Ocypode* WEBER, 1795 are not recommended for aquarium maintenance. The genus name signifies "swift foot", and, as this suggests, these crabs are "sprinters" that populate the dry higher parts of sandy tropical beaches, away from the water. They are thus in no way aquatic and certainly not freshwater denizens. They must even have clean sea water to drink.

Ocypode ryderi Photo: F. Schäfer

The fiddler crabs also live on tropical beaches, but occupying areas of mudflats that remain constantly moist. They need mud to survive, retreating into their burrows when the tide comes in and closing the entrance from inside. Only a few occur in brackish water, and even fewer in fresh. Most crabs of this group offered for sale belong to the genus *Uca* LEACH, 1814. Males of this group develop a single oversized claw, the weight of which may be half that of the entire crab and which in most cases is also strikingly coloured; this claw is waved to attract the attention of females, whose claws are not enlarged. Males thus have one enlarged "signalling claw" and a smaller "feeding claw". In England and France these crabs are called fiddler crabs and crabes-violonistes respectively, because the large claws make them look as if they are carrying a fiddle (violin)! The German popular name of Winkerkrabbe, which means waving crab, alludes to the actual use of the enlarged claw. The gestures of the males vary from species to species, but all look like waving. The genus name *Uca* is supposedly derived from a native name and dates back to the pre-Linnaean work of SEBA (1758), which refers to Cancer uka una, Brasiliensibus (the crab known as uka una among the Brazilians). Anyone who is interested in the systematics and nomenclature of *Uca* is referred to ROSENBERG (2001). Around 100 species are currently regarded as valid. The maintenance of fiddler crabs should be conducted in an aqua-terrarium such as has been described above for jumping and mangrove crabs.

Uca ecuadoriensis is regularly exported from Ecuador. Photo: F. Schäfer

Ocypodoidea: Fiddler crabs – Ocypodidae

Fiddler crabs breed regularly in the aqua-terrarium. This is a gravid female *Uca ecuadoriensis*. Photo: F. Schäfer

Brackish water should be used. If the identity of the species is unknown then it is best to use strongly brackish water (20-25 grams of salt per litre), as many of the species that occur along sea coasts will not tolerate fresh water. The land area for fiddler crabs should consist of fine sand which the crabs will sift through unceasingly for food particles. Fiddler crabs are again omnivores, but the pieces of food offered should be relatively small and of appropriate size for the crabs. The food should be scattered on the land area.

Battles between fiddler crabs are highly ritualised and even in the confines of the aqua-terrarium do not normally lead to injury in the combatants. Hence they can - and should – be kept in groups; an excess of females (2-4 females per male) has proved effective in practice. Unfortunately, in the case of the fabulously colourful species, for example *Uca annulipes*, time and again it is only males that are imported. Once a male has successfully courted a female, mating occurs belly to belly. The copulation may take only a few minutes, but equally more than half an hour. Both partners tenderly hold and touch each other, as if in a warm embrace. At the same time the male repeatedly knocks on the back of the female, using his enlarged claw. The female subsequently carries eggs and eventually washes them off into the water area with vigorous beats of her pleon in the water. The larvae are tiny, pelagic, and pass through several different developmental stages (zoëae). They can be reared as described earlier for the Grapsidae, in brackish or sea water. In a number of species more than 10 generations have so far been bred in captivity, as H.-G. Rupp describes in detail in the Aqualog Mini mentioned earlier. The identification of the individual species is once again far from easy among the fiddler crabs. For this reason it is quite possible that some of the names used here will subsequently need to be corrected.

A species is very frequently imported from Ecuador that may be *Uca ecuadoriensis* Maccagno, 1928. The specific name relates to the provenance of the type material. This is a peaceful species that is easy to maintain and thus also suitable for the beginner. The distribution of the species lies in the eastern Pacific, from Mexico (Kino Bay, Sonora) to northern Peru. This crab attains a carapace breadth of 2-3 cm.

A second, very much larger but attractive species is also sometimes imported from Ecuador, and is probably *Uca ornata* (Smith, 1870). The Latin adjective ornatus means "decorated". Unfortunately only males have been imported to date, and have, moreover, proved tricky to maintain. It is advisable to provide this species with full-strength sea water. This species too is distributed in the eastern Pacific, from El Salvador to northern Peru.

The species *Uca pugilator* (Bosc, 1802) is quite frequently imported from Florida in the U.S.A.; *pugilator* means

Ocypodoidea: Fiddler crabs – Ocypodidae

Uca ornata is a large species, as comparison with the hand demonstrates. Photo: F. Schäfer

"boxer" and is derived from the Latin word pugil with the same meaning. This species is again readily maintained but likes a higher salt content as it normally occurs immediately adjacent to the sea. It is a species of the western Atlantic, and is distributed from Florida to Brazil and in the islands of the West Indies. It attains a carapace breadth of around 3 cm.

Uca rapax (Smith, 1870) is similar in appearance and size and shares the same distribution. The Latin adjective *rapax* means "greedy" or "rapacious". This is the species that H.-G. Rupp bred successfully for well over 10 successive generations. Interestingly individuals with two "fiddles" instead of just one enlarged claw occurred among the offspring. These would have been unlikely to survive in the wild, but were able to attain adulthood in the aquarium.

Fiddler crabs are also occasionally imported from south-east Asia, but unfortunately often only the colourful males are collected and despatched. A species that may well be *Uca vocans* (Linné, 1758) is occasionally imported as a by-catch with *Pseudosesarma moeschi*. The species is widely distributed in the western Indo-Pacific and attains a carapace breadth of around 4 cm. The Latin name *vocans* means "calling", "shouting". This species is a typical inhabitant of mangrove swamps, but will tolerate maintenance in completely fresh water for only a very short time. It requires at least brackish, better sea water.

Uca pugilator Photo: F. Teigler

Uca rapax, specimen with two "fiddles". Photo: H.-G. Rupp

Ocypodoidea: Fiddler crabs – Ocypodidae

Uca vocans Photo: F. Schäfer

Uca annulipes Photo: F. Schäfer

Like all crabs, fiddler crabs are again very variable in colour. Here two female *Uca vocans*. Photo: F. Schäfer

The most spectacular species imported to date is without question *Uca annulipes* (H. Milne Edwards, 1837), which enjoys an enormous distribution region in the western Indo-Pacific: Madagascar, South Africa to Thailand, Indonesia, Malaysia, and the Philippines. The specific name signifies "ring-foot". Unfortunately to date it has invariably been only males that have been exported from Singapore. Breeding this species would certainly be a worthwhile exercise for the aquarium hobby. This species again remains small, with a carapace breadth of 2-3 cm.

The species *Uca perplexa* (H. Milne Edwards, 1852) is similar in size and appearance, and again widely distributed in the western Indo-Pacific. The specific name means "confusing". This species too is occasionally imported via Singapore.

In conclusion it is appropriate to mention the only *Uca* species with a foothold in Europe, specifically in Portugal. This is *Uca tangeri* (Eydoux, 1835), which is distributed in the warmer parts of the eastern Atlantic, including along the entire coast of West Africa. The specific name means "of Tangier" and probably relates to the type locality. The species is regularly imported from Nigeria for the aquarium hobby. Although it has so far hardly ever been seen feeding, H.-G. Rupp has already managed to breed this species successfully as well and recently reported (pers. comm., 8/2007) the metamorphosis of the first megalopae into young crabs. This species grows somewhat larger than the majority of those mentioned above and attains a carapace breadth of easily 5 cm.

Uca perplexa Photo: F. Schäfer

Ocypodoidea: Fiddler crabs – Ocypodidae

Uca tangeri is the only fiddler crab species with a foothold on European soil, although it is imported from Nigeria for the hobby. Photo: F. Schäfer

Ucides occidentalis (Ortmann, 1897) is a very remarkable crab from the fiddler and ghost crab group, which is occasionally imported from Ecuador for the hobby. The species is distributed along the coast of the eastern Pacific from Mexico to Peru and is a typical inhabitant of mangrove swamps, where it performs a similar role in the ecosystem to that of earthworms in Europe. The main food of these crabs consists of dead leaved, which they drag into their up to a metre long underground tunnels, to decompose and be eaten. The breadth of these giant crabs can be up to 40 cm. They are regarded as a delicacy in their native lands and there are size restrictions on their collection. But the appalling destruction of the natural habitat of these and many other species represents a generally greater threat to their survival.

The genus name is derived from *Uca* and signifies "related to Uca", while the specific name (= "western") relates to the fact that these crabs occur to the west of their Atlantic sibling species *Ucides cordatus* (Linné, 1758). Both taxa are sometimes regarded as subspecies of one and the same species (*U. cordatus*). As far as I know *Ucides cordatus* (the specific name signifies "heart-shaped" and refers to the shape of the carapace) has not yet been imported for the hobby. The maintenance of these crabs requires an adequately large container and brackish water. They are relatively tolerant of one another.

Female *Uca tangeri.* Photo: F. Schäfer

Ucides occidentalis Photo: Sch. Nakano

Land crabs – Gecarcinidae

Land crabs

Land crabs of the family Gecarcinidae have also repeatedly been imported. Some of them grow to a respectable size, their shells measuring around 20 centimetres across! They include the American *Gecarcinus* LEACH, 1814 and the Indo-Pacific *Gecarcoidea* MILNE EDWARDS, 1837. Both are totally unsuitable for freshwater aquaria. They are exclusively land-dwellers and populate the upper, dry parts of sand and coral beaches. Adult individuals are the best adapted of all the crabs for life on dry land; they breathe almost exclusively via "lungs" and drown in water! In the wild they find shelter in fissures in rocks and shallow cavities beneath stones and tree roots, where it is cool and dry. Their water requirement is supplied by eating plants, and they also collect dew at night on their hairy legs! In addition they are generally more active in the cool of the night than during the daytime. Both genus names relate to this way of life: *Gecarcinus* is a Latinised combination of the Greek words ge meaning "earth", "land" and karkinos meaning "crab", while *Gecarcoidea* is simply a derived form of the same name. The species contained in this genus were originally assigned by DE HAAN, 1835 to his own genus *Gecarcinus*, erected in ignorance of the fact that a taxon of the same name was already in existence. When this error came to light, MILNE EDWARDS introduced the replacement name *Gecarcoidea,* which remains valid today.

Even though adult crabs of both groups live on land, their eggs develop only in the sea. After copulation the females lay fertilised eggs and carry them about, attached to their hairy pleopods. During their development the eggs change colour from orange or red to a greyish-green. Eventually the females make their way to the sea, often in large groups. This often takes place at full moon, as the timing of the whole procedure is determined by the phases of the moon. Aided by vigorous movements of the abdomen, they rinse their eggs off into the surf – a hazardous process, at least for *Gecarcinus* and *Gecarcoidea*, whose gills are so atrophied that they are at risk of drowning. When the larvae hatch they begin a planktonic life. During their time at sea they develop through a number of stages, some of them reminiscent of shrimps, until finally they leave the water as fully-formed crabs. In captivity rearing can be achieved as described above for the jumping crabs, that is, in full-strength sea water, where the zoëa and megalopa stages can be fed with *Artemia* nauplii.

A number of species of river crabs (q.v.) have also made the transition to a completely terrestrial life and die if compelled to try and live in the aquarium. A notable example is the gorgeous *Demanietta sirikit*. In the wild this species lives in self-dug burrows that are so deep that the lower end always contains a puddle of water. The crabs leave these burrows only at night, to search for food and at mating time. In land-dwelling river crabs the young develop into fully-formed

This attractive land crab is regularly imported from Ecuador for the vivarium hobby under the name *Gecarcinus ruricola*. It is, however, equally possible that it is actually the species *G. lateralis*. Photo: F. Schäfer

Land crabs – Gecarcinidae

White colour variant of the *Gecarcinus* species from Ecuador.
Photo: F. Schäfer

little crabs within the eggs before the latter hatch, and are thus completely independent of the sea.

All land crabs (with the exception of *Cardisoma armatum*, whose care is detailed separately below), regardless of their systematic placement, should be maintained in a terrarium with a deep substrate and a water component consisting only of a dish of water, which should be replaced regularly so it is always fresh. The substrate should be at least 15 cm deep and composed of a mixture of sand, clay, peat, and garden soil. The mixture should be such that the crabs can dig their burrows without the latter caving in, hence the clay component. The sand will keep the mix "open", allowing air and water to permeate, the peat will ensure an acid pH that will inhibit germs and help retain moisture, while the garden soil will introduce micro-organisms that will prevent the substrate from becoming putrid as a result of excreta from the crabs.

All land crabs should be kept singly (except when breeding), with the only exception again being *Cardisoma armatum*, which lives in social communities and can be kept in the same way. While land crabs may look attractive and desirable as pets, it should always be borne in mind that if their accommodation is arranged halfway appropriately then they will hardly ever be visible. They are very retiring in their habits and are also strongly crepuscular or nocturnal. A 60-cm aquarium is adequate for the maintenance of a single such crab.

The land-dwelling river crab species imported for the hobby have already been detailed above (page 147 ff.). When it comes to the true land crabs, four species are occasionally imported for the private hobbyist, but their identification once again involves a number of question marks.

An attractive orange or (more rarely) white *Gecarcinus* species is imported from Ecuador. It was initially identified as *Gecarcinus ruricola* (LINNÉ, 1758). The specific name is

Gecarcinus quadratus is another very colourful land crab. It and its congeners are best kept singly. All these crabs are sold under the name Halloween Crab in the trade.
Photo: F. Schäfer

composed of the Latin rus, ruris = "country(side)" and cola = "inhabitant", hence "country-dweller". But according to other sources the species is *G. lateralis* (Freminville, 1835). The specific name lateralis signifies "lateral". But, both are Atlantic species, with a distribution from Florida to French Guiana, while Ecuador has only Pacific coast. It may be that the species exported from Ecuador has used the Panama Canal to migrate into the Pacific. Both species look rather similar on the basis of photos taken in the field, but the extent of the black area on the carapace is larger in *G. ruricola*; for this reason it is also known as the Black Land Crab.

The second species imported from time to time is *Gecarcinus quadratus* De Saussure, 1895, which is easily recognisable from its incredibly gaudy combination of colours. It is a species of the eastern Pacific and distributed from Mexico to Colombia. The specific name *quadratus* means "rectangular", "with four corners".

All these land crab species are subject to serious pressure from humans, who regard them as delicacies and an important source of protein.

Unlike the air-breathing crabs discussed above, *Cardisoma* species are suitable for maintenance in an aqua-terrarium. In the wild they live in salt marshes, in burrows that they dig themselves. These are sometimes more than a metre deep and always contain the water essential to these crabs, which breathe via gills. An aqua-terrarium for a group of *Cardisoma* should be fairly spacious (e.g. 150 x 70 cm) and not too shallow as a deep layer of sand is required so that the crabs can construct their burrows. Stones and roots can be used to provide additional cavities, but such decor must be well-founded. Part of the sandy area of the aqua-terrarium should be kept covered with fresh leaves (preferably of those of fruit trees) or lettuce. The crabs will feed on them and deposit their excrement on them, so that it is easier to keep the substrate clean. The small water reservoir (at most a quarter of the available space) should be just deep enough for the crabs to be able to breathe without difficulty while resting on the bottom. You will then see how the used water is expelled via the mouth. At the same time the crabs should be able to raise their respiratory openings (which are located at the insertions of the peraeopods) above the water level when they stand up. The lower layers of sand of the land area must be kept moist or wet, and because of the high metabolic rate of the crabs, the water must be changed frequently. It should be brackish, and this is best achieved using some marine salt.

It is also important to cover the aqua-terrarium tightly so that the necessary atmospheric humidity (more than 80%) is maintained. The air temperature should be 28–30°C, higher than that of the water (24–25°C), to avoid chilling. If the air space is too cool then the crabs will seek out a spot in the warmth of the light. But the cover should also be completely crab-proof to prevent the residents from climbing out, as these crabs are skilled escape artists.

Because of their aggressive nature the crab community should consist of individuals matched as closely as possible in size and strength, so that none is easy prey for the rest. Newly-moulted specimens must be able to find shelter or else be separated from the others. These crabs, too, eat almost anything, so you can give them the same food as the river crabs. However, the bulk of their diet should consist of fruit and other vegetable matter, not least because all crabs are sensitive to the breakdown products of animal material, which may cause (auto-)toxicity. Their tolerance of such waste products will generally be greater if the water is mineral-rich or contains salt. Most land crabs can live for more than ten years and become hand tame.

The species most commonly available is *Cardisoma armatum* Herklots, 1851, an eastern Atlantic species that is distributed along the coast of West Africa. The species, whose genus name means "heart-shaped body" and specific name "armed", is imported from Nigeria. The larvae of *Cardisoma armatum* develop in the sea via 5-6 zoëa stages and one megalopa, and can be reared as described above for the Grapsidae.

A second species, formerly also assigned to *Cardisoma*, has now been transferred to the genus *Discoplax* A. Milne Edwards, 1867: *D. hirtipes* (Dana, 1852). The genus name signifies "disc-shaped" and the specific name means "hairy foot". This species is occasionally imported from Japan. In the wild it inhabits the higher parts of beaches and *Casuarina* thickets, and it should be kept in the same way as a land crab. In the pet trade all these species are sold as Halloween Crabs or Harlequin Crabs. The reader is referred to Ng & Guinot, 2001 for an up-to-date summary of the taxonomy of the land crabs.

Egg-bearing female of *Cardisoma armatum*.

Photo: F. Schäfer

Land crabs - Gecarcinidae

Cardisoma armatum is one of the land crabs currently available in the pet trade. It is imported from Nigeria, where these sociable crabs live in large colonies in the mangrove swamps. Photo: F. Schäfer

Discoplax hirtipes is a land crab that is imported from Japan. Photo: F. Schäfer

Appendix 1

Alpheidae – pistol or snapping shrimps

The pistol shrimps of the family Alpheidae are in the main sea-dwellers and many species are well-known to marine aquarists. The symbiosis between pistol shrimp species and sleeper gobies is renowned and can also be seen very nicely in the aquarium. The almost blind pistol shrimp is an indefatigable tunneller that keeps the cave shared by the two species as their home free of the constantly encroaching sand, while the goby, which has good eyesight, acts as guard.

The pistol shrimps received their warlike name because of their ability to make a cracking sound with their greatly enlarged and specially modified claws. This is clearly audible outside of the water, and under water the "crack" can stun a fish. However, the sound is less reminiscent of a pistol shot than of the noise made by an aquarium glass splitting suddenly! I personally rehomed a marine pistol shrimp after I had several times sprinted into my fish room in a panic in the middle of the night to see which aquarium had burst! Every time it turned out to be a false alarm occasioned by the pistol shrimp, but it nevertheless left my nerves in shreds.

True freshwater species are, as mentioned earlier, very uncommon among the alpheids. *Potamalpheops haughi* (Coutiere, 1906) has been reported from completely fresh water in West Africa (Niger Delta and Gabon). The genus name means "river-dwelling *Alpheus*-like (shrimp)"; the specific name is, like that of the following species, an honorific. *P. monodi* (Sollaud, 1932) is a brackish-water species that is widespread in West Africa and sometimes found in almost completely fresh water. Two further species are also found in the Niger area, one of them as yet undescribed. *P. stygicola* (Hobbs, 1973) is a freshwater, cave-dwelling species from Mexico. Its specific name means "Styx-dweller" - in classical mythology the subterranean river Styx was the boundary which the dead must cross to enter the underworld. Further species have only recently been discovered in Australia and south-east and southern Asia, and in some cases also described.

The genus may not have made an appearance in the aquarium hobby so far, but, as can be seen from the above catalogue, is very interesting from a zoogeographical viewpoint (see also Anker, 2005).

The genus *Alpheus* Fabricius, 1798 contains a very small number of brackish-water species and one species that is adapted to completely fresh water. The genus name is again borrowed from classical mythology - Alpheus was a river god. The species *A. cyanoteles* Yeo & Ng, 1996 is an inhabitant of completely fresh water from the Malayan peninsula. The specific name relates to the blue coloration of the telson and uropods. In the natural habitat this shrimp lives in very soft (conductivity < 24 µS) acid water. Before it was realised that this was a distinct species, collections of this pistol shrimp from fresh water were incorrectly identified as *A. paludicola* Kemp, 1915 (*paludicola* (Latin) = "marsh-dweller"). The latter species, a close relative of *A. cyanoteles*, is a brackish-water shrimp with a high tolerance of fluctuations in salinity, but nevertheless seldom or never visits completely fresh water.

The eggs of *Alpheus cyanoteles* are large and it belongs to the specialised reproductive type. This freshwater pistol shrimp has occasionally been imported for aquarium maintenance, but has proved delicate and difficult to keep alive, so it has not yet been possible to establish an aquarium strain. The problem may be unsuitable water chemistry. In the event that the species is imported again it should be maintained in very soft, very acid water. These shrimps are not very tolerant of conspecifics and are always chopping of bits of one another's legs. The species is an omnivore.

Alpheus cyanoteles is an inhabitant of completely fresh water, and thus an exception among the pistol shrimps. Photo: F. Schäfer

Appendix 1

Alpheidae – pistol or snapping shrimps

Pistol shrimps are interesting creatures that can even stun larger fishes with their huge "cracker claws". *Alpheus cyanoteles* are very intolerant of one another.
Photos: F. Schäfer

Appendix 2

Xiphosura - horseshoe crabs

The boom in the maintenance of invertebrates in recent years has spilled over into our aquaria as well, bringing us such strange creatures as the horseshoe or sword-tail crabs. For 300 million years they have remained practically unchanged (by comparison, modern Man has been in existence for barely 40,000 years), they have seen the dinosaurs come and go, and they will probably still be around when the mammals have taken their final curtain call on this planetary stage. They are not in fact closely related to the crabs & co at all, the common name is misleading. Like the crustaceans they are arthropods (Arthropoda), but systematically they are actually closer to the spiders.

There are four species of horseshoe crab, in three genera. The best-known is undoubtedly *Limulus polyphemus* (Linné, 1758) from the North American Atlantic coast. *Limulus* means "sideways", referring to its mode of locomotion, while Polyphemus was a one-eyed giant in classical mythology. *Limulus* is, however, an exclusively marine species, and hence will not be discussed further here. By contrast the three species that occur in southern and south-east Asia, *Tachypleus gigas* (Müller, 1758), *T. tridentatus* (Leach, 1819), and *Carcinoscorpius rotundicauda* (Latreille, 1802), are at home in a brackish environment. The genus name *Tachypleus* signifies "fast mushroom cap", referring to the rapid-beating, round gill lamellae that in horseshoe crabs are located beneath the opisthosoma (the central segment of the body), while *gigas* means "giant", and *tridentatus* "with three teeth" (referring to the three distinctive serrae on the opisthosoma); *Carcinoscorpius* means "crab-scorpion" and *rotundicauda* "with a round tail".

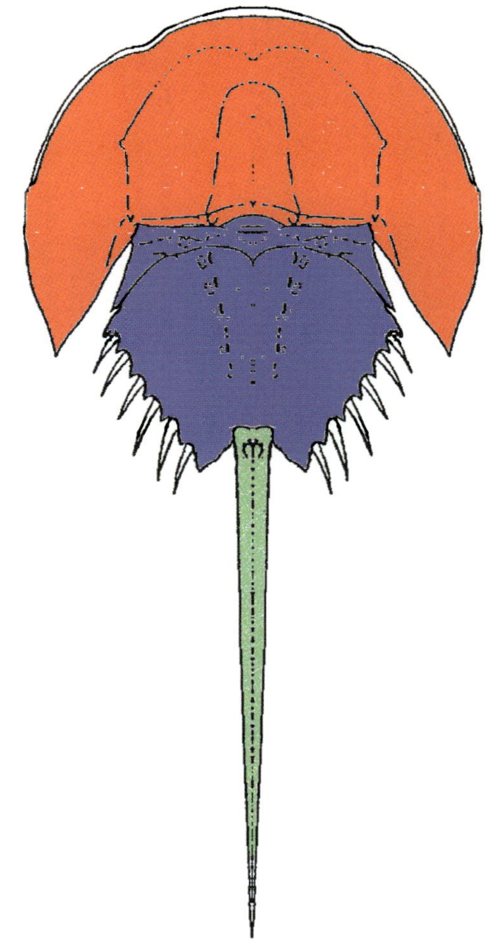

The sections of the body in horseshoe crabs.
Red: prosoma; blue: opisthosoma; green: telson.
after Chiu & Morton, 2003

In fact only *Carcinoscorpius rotundicauda* is truly estuarine and hence the most suitable for freshwater tanks with a little salt added. But they will regard it as a favour if they are provided with a specially set-up brackish-water aquarium. Tachypleus, meanwhile, do best in full-strength sea water.

A few words on distinguishing the three species: in *Tachypleus* the upper edge of the sword-like tail is serrated, in *Carcinoscorpius* the tail is smooth and slightly rounded at the tip. *Tachypleus gigas* has only one distinctive serra on the opisthosoma, *T. tridentatus* has three. *T. tridentatus* is the largest species, with a maximum length of 75 cm, *T. gigas* grows to around 50 cm long, and *C. rotundicauda* is the smallest species at 35 cm maximum.

In horseshoe crabs the female is normally larger and heavier the male. External sexual characteristics become visible only at the onset of sexual maturity and hence it is impossible to tell the sexes apart in sexually inactive juveniles. In mature males the tips of the second and third pairs of legs are modified into claspers while females retain the normal claws. During the mating season these crabs undertake mass migrations into shallow coastal regions, with the females arriving first and excavating nesting pits. During mating the male initially mounts the female from behind. According to Xin (1990), internal fertilisation then

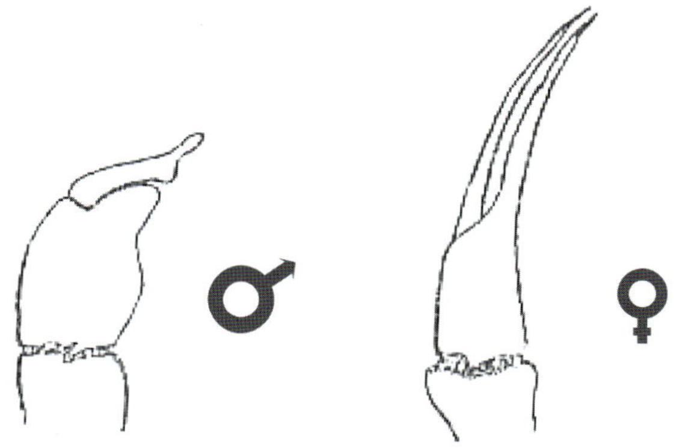

In sexually mature horseshoe crabs (this is *T. gigas*) the male can be recognised by having the claws of the second and third pairs of legs modified into claspers. after Smedley, 1929

Appendix 2

Xiphosura - horseshoe crabs

Carcinoscorpius rotundicauda. Above: a sexually mature male; below: a sexually mature female. The modified second and third peraeopods of the male are clearly recognisable. Photos: F. Schäfer

Appendix 2

Xiphosura - horseshoe crabs

Tachypleus tridentatus can be recognised by the strongly compressed telson with a serrated upper edge. With a maximum length of easily 75 cm and a weight of up to 5 kg, this is the largest species of the family and should be kept in a marine aquarium. Photo: F. Schäfer

In *Carcinoscorpius rotundicauda*, by contrast, the telson is cylindrical and smooth dorsally. This is the smallest species of horseshoe crab and the only one that can be kept long-term in a freshwater aquarium with salt added, or better, a proper brackish-water aquarium. Photo: F. Schäfer

Appendix 2

Xiphosura - horseshoe crabs

Horseshoe crabs are fascinating relics from Earth's remote past. The mouth opening lies in the centre of the underside of the body and is surrounded by yellowish hairs. Photo: F. Schäfer

takes place in a belly-to-belly position. The female then lays her eggs in the nest. The juveniles look similar to the long-extinct trilobites and spend their first few days free-swimming before adopting a bottom-oriented lifestyle and soon coming to look like the adults. I am not aware of any life-span data for *C. rotundicauda*, but *Limulus*, which grows to around 50 cm long and has been fairly well studied, attains sexual maturity at the age of 11 years and lives for a total of 20-25 years.

During the mating period many horseshoe crabs (up to 10%) meet their end through being turned onto their backs by the action of the waves in over-shallow water. They are then unable to regain their normal position and die.

Horseshoe crabs are omnivores with carnivorous preferences. In the aquarium they can readily be fed on all the different types of frozen food that are available for feeding ornamental fishes. In the wild juvenile *T. tridentatus* and *C. rotundicauda* feed by preference on chironomid larvae, and hence should without fail be offered a similar diet in the form of bloodworm (red mosquito larvae) (Zhou & Morton, 2004). If they are provided with a substrate of fine sand then they will happily bury themselves in it – sometimes for days on end. But if the aquarium substrate is gravel or only a thin layer then they will often be seen to lie on their backs, apparently lifeless. This is no cause for concern, however, but completely harmless.

Horseshoe crabs are completely peaceful towards conspecifics, fishes, and other invertebrates (e.g. *Clibanarius* species). On the other hand it is important to make sure that these plump and completely defenceless creatures are not imprisoned in an aquarium containing thugs of any kind, for example some crabs and cichlids.

Unfortunately populations of these "living fossils" are declining worldwide due to environmental pollution. *Tachypleus* are in fact maintained in aquaculture in order to extract their blood, which is the focus of medical research on account of some of its unique features (because of its different chemical composition they have not red but blue blood – genuine ancient royalty!), but they have not yet been bred in captivity – or at least this has not been reported.

Appendix 3
Crayfishes from Madagascar

The occurrence of freshwater crayfishes on the island of Madagascar is a zoogeographical puzzle as freshwater crayfishes are completely absent from Africa. And even on Madagascar the seven endemic species are found only in an area of around 60,000 km^2 in the south-east of the island, at an altitude of between 500 and 2,000 metres. Aquaristik Service Reuter has now imported three of these species to Germany.

All seven species of Madagascan crayfishes are assigned to the genus *Astacoides*. A comprehensive overview of the genus has been given by Hobbs (1987), and two years ago an additional species was scientifically described (Boyko et al., 2005). *Astacoides* belongs to the southern crayfish assemblage (Parastacoidea), which is already known to the aquarium hobby in the form of the genus *Cherax* from New Guinea and Australia.

Although the Madagascan crayfishes are not the largest species of freshwater crayfishes known, they can attain a not inconsiderable size. The largest species of the genus *Astacoides* is *A. madagascarensis*, which can attain a carapace length of almost 9 cm, corresponding to a total length of 19-20 cm. The smallest species is *A. crosnieri* with a carapace length of 5.3 cm (ie around 11-12 cm total length).

In *Astacoides* males and females exhibit very few external differences, and in order to sex them they most be turned onto their backs. The males have their reproductive openings (gonopores) at the base of the fifth pair of walking legs, while in females the gonopores are at the base of the third pair. In specimens of the same size the abdominal segments in females are somewhat shallower in form, but this is difficult to see in live individuals, as *Astacoides* are inclined to carry their tails tucked under.

Hardly anything is known about the lifestyle of Madagascar crayfishes in the wild. It is known that the species *A. betsileonensis*, *A. caldwelli*, *A. hobbsi*, *A granulimanus* and *A. madagscarensis* are typically found in running water with a stony bottom, while the species *A. crosnieri* and *A. petiti* live in swampy regions.

Feeding Madagascar crayfishes in the aquarium presents no problems as they are omnivores like other more familiar crayfishes. But otherwise the maintenance of these crayfishes is still absolutely virgin territory. Cool water (around 12 °C) is better tolerated than when the temperature rises above 25 °C. They are not excessively aggressive among themselves, but housing fluviatile crayfishes together is always a risky business. No species is truly sociable and a newly-moulted conspecific may well be regarded as food.

The importation contained at least three species. The most spectacular is undoubtedly *A. betsileonensis*, an up to 18 cm long species with bizarre, stout spines on its carapace. In addition this species is very attractively coloured in red and blue. The second species is *A. madagascarensis*, which, as already mentioned, is the largest member of the genus. In this species the sides of the carapace are merely granular and not set with spines. And finally the consignment contained *A. granulimanus*, an approximately 14 cm long species. The last two species have appreciably smaller eyes than *A. betsileonensis*, and can be told from it by this feature.

Astacoides granulimanus Photo: F. Schäfer

Astacoides madagascarensis Photo: F. Schäfer

Astacoides betsileonensis Photo: F. Schäfer

Appendix 3

Crayfishes from Madagascar

Red morph (large picture) and blue-red morph of *Astacoides betsileonensis.* Photos: F. Schäfer

Appendix 4
Crustaceans from Sulawesi

Quite recently, Mimbon Aquarium in Cologne, Germany, was able to import crustaceans from the Malili lake system (lakes Matano, Mahalona, and Towoeti) in central Sulawesi (formerly known as Celebes). Some of these animals are really spectacular coloured. Most of the species are still under description, as they are not known to science yet. Due to the shortness of their appearance in the hobby there are hardly any informations availble how to care for them, but it seems necessary to imitate the water chemistry they have in their natural habitat as close as possible. Especially a constantly high pH of 8.3 seems to be of some importance. This importation shows that we just started to discover the diversity of freshwater crustaceans.

Syntripsa flavichela, Malili (lakes Mahalona and Towoeti)
Photo: C. Lukhaup

Parathelphusa pantherina, Malili (lake Matano)
Photo: C. Lukhaup

Syntripsa matannensis, Malili (lake Matano)
Photo: C. Lukhaup

Undetermined crab, Malili
Photo: C. Lukhaup

Parathelphusa ferruginea, Malili (lakes Mahalona and Towoeti)
Photo: C. Lukhaup

Caridina sp., Malili
Photo: C. Lukhaup

Caridina ensifera, blue variety, lake Poso
Photo: C. Lukhaup

Appendix 4
Crustaceans from Sulawesi

Caridina ensifera, red variety, lake Poso

Photo: C. Lukhaup

Caridina sp., Malili

Photo: C. Lukhaup

Caridina sp., Malili

Photo: C. Lukhaup

Caridina sp., Kardinalsgarnele / Cardinal shrimp, Malili

Photo: C. Lukhaup

Caridina cf *spinata*, Malili

Photo: C. Lukhaup

Caridina cf. *spinata*, Malili (lake Towoeti)

Photo: C. Lukhaup

Caridina sp., Malili

Photo: C. Lukhaup

Caridina sp., Malili

Photo: C. Lukhaup

Appendix 4

Crustaceans from Sulawesi

Caridina sp., Malili

Photo: C. Lukhaup

Caridina sp., Malili

Photo: C. Lukhaup

Caridina sp., Malili

Photo: C. Lukhaup

Caridina sp., Malili

Photo: C. Lukhaup

Caridina loehae, Malili

Photo: C. Lukhaup

Caridina sp., Malili

Photo: C. Lukhaup

Caridina lingkonae, Malili

Photo: C. Lukhaup

Caridina lanceolata, Malili

Photo: C. Lukhaup

Picture index

Picture index

Picture index

Literature cited

ALTEVOGT, R. (1971): Unterklasse Höhere Krebse. In: Grzimeks Tierleben 1: Niedere Tiere, Kap. 16: Die Krebstiere. Zürich: 468–506.

AMESBURY, S. S. (1980): Biological studies on the coconut crab (Birgus latro) in the Mariana islands. Agriculture Experiment Station, College of Agriculture and Life Sciences, University of Guam, Technical Report No 17: 37 pp.

ANGER, K. (1995): The conquest of freshwater and land by marine crabs: adaptation in life-history patterns and larval bioenergetics. Journal of Experimental Marine Biology and Ecology 193: 119-145

ANKER, A. (2005): Presence of the Alpheid shrimp genus Potamalpheops Powell, 1979 (Crustacea: Decapoda: Caridea) in south Asia, with description of a new species from Sri Lanka. The Raffles Bulletin of Zoology Suppl. No 12: 31-37

ARBEITSGEMEINSCHAFT Wirbellose im Internet: www.wirbellose.de

ARNOLD, A. (1989): Nochmals zum Kuba-Süßwasserkrebs, Procambarus cubensis. AT 36: 24–26.

BERGER, M. (1985): Cuba-Süßwasserkrebs. AT 32: 153.

BITTER, F. (2000): Fächergarnelen. Aquaristik aktuell 3-4: 74-78.

BOETGER, C. (1949): Das Auftreten des Amerikanischen Flußkrebses in Niedersachsen. Natur und Volk (5/6): 143–146.

BÖNIG, I., Deuss, T. & Reith (2005): www.nachzuchtenregister.de

BOTT, R. (1949): Amerikanische Flußkrebse im Main. Natur und Volk (6/6): 139–143.

BRODIE, R. & A. W. Harvey (2001): Larval developement of the land hermit crab Coenobita compressus H Mline Edwards reared in the laboratory. Journal of Crustacean Biology 21 (3): 715-732

CAI, Y. & N. K. Ng (1999): A revision of the Caridina serrata species group, with descriptions of five new species (Crustacea: Decapoda: Caridea: Atyidae). Journ. Nat. Hist., 33: 1603-1638.

CARROLL, P. N. (Ed.) (1980): A Yabbie Pot Pourri. Vorlesungstexte u. a. d. Hawesbury Agric. Coll. u. d. Univ. New England, Armidale.

CARSON, H. L. (1974): Three flies and three islands: Parallel evolution in Drosophila (Caribbean Sea/Indian Ocean/ecology/land crabs). Proc. Nat. Acad. Sci. USA 71 (9): 3517-3521

CHACE, F. A. Jr. (1983): The Atya-like shrimps of the Indo-Pacific Region (Decapoda: Atyidae). Smithsonian Contributions to Zoology 384.

CHIA, D. G. B. & P. K. L. Ng (1994): Die Riesenlandkrabben von Malaysia. DATZ 47: 30–34.

CHIU, H. M. C. & B. Morton (2003): The morphological differentiation of two horseshoe crab speciers, Tachypleus tridentatus and Carcinoscorpius rotundicauda (Xiphosura), in Hong Kong with a regional Asian comparison. Journal of Natural History 37 (19: 2369-2382

CONVERT, C. (1982): Reproduction de Procambarus clarkii. AQUARAMA 64, 14 ff.

DANIELS, S. R., Cumberlidge, N., Pérez-Losada, M. Marijnissen, S. A. E. & K. A. Crandall (2006): Evolution of afrotropical freshwater crab lineages obscured by morphological convergence. Molecular Phylogenetics and Evolution 40: 227-235

DAVIE, P. J. F. (2003): A new species of Perisesarma (Crustacea: Brachyura: Sesarmidae) from the Bay of Bengal. The Raffles Bulletin of Zoology 51 (2): 387-391

DE GRAVE, S. & D. K. A. Barnes (2001): Ecology of tropical hermit crabs (Crustacea Decapoda) at Quirimba island, Mozambique: a multivariate assemblage perspective. Tropical Zoology 14: 197-209

DOST, U. (1995): Flußkrebse im Aquarium. DATZ 48: 502–508.

ESTERBAUER, H. (1983): Notizen zur Biologie und Pflege der Süßwasserkrabbe Potamon potamios. Das Aquarium 27, Heft 293 (11): 11–14.

FALCIAI, L. & E. Palmerini (2001): Larval developement of the freshwater shrimp, Palaemonetes antennarius (H. Milne Edwards, 1837) (Decapoda, Palaemonidae) reared in the laboratory. Crustaceana 74 (11): 1315-1333

FISHERIES Department Perth (1985): Marron and Marron farming. Ext. Publ. Sect. Fish. Dept. Perth, WA: 39 pp.

FISHERIES of Western Australia, Homepage: http://www.wa.gov.au/westfish/aqua/broc/idfresh/idfresh02.html

FREITAG, H. & D. C. J. Yeo (2004): Two new species of Parathelphusa H. Milne Edwards, 1853, from the Philippines (Crustacea: Decapoda: Brachyura: Parathelphusidae). The Raffles Bulletin of Zoology 52 (1): 227-237

GARCÍA-DÁVILA, C. R., C. Magalhaes, C. & J. C. H. Guerrero (2005): Morphometric vaiability in populations of Palaemonetes spp. (Crustacea, Decapoda, Palaemonidae) from the Peruvian and Brazilian Amazon basin. Iheringia. Série Zoologica 95 (3): 327-334

GILLIKIN, D. P. & C. D. Schubart (2004): Ecology and systematics of mangrove crabs of the genus Perisesarma (Crustacea: Brachyura: Sesarmidae) from East Africa. Zoological Journal of the Linnean Society 141: 435-445

GORTZYTZA, H. (1990): Die Zucht von Süßwassergarnelen – eine Herausforderung? DATZ 43: 599–601.

GÖTHEL, H. (1986): Zwei Süßwassergarnelen für das Gesellschaftsbecken. DATZ 39: 67–69.

GRABOWSKI, T. (1998): Über Krebse. Thannhausen/Mindelzell; 47 S.

GRÜNWALD, H. (1970): Einwanderer aus Amerika. Amerikanische Flußkrebse im Lippe-Seiten-Kanal. Heimatkalender des Kreises Dinslaken (NRW).

HANSON, J. A. & H. L. Godwin (1977): Shrimp and prawn farming in the western hemisphere. Dowden, Hutchinson & Ross, Inc., Pennsylvania: 193 pp

HARRIS, R. R. (1977): Urine production rate and water balance in the terrestrial crabs Gecarcinus lateralis and Cardisoma guanhami. J. exp. Biol. 68: 57-67

HARVEY, A. W. (1992): Abbreviated larval developement in the Australian terrestrial hermit crab Coenobita variabilis McCulloch (Anomura: Coenobitidae). Journal of Crustacean biology, 12 (2): 196-209

HENDRIX, A. N. & W. F. Loftus (2000): Distribution and relative abundance of the crayfishes Procambarus alleni (Faxon) and P. fallax (Hagen) in southern Florida. Wetlands 20, 1: 194-199.

HOBBS, H. H. Jr. (1972): Crayfishes (Astacidae) of north and middle America. Biota of Freshwater Ecosystems 9: 173 pp.

HOLTHUIS, L. B. (1949): Decapoda macrura. With a revision of the New Guinea Parastacidae. Zool. Res. Dutch New Guinea Exp. 1939, 3: 37-329 + Plates. In: Nova Guinea, Ne Series V. Leiden.

ICZN (2002): Case 3183: 59 (1)

ICZN (2003): Opinion 2052 (Case 3183): 60 (3)

JORDAN, F., J. B. Kimberly, C. C. McIvor & S. J. Miller (1996): Spatial ecology of the crayfish Procambarus alleni in a Florida wetland mosaic. 21 pp.

KADEN, J. (1991): Strandläufer. DATZ 44: 22–27.

KARGE, A. & W. Klotz (2007): Süßwassergarnelen aus aller Welt. Dähne Verlag, Ettlingen, 200 pp.

KUPFERER, R. (1991): Mangrovekrabben (mit einer Anmerkung von D. Schaller). DATZ 44: 492–493.

KURIAN, C. V. & V. O. Sebastian (1982): Prawns and prawn fisheries of India. Hindustan Publ. Corp. (India), Delhi-110007: 62 ff.

LECHLEITER, S. (1995): Flußkrebse im Aquarium. DATZ 48: 745.

LEHMANN, H. (1986): Erfahrungen mit Kuba-Süßwasserkrebsen. AT 33: 102.

LEIENDECKER, E. & U. (1982): An ihren Scheren kann man sie erkennen: Süßwassergarnelen. Aquarien-Magazin, Heft 3: 167–172.

LIETSCH, P. (1984): Zur Pflege und Zucht des südamerikanischen Sumpfkrebses (Procambarus troglodytes). AT 31: 313.

LING, Shao-Wen (1977): Aquaculture in Southeast Asia. Wash. Sea Grant Publ., Seattle & London: 94-101.

LUKHAUP, Ch. & R. Pekny (2005): Krebse im Aquarium. Haltung und Pflege im Süßwasser. Dähne Verlag, Ettlingen, 158 pp.

LUKHAUP, Ch. (2000): Florida-Lobster, Blickfang im Süßwasseraquarium. Aquaristik aktuell 8: 32-36.

LUKHAUP, Ch. (2001): Procambarus milleri, der Mandarinenkrebs. Aquaristik aktuell 3-4: 70-73.

LUKHAUP, Ch. (2003): Süßwasserkrebse aus aller Welt. Dähne Verlag, Ettlingen, 256 pp.

LUKHAUP, Ch. (cont.): www.crusta10.de

MANCINI, A. (1989): Les Ecrevisses (Crustacea: Decapoda: Astacoidea, Parastacoidea) dans l'aquarium. Revue fr. Aquariol., 16 (1), 7:11–21.

MANCINI, A. (1995): Crabes et pagures d'eau douce, d'eau saumâtre et...de terre. AQUARAMA 142: 16–22.

MARIJNISSEN, S. A. E., Michel, E., Daniels, S. R., Erpenbeck, D., Menken, S. B. J. & F. R. Schram (2006): Molecular evidence for recent divergence of lake Tanganyika endemic crabs (Decapoda: Platythelphusidae). Molecular Phylogenetics and Evoltion 40 (2): 628-634

Literature cited

MARTIN J. W. & G. E. Davis (2001): An updated classification of the recent Crustacea. Natural History Museum of Los Angeles County, Sience Series. Contribution in Science 39: 124 pp

MCLAUGHLIN, P. (2001): Illustrated keys to the families and genera of the superfamily Paguroidea (Crustacea: Decapoda: Anomura), with diagnoses of genera of Paguridae. Memoirs of Museum Victoria 60 (1): 111-144

MERRICK, J. R. & C. N. Lambert (1991): The Yabby, Marron and Red Claw. Production and marketing. Nat. Lib. Austr., 175 pp.

MORI, F. (1998): Asiatische Süßwassergarnelen. Aquaristik aktuell 7-8: 6-11.

MÜLLER, H. (1973): Die Flußkrebse. Die langschwänzigen Decapoda Mitteleuropas und ihre wirtschaftliche Bedeutung. Brehm-Bücherei Nr. 121, Wittenberg-Lutherstadt, 2. bearb. Aufl..

NAKASONE, Y. (1988): Land hermit crabs from the Ryukyus, Japan, with a description of a new species from the Philippines (Crustacea, Decapoda, Coenobitidae). Zoological Sciences 5 (1): 165-178

NARUSE, T., Shih, H.-T., Ng, N. K. & H.-L. Hsu (2004): On two new records of Varunid crabs (Crustacea: Brachyura: Varunidae) from southern Taiwan. Coll. And Res. 18: 69-79

NG, P. K. L. & C. D. Schubart (2002): Haberma nanum, a new genus and new species of mangrove crab (Crustacea: Decapoda: Brachyura: Sesarmidae) from Singapore. The Raffles Bulletin of Zoology 50 (2): 437-442

NG, P. K. L. & C. D. Schubart (2003): On the identities of Sesarma obesum Dana, 1851, and Sesarma eydouxi H Milne Edwards, 1853 (Crustacea, Decapoda, Brachyura, Sesarmidae). Zoosystema 25 (3): 425-437

NG, P. K. L. & D. G. B. Chia (1994): Die Riesenbachgarnele. DATZ 47: 644–648.

NG, P. K. L. & D. Guinot (2001): On the land crabs of the genus Discoplax A. Milne Edwards, 1867 (Crustacea: Decapoda: Brachyura: Gecarcinidae), with description of a new cavernicolous species from the Philippines. The raffles Bulletin of Zoology 49 (2): 311-338

NOLTE, A. (1996): Der Zwergflußkrebs Cambarellus shuffeldtii. DATZ 49: 567–569.

ÓLAFSSON, E., Buchmayer, S. & M. K. Skov (2002): The East African decapod crab Neosarmatium meinerti (de Man) sweeps mangrove floors clean of leaf litter. AMBIO: A journal of the human environment 31 (7): 569-573

OSAWA, M. & N. Ng (2006): A new species of Ptychognathus Stimpson, 1858 (Crustacea: Decapoda: Brachyura: Varunidae) from the Ryukyu Islands, southwestern Japan. Zootaxa 1260: 57-66

OSAWA, M. & Y. Fujita (2005): Clibanarius ambonensis (Crustacea: Decapoda: Anomura: Diogenidae) from the Ryukyu Islands, south-western Japan. JMBA2 - Biodiversity Records: 1-8

OTT, G. (1990): Flußkrebse. Der Amerikanische Flußkrebs, Orconectes limosus, ist meist nur aus dem Kochtopf bekannt. Das Aquarium, Heft 8: 5–10.

PARRY, G. & W. T. W. Potts (1965): Sodium balance in the freshwater prawn, Palaemonetes antennarius. J. Exp. Biol. 42: 415-421

PÉREZ-BOTE, J. L. (2006): Summer diet of the adult freshwater prawn Palemonetes zariquieyi Sollaud, 1939 (Decapoda, Palemonidae) in the Jerte river (SW Iberian Peninsula). Crustaceana 79 (3): 363-370

RAHAYU, D. L. (2004): Hermit crabs (Crustacea: Anomura) of the Anambas expedition 2002. The Raffles bulletin of Zoology, Suppl. No 11: 73-78

RASCH, P. (1985): Ritter ohne Furcht und Tadel. Pflege und Zucht des Amerikanischen Teichkrebses. Aquarien-Magazin 10: 428–433.

RATHBUN, M. J. (1921): The brachyuran crabs collected by the American museum Congo expedition, 1909-1915.Bulletin American Museum of Natural History 43: 379-481 + pl. 15-64

REED, S. K. & N. Cumberlidge (2006): Taxonomy and biogeography of the freshwater crabs of Tanzania, East Africa (Brachyura: Potamoidea: Potamonautidae: Platythelphusidae: Deckeniidae). Zootaxa 1262: 1-139

RENNER, M. (1967): Leitfaden für das Zoologische Praktikum, Stuttgart: 223–244

ROCHARD, Chr. & E. (1984): Contribution à la maintenance et la reproduction de la crevette d'eau douce Macrobrachium lanchesteri. AQUARAMA, Heft 79, 21 ff.

ROUSE, D. B & I. Kartamulia (1992): Influence of salinity and temperature on molting and survival of the Australian freshwater crayfish (Cherax tenuimanus). Aquaculture 105: 47-52.

SCHÄFER, F. (2005): Die Grünen aus Paraguay. Aegla platensis erstmals importiert. AqualogNews 64: 18

SCHÄFER, F. (2006): Süßwasser-Krabben. Liebenswerte Minimonster. Aqualog Verlag, Rodgau, 72 pp.

SCHLÜTER, M. (1989): Flußkrebse aus Australien. Ritter in farbenfroher Rüstung. DATZ 42: 526–528.

SCHMIDT-HERZER, K. (1999): Die Krebspest - eine unendliche Geschichte? Das Aquarium 361: 3-9.

SKINNER, D. M., Marsh, D. J. & J. S. Cook (1965): Physiological salt solution for the land crab, Gecarcinus lateralis. The Biological Bulletin 129: 355-365

SMEDLEY, N. (1929): Malaysian King-Crabs. The Raffles Bulletin of Zoology 2: 73-78

SPIVAK, E. D. & J. A. Cuesta (2000): Larval developement of Cyrtograpsus affinis (Dana) (Decapoda, Brachyura, Varunidae) from the Rio de la Plata estuary, reared in the laboratory. Scientia Marina 64 (1): 29-47

STRACHAN, P. H., Smith, R. C., Hamilton, D. A. B., Taylor, A. C. & R. J. A. Atkinson (1998): Studies on the ecology and behaviour of the ghost crab, Ocypode cursor (L.) in northern Cyprus. Scientia Maritima 63 (1): 51-60

SUBRAHMANYAM, M. (...) : Studies on growth of the giant freshwater prawn Macrobrachium rosenbergii (De Man). Prawn Breeding Unit CIFA, Andhra Pradesh, India: 340-351.

TAN, C. G. S. & P. K. L. Ng (1999): A revision of the genus Camptandrium Stimpson, 1858 (Crustacea: Decapoda: Brachyura: Camptandriidae). The Raffles Bulletin of Zoology 47 (1): 193-219

TAYLOR, A. C. & P. S. Davies (1981): Respiration in the land crab, Gecarcinus lateralis. J. exp. Biol. 93: 197-208

VARADARAJAN, S. & T. Subramoniam (1982): Reproduction of the continuously breeding tropical hermit crab Clibanarius clibanarius. Marine ecology - progress series 8: 197-201

VON HAGEN, H.-O. (1983): Vom Strand auf den Markt. Südamerikas Landkrebse leben gefährlich. Das TIER: 72–75.

WERNER, U. (1987): Eine Garnele mit 'Fächerhänden': Atya moluccensis. DATZ 40: 283–284.

WERNER, U. (1987): Gaumenfreude-Augenweide: Procambarus clarkii, der Nordamerikanische Teichkrebs. DATZ 40: 529–531.

WERNER, U. (1987): Mehr als nur kulinarische Köstlichkeit – Süßwassergarnelen der Gattung Macrobrachium Bate, 1868. TI 84: 37–39.

WERNER, U. (1993): Ausgefallene Aquarienpfleglinge, Landbuch-Verlag Hannover, 191 S

WERNER, U. (1997): Die Blaue Fächergarnele. Eine neu eingeführte Atya-Art aus Westafrika. Das Aquarium 337: 12–15.

WERNER, U. (1999): Biologie und Pflege von Cherax-Arten (Parastacidae, Crustacea) im Aquarium. In: Riehl, R. & H. Greven (Hersg.): Fortpflanzungsbiologie der Aquarienfische. Symposiumsband. Bornheim: 240 S.

WERNER, U. (1999): Neue Garnelen für das Süßwasseraquarium. Das Aquarium 363: 22-28.

WERNER, U. (2001): Der "Marron", Cherax tenuimanus, ein australischer Krebs, neu für das Süßwasseraquarium eingeführt. Das Aquarium 386: 8-12.

WERNER, U. (2001): Die Maya-Garnele aus Palenque. TI 159: 47-48.

WERNER, U. (2001): Zwergkrebse. Die Arten der Gattung Cambarellus sind in Mexiko heimisch. Das Aquarium 383: 16-19.

YEO, D. C. J. & P. K. L. Ng (1996): A new species of freshwater snapping shrimp, Alpheus cyanoteles (Decapoda: Caridea: Alpheidae) from Peninsular Malaysia and a redescription of Alpheus paludicola Kemp, 1915. The Raffles Bulletin of Zoology 44 (1): 37-63

ZHOU, H. & B. Morton (2004): The diets of juvenile horseshoe crabs, Tachypleus tridentatus and Carcinoscorpius rotundicauda (Xiphosura), from nursery beaches proposed for conservation in Hong Kong. Journal of Natural History 38 (15): 1915-1925

Eine klare Sache...
REISER systems – aquaristic
Pure, clear water for animals and plants
Environment friendly, no need of external energy, no chemicals
• changing water without any risk
• improved care of shrimps and other crustaceans
• better growth of plants
• protection against algea
• more comfort for all animals
• higher hatching rate
The REISER BLOCKFILTER® removes
depending on the filter fineness:
• particles of lime and rust
• dirt and floating particles
• sand and mud
• chlorine, chlorine gases and chlorinated hydrocarbons
• organic pollutants
• germs, bacteria and drugs
• pesticides, herbicides and fungicides
• copper and lead
• odour and colouration
AK-1M
Cloudy water and algae pests become occurences of the past........
REISER®
Filter technique
Water processing
D-63500 Seligenstadt · Telefon +49(0)6182 7875991 · Telefax +49(0)6182 7875993
e-Mail: reiser@reiser-filtertechnik.de · Internet: www.reiser-filtertechnik.de

eSHa®
Präparate für Aquarien
EXIT Gegen alle Pünktchen-Krankheiten
EXIT unterscheidet sich vor allem durch die ausgezeichnete Wirkung gegen Ichthyo aber ist auch hochwirksam gegen Süßwasser Oodinium und Import-Ichthyo. EXIT wird auch von sehr empfindlichen Fischen gut vertragen.
EXIT™
Breitenwirkung
Spreading effect
EINFACH SICHER LEICHT
eSHa-OPTIMA
Enthält Bestandteile von "Tropischem Wasser" mit Spurenelementen, Mineralien und Vitaminen.
eSHa-OPTIMA fördert die Erholung nach Krankheit und Verletzung. Und sorgt für eine optimale Kondition und besonderen Widerstand gegen Krankheiten und Parasiten.
eSHa OPTIMA™
für max. 2000 ltr.
SIMPLE SAFE EASY
ZUSAMMEN FINDEN WIR DIE LÖSUNG
©2008 eSHa lab - P.O Box 431 - NL 6200 AK Maastricht

ZOO ZAJAC
Das größte Zoofachgeschäft der Welt
• 8.000 m² Erlebnisfläche
• Aquarienabteilung mit 1.000 Aquarien
• Terraristikabteilung mit 500 Terrarien
• Große Auswahl an Garnelen und Krebsen
• Zubehör und Futter in riesiger Auswahl
• Fachliteratur zu allen Themen
• Erstklassige und fachkundige Beratungen
Fordern Sie noch heute kostenlos unseren über 550 Seiten starken Katalog an!
Zoo Zajac GmbH, Konrad-Adenauer-Ring 6, 47167 Duisburg, Tel.: 0203 45045-0, Fax: 0203 45045-45, E-Mail: info@zajac.de, Online-Shop: www.zajac.de
Öffnungszeiten
Montag bis Freitag 10:00 – 20:00 Uhr
Samstag 9:00 – 20:00 Uhr
www.zajac.de
Alles für Ihr Hobby | Über 20.000 Artikel | Tolle Sonderangebote
Informative Ratgeber rund ums Thema Haustier | Aktuelle Veranstaltungshinweise
Hier bleiben keine Wünsche offen

Die einzige Zeitschrift über
Wirbellose im Süßwasser
• Haltung und Pflege im Aquarium, Nachzucht und Fütterung
• Alles zur Technik: Filter, Beleuchtung, Heizung, Regeltechnik
• Veranstaltungen, Bezugsquellen, Leserfragen und vieles mehr
• Caridina erscheint dreimal jährlich
Garnele, Krebs & Co.
caridina
Raubschnecken
Ninja-Garnelen
Edelkrebse im Aquarium
Maximal-Filter zu gewinnen.
Garnele, Krebs & Co.
caridina
Vampir-krabben
Erstmals vermehrt
Wirklich ein Zerstörer?
Cherax destructor
Jetzt im Trend:
Blaue Tigergarnelen
Designer-Rückwand zu gewinnen.
Garnele, Krebs & Co.
caridina
Weißperlen-Garnelen
Zwerg-flusskrebse
Pagoden- und Apfelschnecken
10 Aquarien und Futter zu gewinnen.
3x jährlich alles Wissenswerte rund um Garnelen,
Krebse, Krabben, Schnecken und Pflanzen.
Einfach telefonisch oder online bestellen
LeserService 0 72 43 / 575-143
service@daehne.de · www.caridina.eu
Dähne Verlag
Ich weiß.
Dähne Verlag GmbH
Postfach 10 02 50
76256 Ettlingen
Tel. 0 72 43 / 575-143
Fax 0 72 43 / 575-100

APS-Center
Ihr Süßwasserspezialist
APS-Center
Kasinostraße 26
65929 Frankfurt
(069) 33 33 44
(069) 33 33 43
(0700) 55 33 88 33
(069) 33 12 48
Aquarien-Notdienst:
(0171) 5 33 88 33
Notdienst-Center:
(0171) 269 269 2
Pflege - Service:
(0171) 19 19 777
info@aquarien-notdienst.de
www.aquarien-notdienst.de
- Zierfische und Wasserpflanzen – über 100 verschiedene Panzerwelse sowie L-Welse auf Leitungswasser (GH 18°-25°dGH, pH 7,5 - 8,5)
- Großes Garnelen- sowie Krebsangebot (ständig wechselnde Tiere)
- Eine reichhaltige Auswahl an Aquarienmöbel, Aquarien, sowie Abdeckungen, Aquarienverklebung vor Ort, jedes Sondermaß ist möglich. Spezialisiert auf Giesemann, Eldorado sowie Müller und Pfleger
- komplettes EHEIM - Ersatzteileprogramm (über 400 verschiedene Ersatzteile vorrätig und über 100 weitere EHEIM - Produkte)
- Kostenloser Reparaturservice und Beratung, kostenloses Parken
- auf 70m² Außengelände alles rund um den Teich (Koikarpfen, Störe, Orfen, Goldfische, Löwenköpfe....usw., Wasserpflanzen, SÖLL - Pflegeprodukte)
- Kompletter Terrarienzubehör sowie wöchentlich frisches Lebendfutter
Besuchen Sie auch unsere Welsgrotte!

animalbook.de
your #1 bookstore for pet literature
▪ We have a large assortment of german, english, spanish and french pet literature.
▪ Delivery worldwide! Fair prices guaranteed.
▪ PayPal, Visa/Mastercard accepted!
▪ Visit our website: www.animalbook.de
We also supply the retail market!
Conditions on request.
Animalbook.de
D-63110 Rodgau - Liebigstr. 1
Tel: +49 (0)6106 / 697977
Fax: +49 (0)6106 / 697983
info@animalbook.de - www.animalbook.de

Milliarden für sauberes Wasser!
amtra system
clean procult
auf MK-19 Sediment
Lebend-Impfkulturen für ein gesundes Aquarium
Verwandeln Sie Ihr gesamtes Aquarium in einen hochaktiven Filter
Die biologische Grundreinigung gegen organische und anorganische Schadstoffe.
• clean procult besteht aus Milliarden hochaktiven schadstoffabbauenden Bakterien, die auf einem natürlichen, speziell entwickelten Mineralgranulat (Mk-19 Sediment) siedeln.
• Das Besiedlungssubstrat bindet gleichzeitig große Mengen von Schadstoffen, die so direkt dem bakteriellen Abbau zugeführt werden.
• Fische zeigen mehr Farbe und Vitalität, Algenwuchs wird reduziert, der Keimgehalt im Wasser wird positiv verändert, das Mk-19 Sediment dient auch als Pflanzennährstoff.
Das Wasser wird glasklar.
amtra Aquaristik GmbH • 63110 Rodgau • info@amtra.de • www.amtra.de

Aqualog Reference books

reference fish of the world

2008

The world-wide unque books with pictures of all known fishes!

Aqualog Verlag • Liebigstraße 1 • D-63110 Rodgau
Fax: + 49 (0) 6106 644692 • Tel: + 49 (0) 6106 644691
e-mail: info@aqualog.de • web: www.aqualog.de
Alle Produkte im Zoofachhandel und Buchhandel erhältlich

South American Cichlids I
(U. Glaser sen.)

Excellent colour photographs show all Cichla, Crenicichla, Teleocichla, Guianacara, Geophagus, Gymnogeophagus, Satanoperca, Acarichthys, Uaru, Biotodoma, Astronotus, Retroculus and Chaetobranchopsis.

(112 pages, 500 colour photos)
ISBN 978-3-931702-04-5
article no. B002

Southamerican Cichlids II
(U. Glaser sen.)

Vol. 2 contains phantastic photos of renowned photographers all dwarf cichlids like Apistogramma, Biotoecus, Crenicara, Dicrossus, Nannacara, Taeniacara und Microgeophagus, previously known as Papiliochromis.

(112 pages , 500 colour photos)
ISBN 978-3-931702-07-6
article no. B003

All Corydoras
(U. Glaser sen.)

All known plated catfish are presented. Besides the genera Aspidoras, Brochis, Callichthys, Corydoras, Dianema, and Hoplosternum all variants, mutants, hybrids, breeding forms, and undescribed forms ("C-numbers") are shown

(144 pages, 650 colour photos)
ISBN 978-3-931702-13-7
article no. B004

Southamerican Cichlids III
(U. Glaser sen.)

In diesem Band finden Sie die Sammelgattungen Aequidens, Cichlasoma und deren Verwandte Acaronia, Caquetaia, Petenia und Herotilapia. Wissenschaftliche Namensänderungen bis 1998 sind bereits berücksichtigt.

(144 pages, 650 colour photos)
ISBN 978-3-931702-10-6
article no. B005

African Cichlids I
MALAWI MBUNA
(E. Schraml)

This book actually shows all the Mbuna species that have been discovered in the Lake Malawi so far

(240 pages, approx. 1500 colour photos)
ISBN 978-3-931702-79-3
article no. B012

All Labyrinths
(F. Schäfer)

The first comprehensive book with all anabantoid fishes, plus all snakeheads, nandids, and related families that show many behavioural parallels to labyrinths or anabantoids. Furthermore, this book provides a determination key to the genus Betta. It became immediately the number 1 identification lexicon of the Betta societies all over the world!

(144 pages, 650 colour photos)
ISBN 978-3-931702-21-2
article no. B006

All Rainbows
(H. Hieronimus)

The name already says it: colourful like a rainbow. All rainbow fishes known today are described. A lot of these beauties still live undiscovered in their biotopes, because in many countries, like for example Papua New Guinea, collectors have to work under extremely difficult conditions.

(176 pages, approx. 700 colour photos)
ISBN 978-3-931702-80-9
article no. B013

Killifishes of the world – New World Killis
(L. Seegers)

This book adds to the series on killifishes the groups from the New World: Rivulus, Cynolebias, Fundulus, Pterolebias, and others.

(224 pages, 1200 colour photos)
ISBN 978-3-931702-76-2
article no. B014

Freshwater Rays
(R. A. Ross / F. Schäfer)

This unique lexicon covers all known species of freshwater stingrays in their entire variety. For the first time you now have a complete reference work in which the South American river stingrays, as well as the Asian, African, Australian, and North American freshwater species are presented. Also the sawfishes are included.

(192 pages, approx. 400 colour photos)
ISBN 978-3-931702-93-9
article no. B015

The puffers of fresh and brackish waters
(K. Ebert)

This book shows 300 brilliant photos of all the puffers around the world, and also a vast knowledge in keeping these outragious and colourful animals, which the author experienced over 40 years. A unique Lexicon for beginners in the hobby, as well as for specialised aquarists and scientists..

(96 pages, 300 colour photos)
ISBN 978-3-931702-61-8
article no. B016-GB

Killifishes of the World – Old World Killis I
(L. Seegers)

"Freshwater Jewels" is another name for the beautiful killis – you will know why after having seen the amazing array of colours displayed by the fishes of the group presented in this book: Aphyosemion, Lampeyes und Ricefishes

(160 pages, more than 890 colour photos)
ISBN 978-3-931702-25-0
article no. B007

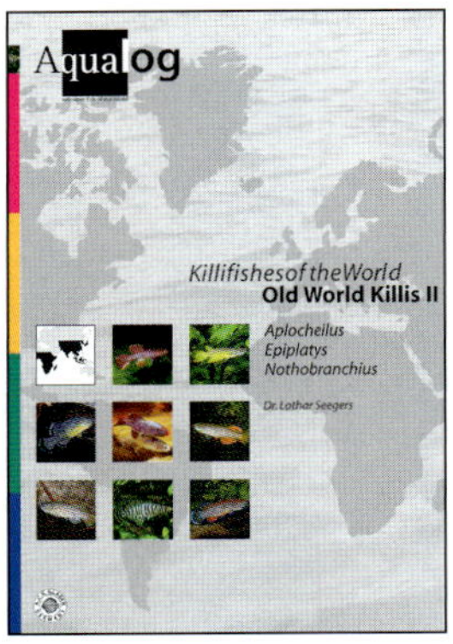

Killifishes of the World – Old World Killis II
(L. Seegers)

This sequel introduces the groups of Panchaxes, Aplocheilus, Epiplatys, Nothobranchius, Aphanius, and others. Their colours and size (they reach only 3–8 cm) make them the ideal aquarium inhabitants.

(112 pages, 550 colour photos)
ISBN 978-3-931702-30-4
article no. B008

All Livebearers and Halfbeaks
(M. Kempkes, F. Schäfer)

The first reference book not only show the well known guppies, mollies, swordtails, platies, etc., but also all the others wild and breeding forms and colour variants as well als Halfbeaks..

(352 pages, 2000 colour photos)
ISBN 978-3-931702-77-9
article no. B009

Southamerican Cichlids IV – Discus & Scalare -
(M. Göbel, H. J. Mayland)

Volume 4 shows beautiful discus and angels. Wild caughts, German, other European and Asian breeding forms plus all variants, colour and breeding forms.

(240 pages, more than 900 colour photos)
ISBN 978-3-931702- 75-5
article no. B010

All Goldfish and Varieties
(K. H. Bernhardt)

Goldfish are the oldest ornamental fishes of the world. Everybody knows them, but did you know that there are so many different varieties? This book presents all colour and shape varieties on excellent colour photos.

(160 pages, 690 colour photos)
ISBN 978-3-931702-78-6
article no. B011

African Cichlids III
Malawi II
(E.Schraml)

The Aulonocara have their common name "Peacocks" because of their beauty in colours and their unbelievable beautiful appearance. So you can imagine that our new book will definitely be a "feast for the eyes"..

(128 pages, 470 colour photos)
ISBN: 978-3-936027-59-4
article-No: B017

Polypterus
Flösselhechte/Bichirs
(F. Schäfer)

It contains all Polypterus described and pictures. These fish may not be colourful, however, with enough space they are unbelievably interesting animals in the aquarium. It is the standard work on this group of fish, without any competition worldwide

(A4 size, 128 pages, 180 colour photos)
iSBN 978-3-936027-39-6
article No. B018

African Cichlids II
Tanganjika I Tropheus
(P. Schupke)

As known from AQUALOG, also this Reference book contains absolutely all species and varieties of this genus. For the first time, all Tropheus are described and brilliantly pictured. Included in the book is a poster of the lake with colour drawings of the fish with prices origins of the varieties.

(A4 size, 192 pages, 300 colour photos)
ISBN 978-3-936027-37-2
article No. B019-GB

AQUALOG Loricariidae
alle L-Welse / all L-numbers
(E. Schraml , F. Schäfer)

This world-wide unique standard work of L-numbers is indispensable for fishermen, import and export companies, professional breeders, wholesalers, shopkeepers and hobbyists all over the world.

(272 pages, 1.800 colour photos)
ISBN 978-3-936027-51-8
article No. B021

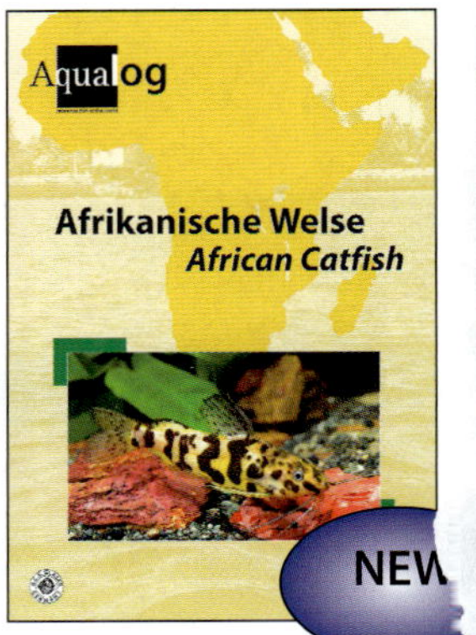

African Catfishes

(U.Glaser sen.)

article-no.: B020

Turtles of the World Vol.2
North America
(H. Vetter)

With more then 500 colour photos this second volume is the reference work for scientist and hobbyists. This unique book impressively shows the variety of turtles of North America including detailed maps of the distribution.

(137 pages, 500 colour photos)
ISBN 978-3-936027-52-5
article no-T002

Turtles of the World Vol.3
Central and South America
(H. Vetter)

Central and South American turtles - including the impressive Galapagos tortoises as well as the various genera of the family Chelidae - are covered in this third volume of TERRALOG. A unique reference for everyone - from the hobbyist to the scientist..

(127 pages, 500 colour photos)
ISBN: 978-3-936027-60-0
article-No: T003

Turtles of the World Vol.4
East and South Asia
(H.Vetter, P. Paul van Dijk)

This volume of TERRALOG is a portrayal of the chelonians of East and South Asia.With a total of 600 color photographs and color distribution maps for all species, this volume of TERRALOG is a unique reference for everyone - from the hobbyist to the scientist.

(144 pages, 600 colour photos)
ISBN: 978-3-936027-92-1
article-No: T004

Venomous snakes of Asia
Giftschlangen Asiens
(G. Vogel)

This volume of TERRALOG is a presentation of the venomous snakes of Asia. It portrays about 165 taxa and forms of the familie Elapidae and Viperidae, and covers a geological range from Pakistan to China and Japan to Indonesia.

(144 pages, 600 colour photos)
ISBN: 978-3-936027-93-8
article no. T014

Venomous snakes of Africa
Giftschlangen Afrikas
(M. Dobiey, G. Vogel)

This volume of TERRALOG is a presentation of the venomous snakes of Africa. It portrays about 136 taxa and forms of the families Atracaspidae, Elapidae and Viperidae. Several species are illustrated for the first time ever!

(148 pages, 470 colour photos)
ISBN: 978-3-939759-04-1
article no. T015